THEY AND We

Racial
and
Ethnic Relations
in
the United States

THEY

AND

We

**Racial
and
Ethnic Relations
in
the United States**

Fourth Edition

PETER I. ROSE

McGRAW-HILL PUBLISHING COMPANY
New York   St. Louis   San Francisco   Auckland   Bogotá
Caracas   Hamburg   Lisbon   London   Madrid   Mexico
Milan   Montreal   New Delhi   Oklahoma City   Paris
San Juan   São Paulo   Singapore   Sydney   Tokyo   Toronto

1 2 3 4 5 6 7 8 9 0 FGR FGR 9 5 4 3 2 1 0

ISBN 0-07-053640-6

Acknowledgments appear on pages 233–234;
copyrights included on this page by reference.

This book was set in Melior by J.M. Post Graphics, Corp.
The editors were Phillip A. Butcher and Peggy C. Rehberger;
the production supervisor was Louise Karam.
The cover was designed by Karen K. Quigley.
Arcata Graphics/Fairfield was printer and binder.

Library of Congress Cataloging-in-Publication Data

Rose, Peter Isaac, (date).
    They and we: racial and ethnic relations in the United States /
Peter I. Rose.—4th ed.
        p.   cm.
    Includes bibliographical references.
    ISBN 0-07-053640-6
        1. Minorities—United States.   2. Discrimination—United States.
    3. United States—Race relations.   4. United States—Ethnic
    relations.   I. Title.
    E184.A1R72   1990
    305.8'00973—dc20   89-77429

ABOUT THE AUTHOR

Peter I. Rose (Cornell Ph.D., 1959) is Sophia Smith Professor of Sociology and Anthropology and Director of the American Studies Diploma Program at Smith College. He has been a visiting professor at the University of Colorado, Wesleyan, Yale, Clark, Harvard, and the University of Massachusetts, where he continues to serve as a member of the Graduate Faculty. He has also been a Fulbright Professor in England, Japan, and Australia; Oldendorff Lecturer in The Netherlands; Visiting Scholar at the Chinese Academy of Social Sciences; Resident Scholar at the Rockefeller Study Center in Bellagio, Italy; and Visiting Senior Fellow in the Refugee Studies Program at Oxford University. He has lectured at universities in over forty other countries.

In addition to *They and We*, Mr. Rose is the author of *The Subject Is Race*, *Strangers in Their Midst*, and *Mainstream and Margins*, and co-author of two introductory sociology textbooks. He is the editor of *The Study of Society*, *The Ghetto and Beyond*, *Americans from Africa*, *Nation of Nations*, *Seeing Ourselves*, *Views from Abroad*, *Socialization and the Life Cycle*, and *Working with Refugees*, and co-editor of *Through Different Eyes: Black and White Perspectives on American Race Relations* and *Over Vreemdeling en Vluchteling [About Strangers and Refugees]*. He was General Editor of the Random House Series, *Ethnic Groups in Comparative Perspective*, and General Consultant on the fourteen volume Time-Life Series, *Human Behavior*.

For Hedy

CONTENTS

PREFACE

The first edition of *They and We* was completed in 1963, the year the civil rights movement reached its zenith. Black Power was but a hushed whisper then. Few who listened to the Reverend Martin Luther King, Jr. address a quarter of a million Black and White Americans assembled on the Mall in front of the Lincoln Memorial on August 28, 1963 realized that he, his people, and their allies in the struggle—and their enemies— were about to enter a new era. The whisper was to become a roar.

Those days, just a quarter of a century ago, now seem light-years away. In the period before the March on Washington thousands participated in a movement marked by righteousness and perseverance, liberal faith and Judeo-Christian principles, justice and love, and a great deal of confidence in the American system. It was oriented primarily toward forcing the country to honor its own vaunted ideals and to win for all the rights most White Americans took for granted. But by 1964 the tone, temper, and orientation began to change. Many Whites were eased or pushed from positions of leadership; many Blacks (and brown and red Americans in their own fashion) eschewed the rhetoric of integration for the rhetoric of revolution. In many ways the rhetoric was reified. In a real sense there was a revolution.

First, the members of the dominant White majority were told over and over that they, all of them, were racists. A spate of books hammered home the theme. Many black people who, for any number of reasons, had not organized themselves before began to add action to their verbal attacks. Demands were made, met, escalated, and often met again. The litany began where the old civil rights leaders had left off: "Freedom Now" and "We shall Overcome" to "Look Out, Whitey, Black Power's Gon' Get your Momma." Then came the call for recompense, for special treatment. Ultimately, in what many saw as justified and others saw as racism-in-reverse, the pleas for admission and fairness became a cry for affirmative action, even for favoritism. As the demands, particularly of college students, were beginning to be responded to by frightened faculties and baffled administrators (often liberal and therefore highly vulnerable to the accusations of the young), more conservative organizations began making their own concessions. For example, large industries increased the level of tokenism to include more Black and Hispanic workers, especially in places where they would be seen. Television networks and local stations began to employ them, too. (It was fascinating to note how many minority people were available as potential freshmen in Ivy League colleges, as workers in various Fortune 500 companies, as TV announcers and print media commentators, when the threat of disruption loomed on the horizon.) As the disaffected members of the civil rights movement were beginning to rally their troops for assaults on the academy and the factory, the people in the streets became involved, too—some in organized fashion, others more spontaneously. Dozens of urban riots flared up in cities as different as New York, Detroit, Cleveland, and Los Angeles as poor folks (though not always the poorest) joined in the burning and looting and pillaging in a frenzied expression of frustration, bitterness, and, for some, short-lived pleasure as "Whitey" seemed to be getting his come-uppance. Other people engaged, in more organized political activities, many of them centering on the issue of community control, particularly of schools. And still others simply took renewed pride in who they were, if not in where they found themselves.

All this—the rhetoric, the organizing, the planned attacks on the system, and the spontaneous outbursts—shook the entire society. Many White Americans reeled in disbelief and then, in a variety of ways, they reacted.

Part of the reaction came from the traditional right wing whose preeminent theme was "We told you so." But more significant, and far greater in the numbers involved, was the reaction of two overlapping categories: white, Protestant, lower-middle class Middle Americans, and working-class, predominantly Catholic "ethnics." The latter group, often but a generation or two from ghetto living themselves, began to feel that they, in particular, were being asked to pay for the sins of other peoples' fathers. Backlash became a reality though, save for widespread reaction to forced school busing, it was far less blatant than many, including a number of social scientists, had predicted.

Parallel to the growing resistance to the pressures being exerted by black and brown and other minority Americans was a reexamination of the "ethnics' " own place in the society, and their own history as well. In fact, as several have suggested, the Black Power movement was responsible for ethnic communalism becoming legitimated, then institutionalized, in a manner unprecedented in our history. By the early 1970s the bookstores had another section to add to the one that shelved Angelou, Baldwin, Cleaver, Donaldson, Ellison, Fanon, and on through the rest of the alphabet of black writers or writers on black themes. The new shelf (not yet so long) included Louise Howe's *The White Majority*, Andrew M. Greeley's *Why Can't They Be Like Us?*, Peter Schrag's *Out of Place in*

America, Michael Novak's *The Rise of the Unmeltable Ethnics*, Murray Friedman's *Overcoming Middle Class Rage*, Nathan Glazer's *Affirmative Discrimination*, and many more with similar themes.

The period from 1963 to 1973 was quite a volatile decade on the ethnic front. The period from 1973 to 1980 was very different. Race was not the number one issue, nor was American involvement in Vietnam, the war having ended in 1975. From that time through the rest of the decade, economics and energy took center stage, dominating foreign affairs and domestic debates.

This is not to say everything was settled in the realm of race relations. It wasn't. In fact, the energy crisis served to accentuate the plight of the poor who had the most to lose by rising prices and increasing shortages of fuel to say nothing of the growing scourge of unemployment as the economy slowed and lay-offs became the order of the day.

At the same time, the general economic downturn led increasing numbers of Middle Americans and white ethnics to take even more conservative stances regarding bread and butter issues. Concerned about where tax dollars were going, the cry about "give aways" and "welfare chiselers" was heard again and again. Many voiced the opinion that minorities seemed to get too much of the public monies and too many of the private positions and jobs. Court decisions, as in the Bakke Case, gave additional support to those opposed to affirmative action and quotas, however "benign."

By the end of the 1970s the strains of economic and political problems were deeply etched on the face of America. Unemployment reached a forty-year high and, as always, non-Whites bore the brunt of the burden. Riots in Miami, Orlando, and Chattanooga in the summer of 1980 were an ugly reminder of the depth of hostility still extant in the urban ghettos.

International conflicts influenced many domestic debates as well, and many began choosing sides over U.S. policies in southern Africa and in the Middle East. Moreover, increasing numbers of citizens expressed resentment over the influx of thousands of Cubans and Southeast Asians, who were seen not just as refugees from Communism but as potential usurpers of jobs and benefits of Americans (including many who were but a generation or two away from immigrant status themselves).

With the depressed economic situation, the increase of racial tension, the rising tide of conservatism, and the dearth of strong leadership, many feared that the gains made by minorities in the 1960s and 1970s would prove to be Pyrrhic victories. They were not far off the mark. One reason is that, for all the changes—not least the institutionalization of affirmative action programs—certain underlying structural characteristics of our society remained relatively constant. Among the most enduring of certain seemingly endemic traits was that of a nation that remained hierarchically divided in terms of social class. While it is true that those in the upper echelons were better off than ever before (this was a time when a new and colorful term, "yuppie"—young, urban professional—took on special meaning) and increasing numbers of minority group members joined the ranks of the middle class (often as the result of special efforts to recruit them), many black and brown as well as white working-class Americans found they were treading water just to stay afloat in a highly volatile economic sea. This was also true of the hundreds of thousands of new Americans who entered the country as refugees or immigrants looking for chances to benefit from the promise of the still-touted "American Dream." They often found themselves viewed as interlopers by those who perceived them as additional competitors. Many others, known in the press and in the sociology classroom by the generic label "underclass"—many of them members of nonwhite minorities, especially Blacks, Hispanics, and Native Americans—were found to be falling farther and farther behind. The social profiles of these truly disadvantaged people belied any claims, even by the most progressive of our political leaders, that dramatic progress had been made in dealing with one of the most basic domestic problems in our society.

While in many ways we can point to significant changes in social policy and definitive gains on the "race relations front" in the nearly 30 years since I first began the series of essays which comprised the first edition of this book, much of what I said about the character of American society and about ways of studying it still seem appropriate.

In that first edition, I sketched out the ways sociologists looked at what was then called "intergroup relations," at America's ethnic history, at the various theories put forth to handle the flow of newcomers into the nation, at prejudice and discrimination, and at minority responses. The second edition included a reassessment and expansion of each of these topics and the addition of two new essays, one on "Black Consciousness" and its significance for Blacks and other non-White minorities, the other on reactions to the challenge of their ethnic assertiveness, including "The Resurgence of Ethnicity" among other groups.

Shortly after the second edition was published, I became interested in yet another dimension of the overall problem. It was a logical outcome of several decades of studying and teaching about these matters in various American universities and abroad. It involved an epistemological question about an empirical problem: Who is the better judge of social behavior, the "insider-member" or the "outsider-expert"? In the present context, the question is more than a philosophical one; it has serious political undertones.

In the third edition of They and We, I revised almost a third of the material in the second edition; added text on a variety of subjects, including the debates over "Jensenism" and affirmative action; and also offered a new chapter which outlined my attempts to pose questions to myself about the "insider-outsider debate" and then try to answer them.

This latest edition goes to press a little more than a quarter of a century after the first one and, I believe, at an equally critical juncture. It is a time for stock-taking about gains and losses and, especially, about what happened in the period that will be forever known as "The Reagan Era." A new chapter looks specifically at those years, between 1980 and the present. In addition to minor emendations, in this latest edition I have attempted to bring the story of this "Nation of Nations" up to date and to provide some further thoughts about the meaning of ethnicity for those called minorities and those who, by virtue of their own dominant place in the status hierarchy, often determine that others maintain such a differentiating designation.

Like its earlier versions, *They and We*, fourth edition, is not a blueprint for change. It is, however, a guide for study and reflection. As I explained in the Preface to the original volume: While organized efforts to bring about a reduction in racial and ethnic tension represent an important part of contemporary life, and the tactics and strategies employed are a matter of great concern to many social scientists, including me, they can only be introduced within the compass of this small book. It is hoped, however, that what is presented here will help to replace some of the popular misconceptions of the problems discussed and will thus serve as a basis for understanding—the first step toward change.

As I have before, I welcome the chance to thank many teachers, colleagues, students, and friends who have taught me, encouraged me, offered assistance, offered advice, offered criticism. There are many to whom I am deeply indebted, but I would like especially to acknowledge a baker's dozen of individuals who have had a special influence on my thinking and, directly and indirectly, on my professional life: Nathan Goldman, Robin M. Williams, Jr., John P. Dean, Edward A. Suchman, Oscar Cohen, Alan Holmberg, Melvin M. Tumin, David Riesman, Milton M. Gordon, Lawrence Fuchs—all, in very different ways, models and mentors; also Charles D. Lieber, an editor's editor who "commissioned" a small book on American minorities (that became *They and We*) for Random House in 1960 and, later, as president of Atherton Books, published my two-volume collection, *Americans from Africa*; Charles H. Page, who, as a Consulting Editor in Sociology at Random House, taught me much about writing and editing and, as a former Professor of Sociology at Smith College and current neighbor in Northampton, has continued to be a trusted adviser and close friend; and, my late colleague, Ely Chinoy, a superb sociologist, a sensitive critic, and a wonderful companion.

I also offer my appreciation for the support and guidance of Ted Caris, David Bartlett, Philip Metcalf, Phillip A. Butcher, and Peggy C. Rehberger, editors of the first, second, third, and fourth editions, respectively; for the secretarial assistance of the late Marge Erickson and for that of Agnes

Shannon, Norma Lepine, and Nancy Hill; and for the research assistance of Benjamin F. Samuel.

Finally, I happily repeat what I have written thrice before. Most important of all is my wife, Hedy, to whom this book is dedicated. She knows best what has been involved. So, too, do our children, Lies and Dan.

Peter I. Rose

THEY

AND

We

Racial
and
Ethnic Relations
in
the United States

1

RACE, ETHNICITY, AND THE SOCIOLOGICAL PERSPECTIVE

Introduction

They and We is a book about intergroup relations. It is about the complex distinctions that have long existed in our society, the treatment that has been the fate of various minorities, and the different ways individuals and groups have tried to cement the cracks in the mosaic that is the United States.

They and We is neither a celebration of the triumph of reason over the scourges of racism nor a blanket indictment of "Amerikkka," as the young radicals of the 1960s were wont to spell it. Rather it is an attempt to discuss and debate the meaning of such ideas as democracy, meritocracy, and pluralism; such concepts as prejudice, discrimination, and group rights; such processes as assimilation, amalgamation, and accommodation; and such slogans and expressions as "Freedom Now," "Black Power," and "Why can't they be like us?" within a framework of sociological inquiry.

The Sociologist and Intergroup Relations

Sociologists are primarily investigators, social scientists concerned with the study of social relationships and variegated patterns of social behavior. They share with other scientists the fundamental view that only through the systematic accumulation of empirical evidence and rigorous analysis can the realities of the physical and social world be revealed. Their commitment is to the investigation, description, and analysis of what is—to social realities. In seeking to uncover the complexities of social life there is the ever-present conviction that human beings may benefit from greater knowledge of themselves. Scientific research may thus serve a dual purpose: science for the sake of understanding, and understanding for the sake of providing solutions to social problems.

Often sociologists study those aspects of behavior that many people consider to be detrimental to the functioning of society or injurious to some or all of its members. In examining such phenomena as crime and delinquency, political upheaval, family disorganization, or race relations, it is a difficult but necessary task to maintain the principle of scientific objectivity. It is difficult because such aspects of social life are studied precisely because they are considered problems; it is necessary because, as the late Robert M. MacIver observed, "A moral judgment—no matter how much we may agree with it, cannot be a substitute for the proper study of causes."[1]

Few problems of contemporary life are more in need of continuous sociological investigation than the tensions and cleavages that exist between racial and ethnic groupings. One need look no further than the pages of a daily newspaper or a television screen to see evidence of this fact. In America the persistence of racism, manifest most clearly in continued *de facto* segregation of black people in both northern and southern areas, is only the most obvious case. Puerto Ricans, Mexican-Americans, people from Asia and the Middle East, Native Americans and other non-Whites are still subject to stereotyping and discriminatory treatment. So, too, are members of certain religious groups and atheists as well as political dissenters and dissidents and women in every ethnic, religious, and racial category. Sometimes even members of old immigrant groups, the so-called "white ethnics," still face abuse and discrimination, especially by those who engage in what has been called the "respectable bigotry" of the elite—those upper-class radicals who have great sympathy for the "lumpen proletariat" (the underclass) but cannot abide those in the working class.[2]

While examples of the overt manifestations of intolerance are readily observed, the forces that create, maintain, perpetuate, or alleviate intergroup tensions are highly complex. For many years sociologists have been investigating the causes and consequences of intergroup conflict.[3] A growing body of knowledge and theory now provides important insight into the dynamics of prejudice and discrimination.

In the pages to follow the reader is introduced to some of the principal methods and findings of these researchers. This first chapter contains the definition and explication of several relevant sociological concepts. Chapters Two and Three offer a brief summary of the history of immigration in the United States and a critical evaluation of the theories and processes of adjustment and assimilation. In three succeeding chapters the nature of prejudice, the varied ways in which ethnic minorities have been treated in this society, and the responses of those in minority communities are considered. Chapters Seven and Eight address the issues of Black Power and the resurgence of ethnicity, respectively. Chapter Nine considers that period best known as "the Reagan Years." The last chapter asks the question of whether Outsiders can ever penetrate the veil of Insiders (or get behind their masks) and, if so, how the meaning of minority status and ethnicity may best be conveyed.

Differentiation and Discrimination

In all societies individuals are differentiated by biological and social criteria. People are ranked in hierarchical fashion, as superior or inferior, according to those attributes that are considered important. Even in the simplest, most isolated societies—where subsistence is apt to be the primary concern—distinctions are made on the basis of age groupings, sex roles, and kinship ties. More advanced societies are divided into distinct social classes, and those higher on the scale have access to greater opportunities for wealth, prestige, and social control. The discrepancy between those in superior and subordinate positions is generally quite evident. There is an obvious disparity in the life styles and material possessions of parvenus and peasants, gentlemen and yeomen, bosses and workers. No less significant is the differential access to political and economic power of those on top and those below. Such social stratification often accounts for intense feelings of intraclass identification and interclass rivalry. The rich and powerful seek to maintain their positions; those below try to raise themselves in the status hierarchy or, in some instances, to turn the entire system upside down.

Opportunities for improving one's position largely depend upon a socially defined system of social stratification. Where a rigid *caste system* exists, there is little hope for individual advancement, for status is fixed by birth and marriage is endogamous (within the caste group). In societies with a feudal social structure, placement is determined largely by heredity. The *estate system*, however, does provide limited channels for mobility and individuals are sometimes able to change their estate by royal decree, by marrying someone of higher status, by entering the clergy or military service, or by becoming artisans or tradesmen. The estate system is most prevalent in agricultural societies, where status is directly related to the ownership and use of land. In agricultural societies with socialist governments heredity is largely replaced as a basis for status, but not without upheaval. One thinks of the post-World War II changes in China, beginning with the civil war, the ouster of the Kuomintang, the development of the communist regime, and the cultural revolution, all ostensibly designed to rid the society of its feudal character.

In industrial societies, where land tenure is relatively unimportant, wealth and income become the relevant measures of social position. In such societies an *open class system* is said to prevail. Ideally, every individual should be able to gain recognition based upon personal ability and performance, regardless of birth or previous condition of inequality.[4] While greater opportunities do exist for movement up and down the ladder of social mobility within a class system, there is no society where individual merit is the sole criterion for determining status. In the United States, for example, several factors have long served to inhibit full realization of the traditional ideal of equal opportunity; not the least of these factors is membership in a particular "minority" group. Foreign-born persons, members of certain religious groups, individuals with dubious political affiliations, and, especially, those with dark skins are often handicapped in their attempts to advance on the basis of personal ability. Many members of such groups are categorically denied the right to fulfill their own potentialities in the "pursuit of happiness." In fact, as Kurt Mayer has said, "If the absence of estate-like characteristics makes the American class system unique, it is likewise true that the intrusion of racial caste-like features is almost without parallel in modern Western experience."[5] Thus, a critical aspect of placement in the status hierarchy of American society is that of ethnic and racial group membership.

Race and Culture

Culture and race are two words that are widely misused and often misunderstood. *Culture* refers to the way people live, the rules they set for themselves, the general ideas around which they organize their lives, the things they feel are good or bad, right or wrong, pleasurable or painful. Cultural norms or standards for behavior are learned from those around us: relatives, teachers, friends. We often speak of "Western culture" as the principal source of the American heritage. And this concept is quite accurate for, despite many modifications, our society is largely a product of European values and attitudes.

From ancient times to the present people in the so-called Western World have tended to divide the human species into such separate and visually distinct "races" as "black," "white," "red," and "yellow." Sometimes, when referring to persons of certain mixtures—"white" Spaniards and "red" Indians, for example—the term "brown" has been employed. Although there is no such thing as a "pure" race, various peoples have found it useful to divide humans into racial categories.

It is not illogical to want to group people according to gross similarities and not surprising that such external criteria as skin color, head form, facial features (like broad or narrow noses), stature, and color, texture, and distribution of body hair are used as variables. Indeed, some anthropologists define a *race* as a statistical aggregate of persons who share a composite of genetically transmissible physical traits.[6] Without spelling it out, most Americans would agree.

It is not difficult for most Americans to pick out an "Asian," a "Caucasian," or a "Black" on a crowded street in San Francisco, Chicago, or New York; a set of criteria is associated with each category. A person with brownish-yellow skin, straight black hair, almond-shaped eyes, and a nose that seemed to lack a pronounced bridge would, most likely, be considered Asian or "Yellow." A person with whitish, pinkish, or ruddy skin, blond or brunette, wavy or straight hair, blue or green eyes, a straight, hooked, or pug nose would fall in the category "White." A person with dark brown or brown skin, kinky black hair, brown eyes, a rather broad nose, and thick lips undoubtedly would be seen as a "Black" person.

Of course, it is harder to categorize someone who has a straight high-bridged nose, dark wavy hair, and a dark brown complexion. In the United States, most people would probably say such an individual "must be Black." Why? Because in this society, like many others, racial designations are not merely simple ways of classifying people according to their genetic make-up. Rather, "race" is used for locating or placing people according to culturally defined social positions.[7]

American history is filled with instances of "race mixing." Mexican-Americans are largely the children of Spanish and Indian parentage; Puerto Ricans are the offspring of White and Black as well as Indian ancestors; and many people whom we call "Black" are actually very white indeed. In fact, to find pure-Negroid types is very difficult in this country (as compared with almost any place in sub-Saharan Africa). Even so, until 1960, the United States Census Bureau gave instructions to its enumerators to include the following criteria for designating Negroes:

In addition to persons of Negro and mixed Negro and white descent, this category includes persons of mixed American-Indian and Negro descent, unless the Indian ancestry very definitely predominates or unless the individual is regarded as an Indian in the community.[8]

Many so-called non-White Americans long have been aware of the fact that racial labels mean something special.

If you're white, you're right,
If you're brown, hang aroun'
But if you're black, brother,
Get back, get back, get back.

If no cultural value were placed upon ancestry—whether "pure" or "mixed"—it would matter very little what one was called or in which pigeonhole one was placed. In a race-conscious society like the United States, those who are "colored" (as opposed to "white") have generally been put in inferior positions and treated accordingly. In almost every American town there has long been a close connection between the tasks people perform and the place in which they live, and the color of their skin. Menial work is disproportionately the province of "colored" citizens, the shabbier neighborhoods being their domain. White people have tended to have a greater percentage of better and more varied jobs and, in many instances, finer homes in better neighborhoods. The sociological importance of such a correlation lies in the fact that it is culturally, not biologically, determined. There is nothing in their nature that predisposes non-White citizens to a life of inferior status. There is much, however, in the *social image* of their nature, which largely determines their place in the social structure. In the minds of some Americans:

> A black-type person and a white-type person, they ain't alike. Now the black-type person, all they think about is fighting and having a good time and you know what. Now the white-type person is more the American-type. . . . [9]

As W. I. Thomas has written, "If men define situations as real, they are real in their consequences." When given inferior positions in the social order, individuals often reflect in their attitudes and behavior the status imposed upon them.[10] Shingoro Takaishi, the Japanese writer, discussing the subordinate status of Japanese women, illustrates this notion of the self-fulfilling prophecy:

> The education of our women was neglected, and her intelligence became more and more narrow owing to there being little or no chance for her to see things in the outer world. The next thing which was bound to happen was man's contempt and disdain for her narrow-mindedness and stupidity.[11]

In similar fashion, certain people considered by many to have lower potentialities than others are given low-status, poor-paying jobs, and are denied equal opportunities for achievement. Excluded and often embittered, lacking in advantages and limited in their access to employment and schooling, they may in fact reflect in their behavior and attitudes the stereotypes held by those in dominant positions.[12]

Ethnic Groups

It has been said that "man is separated from man, not only by real or assumed physiological traits, but by differences of group traditions, national or regional or religious, that may or may not be associated with biological distinctions."[13] Groups whose members share a unique social and cultural heritage passed on from one generation to the next are known as *ethnic groups*. Ethnic groups are frequently identified by distinctive patterns of family life, language, recreation, religion, and other customs that cause them to be differentiated from others.[14] They often live—by choice or because of the requirements of others—in their own enclaves, ghettos, or neighborhoods. Above all else, members of such groups feel a consciousness of kind[15] and an interdependence of fate[16] with those who share the customs of the ethnic tradition. Members of different ethnic groups may look very much alike (think of the Catholics and Protestants in Northern Ireland or the Arabs and Jews in Jerusalem) but have very different views of the world and of their roles in it.

In America, members of some ethnic groups or their ancestors may have come from a common homeland, as in the case of Italian-, Irish-, and Mexican-Americans. Such groups are often referred to as "nationalities." Some ethnic-group members, however, like Jews or Gypsies, are joined by common traditions and experiences that cut across political boundaries; they are frequently known as "peoples."

In some societies distinctions are even more complicated. In Israel nationality officially denotes ethnic background. An Israeli citizen may be an Arab or a Jew by nationality; an Arab may be a Moslem or a Christian by religion. However, it is argued that Judaism is the only religion whose adherents belong to a single "nation" and Jews are the only "nation" with a single religion; some say that Jews *anywhere* belong to one nation while holding citizenship in a particular country like Israel or the United States or the Soviet Union.

In a society made up of many cultural groups, like the United States, the intensity of ethnic identity or *ethnicity* is apt to be determined by the attitude of the members of the "host" society toward the "strangers" in their midst. This attitude, in turn, is often dependent upon how closely the ethnic group approximates the culture of the dominant society. Acceptance may loosen the bonds of ethnic identity, as in the case of Scottish and German immigrants to America; rejection and subordination may strengthen them,[17] as among Mexican-Americans or African-Americans today.

The relationship between membership in an ethnic group and social acceptance has been studied by many sociologists. They concur in the conclusion that "when the combined cultural and biological traits [of the ethnic group] are highly divergent from those of the host society the subordination of the group will be very great, their sub-system strong, the period of assimilation long, and the processes slow and usually painful."[18] (It should be noted that this widely expressed view is based on the assumption that "assimilation" is the goal of most minority peoples. As shall be pointed out, many voices recently have been raised seriously questioning the ideology that underlies what the critics would see as a classic case of liberal dogma.[19])

Minorities

In 1932, Donald Young, writing about group relations in the United States, stated: "There is, unfortunately, no word in the English language which can . . . be applied to all these groups which are distinguished by biological features, alike national traits, or a combination of both."[20] He proposed "minority," a term that had been used in a related but different context. Earlier, "minority group" had been applied to subsegments of European societies inhabited by conquered persons or those incorporated by annexation to another national group. The multifarious peoples of the Soviet Union and many Western European countries represent such minorities.

Since Young's adoption, the term *minority* has been used by sociologists to refer to those groups whose members share certain racial or ethnic similarities that are considered to be different from or inferior to the traits of the dominant group and who are thereby "singled out for differential and unequal treatment."[21] In recent years the term has been used in a related but more limited sense. The U.S. government, and its various agencies, label only those in specified categories—African-Americans, Asian-Americans, Hispanic-Americans, and Native Americans—as "minorities." In this book, while we will discuss the reasoning behind such arbitrary designations, the term wil be used much in the manner Young intended.

A decade ago, Graham Kinloch suggested the mere existence of racial and ethnic minority groups raises a number of issues relating to their relationship to those in the dominant society in terms of social organization, patterns and mechanisms of social control, basic cultural values, levels of societal development, and indices of social change.[22]

To be sure, racial and ethnic groups are not the only ones "singled out for differential and unequal treatment." Of late, many people have been categorized in similar fashion—women, children, the aged, the poor, the disabled, homosexuals, and various types of social deviants, sometimes called "behavioral minorities."[23] While fully cognizant of the problems encountered by those groups and the many similarities relating to their treatment—including the phenomena of being variously stigmatized, criticized, ostracized, and discriminated against in different ways, our attention is focused on those originally considered by Donald Young, the members of racial and ethnic bodies.

Statistical underrepresentation does not, in itself, explain why a racial or ethnic group is considered a minority in the sociological sense. It is not even a necessary condition. In the Republic of South Africa, for example, the black minority far outnumbers the white rulers. Prior to independence in Algeria the community of colonists was very small compared with the native "minority" group. Until recently, a limited number of Europeans dominated "minority" peoples in the Dutch East Indies (now Indonesia), in the Belgian Congo (now the Republic of Zaire), and in the tiny Portuguese outpost of Goa on the western coast of the Indian subcontinent. In many towns in the southern states of this country Black people constitute the largest ethnic element in the population but remain a sociological minority.

R. A. Schermerhorn has suggested that to understand best what he calls "dominant-subordinate relationships" it is useful to consider two main issues: relative size and relative power.[24] Schermerhorn divides both dominant and subordinate groups into sub-categories. In the first, there are mass subjects and minorities. These are graphically portrayed in the following diagram:

	Dominant Groups		
	Size	Power	
Group A	+	−	Majority
Group B	−	+	Elites
	Subordinate Groups		
Group C	+	−	Mass subjects
Group D	−	−	Minority[25]

While extremely useful, there is one problem with the Schermerhorn typology. Neither dominant nor subordinate status is fixed or immutable. Not only is it possible that a majority group (in his terms) in one place may be a strategic elite in another (one thinks of Chinese on the mainland and in Malaysia) but a subordinate group in one country may itself be dominant in another. The position of Jews in the Soviet Union and in Israel, of French-Canadians living in New England and in the Province of Quebec, and of "ethnic" Chinese in Jamaica, the Philippines, and Vietnam, compared to those in the People's Republic of China, are cases in point.

In most Western societies the power-holding group is made up of persons having "white" skins and professing a belief in Christianity. In the United States the dominant group consists largely of white individuals of North European background who belong to one of the Protestant denominations (people sometimes referred to as WASPs—white, Anglo-Saxon Protestants). This "majority group" has traditionally been the determining element in public policy. In language, customs, and moral codes, these descendants of early settlers have set the standards for American behavior. Moreover, they have generally determined which groups are to be considered minorities and how each shall be treated.

The American Case

There is good reason for choosing the United States as the focal point for a study of racial and ethnic relations. Few nations can match the heterogeneous quality of American society. No other modern society can claim a history characterized so markedly by the importation of foreign ways and ideologies. All Americans (including the Indians) are of immigrant origin. In Walt Whitman's terms, America is truly "a nation of nations."

The history of this country bears witness to the fact that the accommodation of many racial and ethnic groups has been an essential element in developing and perpetuating the spirit of democracy.[26] Ralph Linton once described the extent of foreign influence when he wrote: "Our solid American citizen . . . reads the news of the day, imprinted in characters invented by the ancient Semites upon a material invented in China by a process invented in Germany . . . and as he absorbs the accounts of foreign troubles he will, if he is a good conservative citizen, thank a Hebrew deity in an Indo-European language that he is 100 percent American."[27]

The influence of European (and, to a lesser extent, Asian and African) culture on America is easy to recognize. This is, however, but one side of the picture, for the very presence of newcomers has, in each generation, often provoked the resentment and suspicion of those already here. America has not been immune from group hatred and discrimination. Throughout its history there have been those who have persisted in denying their fellow citizens the right to full participation in American life, who wished to maintain a society where the "right" skin color or religious preference or cultural heritage was considered to be an essential requisite to acceptance on an equal basis.

Gunnar Myrdal, the Swedish social scientist, thus characterized the United States as a nation possessing a wide gulf between the democratic ideal of brotherhood and the overt manifestations of intergroup conflict.[28] The American creed of freedom and equality of opportunity for all has been, and continues to be, violated by the acts of many citizens. This "American dilemma" remains evident; but the problems that beset minorities in this country are far more complex than the simple discrepancy between the national ethos and individual behavior. As sociologist Robert K. Merton has suggested, the failure to recognize the intricacies of these problems tends so "to simplify the relations between creed and conduct as to be seriously misleading both for social policy and for social science."[29]

Between the prescription set forth in the Preamble to the Constitution and the Bill of Rights and the actual behavior of many people, there exists a wide range of standards for behavior, which vary markedly from group to group, from place to place, and from time to time. The formal and informal policies of a region, state, and local community; the social, economic, religious, and political groups to which one belongs; the attitudes of parents, teachers, and peers; and the demands of particular intergroup and interpersonal situations *all* greatly influence the way in which individuals act towards others. Some of these complexities are analyzed in the following chapters.

NOTES

1. Robert M. MacIver, *Social Causation* (Boston: Ginn, 1942), p. 148.
2. Michael Lerner, "Respectable Bigotry," *American Scholar* (August 1969), and John McDermott, "Laying On of Culture," *The Nation* (March 10, 1969).
3. For a summary of sociological approaches see Peter I. Rose, *The Subject Is Race* (New York: Oxford University Press, 1968), pp. 3–80. See also Michael Banton, *Race Relations* (New York: Basic Books, 1967), pp. 1–77 ff.; and James W. Vander Zanden, *American Minority Relations* (New York: Knopf, 4th edition, 1983) pp. 3–31.
4. For a good summary of varied systems of social stratification, see Kurt B. Mayer and Walter Buckley, *Class and Society*, 3rd ed. (New York: Random House, 1970), Chaps. 1 and 20.
5. Kurt B. Mayer, *Class and Society*, rev. ed. (New York: Random House, 1955), p. 30.
6. See, for example, Douglas G. Haring, "Racial Differences and Human Resemblances," in M. L. Barron (ed.), *American Minorities* (New York: Knopf, 1957), pp. 33–39.
7. For some further views on the use of the term "race" see Ashley Montagu, "The Concept of Race," *American Anthropologist*, 64 (October 1962), 919–928; Juan Comas, "Scientific Racism Again?" *Current Anthropology*, 2 (October 1961), 303–340; Manning Nash, "Race and the Ideology of Race," *Current Anthropology*, 3 (June 1962), 285; and Marvin Harris, "Race," in *International Encyclopedia of the Social Sciences* (New York: Macmillan, 1968), Vol. XIII, p. 263.
8. U.S. Bureau of the Census, 1960 *Census of Population, Supplementary Reports*, PC (S1)-10, Washington, D.C., September 7, 1962, p. 2.
9. Robert Penn Warren, quoting a Nashville taxi driver, in *Segregation: The Inner Conflict in the South* (New York: Random House, 1956), p. 11. See also Ruth Landes, "Biracialism in American Society," *American Anthropologist*, 57 (December 1955), 1253–1263.
10. See Robert K. Merton. "The Self-Fulfilling Prophecy," *The Antioch Review*, 8 (Summer 1948), 192–210. Merton says that "the public definitions of a situation (prophecies and predictions) become an integral part of the situation and thus affect subsequent developments."
11. The original source of this quotation appears in the Introduction to Kaibara Ekken, *Greater Learning for Women*, and appears in David and Vera Mace, *Marriage East and West* (New York: Doubleday, 1960), p. 78.
12. The effect of this situation on the development of anti-black sentiments is, in part, the basis of Norman Podhoretz's controversial essay, "My Negro Problem—And Ours," *Commentary*, 35 (February 1963), 93–101. Also see "Letters from Readers," *Commentary*, 35 (April 1963), 338–347.
13. Robert M. MacIver and Charles H. Page, *Society: An Introductory Analysis* (New York: Rinehart, 1949), p. 386. See also Robin M. Williams, Jr., *The Reduction of Intergroup Tensions* (New York: The Social Science Research Council, 1947), p. 42.
14. Max Weber, *Economy and Society*, Guenther Roth and Claus Wittich (eds.) (New York: Bedminster Press, 1968), pp. 387–398. For discussions of Weber's

views of ethnicity, see Howard M. Bahr, Bruce A. Chadwick, and Joseph H. Stauss, *American Ethnicity* (Lexington, Mass: D. C. Heath, 1979), pp. 4–6.

15. See Andrew M. Greeley, *Why Can't They Be Like Us?* (New York: Dutton, 1971), pp. 120–121.
16. See Kurt Lewin, *Resolving Social Conflicts* (New York: Harper, 1948), Chaps. 10 to 12.
17. See, for example, J. Milton Yinger, "Social Forces Involved in Group Identification and Withdrawal," *Daedalus*, 90 (Spring 1961), 247–262; and Charles F. Marden and Gladys Meyer, *Minorities in American Society*, 2nd ed. (New York: American Book Company, 1962), p. 26.
18. Lloyd Warner and Leo Srole, *The Social System of American Ethnic Groups* (New Haven: Yale University Press, 1954), p. 286.
19. See L. Paul Metzger, "American Sociology and Black Assimilation: Conflicting Perspectives," *American Journal of Sociology*, 76 (January 1971), 627–647.
20. Donald Young, *American Minority Peoples* (New York: Harper, 1932), p. xiii.
21. Louis Wirth, "The Problems of Minority Groups," in Ralph Linton (ed.), *The Science of Man in the World Crisis* (New York: Columbia University Press, 1945), pp. 3–7. MacIver and Page state that "even when mere recognition of difference is all that marks the relationship between groups—an inevitable situation in complex society—there is a necessary antithesis between the 'they' and the 'we,' between in-group and out-group." See MacIver and Page, *op. cit.*, p. 387.
22. Graham C. Kinloch, *The Sociology of Minority Groups* (Englewood Cliffs, N.J.: Prentice-Hall, 1979), pp. 11–13.
23. For a more detailed discussion see Kinloch, *op. cit.*, esp. pp. 33–46.
24. R. A. Schermerhorn, *Comparative Ethnic Relations: A Framework for Theory and Research* (New York: Random House, 1970), pp. 12–13.
25. *Ibid.*, p. 13.
26. See, for example, Oscar Handlin, "Historical Perspectives on the American Ethnic Group," *Daedalus*, 90 (Spring 1961), 220–232. See also Maxine Seller, *To Seek America* (Englewood, N.J.: Jerome S. Ozer, 1977), pp. 1–13.
27. Ralph Linton, *The Study of Man* (New York: Appleton-Century-Crofts, 1936), pp. 326–327.
28. Gunnar Myrdal, *An American Dilemma* (New York: Harper 1944), Chap. I.
29. Robert K. Merton, "Discrimination and the American Creed," in Robert M. MacIver (ed.), *Discrimination and National Welfare* (New York: Harper, 1949), p. 99. See also Ernest Q. Campbell, "Moral Discomfort and Racial Segregation—An Examination of the Myrdal Hypothesis," *Social Forces*, 39 (March 1961), 228–234; and Nahum Z. Medalia, "Assumptions on Race Relations: A Conceptual Commentary," *Social Forces*, 40 (March 1962), 223–227.

2

A NATION OF IMMIGRANTS

Origins

While a detailed description of the origins of the American people is not an aim of this volume[1] a brief review of American racial and ethnic history and the kaleidoscopic changes that have occurred since the days of the first settlement should help to provide a baseline for analysis of the contemporary scene. This chapter presents brief résumés of the experiences of American Indians, European colonists, Africans, and the more recent immigrant groups from across the Atlantic, the Pacific, and the Rio Grande.

The First Americans

All Americans are of immigrant stock, including the "indigenous" Indian population. The ancestors of today's American Indians were Mongolian migrants who crossed over from Asia and began to disperse in a southward and southeastward direction about 20,000 years ago. For many centuries they were the sole inhabitants of the land taken over and, in time, overrun by Europeans.

It is estimated that in the days before the conquests began 1,500,000 Indians occupied the territory now comprising the United States and Canada and that as many as 30 to 40 million Indians were living in the Western Hemisphere.[2] Hundreds of different tribal groups speaking many different tongues inhabited the forests, plains, deserts, and mountain ranges of the Americas. A wide range of culture patterns marked their differing social structures, and their political organizations were as divergent as those of modern industrial societies.[3] There never was a characteristic or single Indian culture of the kind frequently fictionalized by novelists and scenario writers.

The vast majority of Native Americans did, however, share in common the fact that the conquerers—who often treated them as one people (misnamed "Indians" by Columbus, who thought he was somewhere else)—markedly influenced their customary ways, and many tribes suffered the humiliation of being dispossessed from their traditional areas of domain. From almost the first excursions to the New World, many tribal groups were mistreated and abused by Whites—first by Spaniards seeking to extort riches from them and to convert them to Christianity, later by Englishmen who initially placated and then coerced them into retreating from their lands.

In many ways, Spanish policy, in North America at least, was more benign than that of the English. Spanish *conquistadores* and their cadres consisted of single men who came from a part of the world where racial mixing was not uncommon and fraternization with native women was not at all repugnant. Moreover, as Catholics, they felt an obligation to urge the Indians to accept Christianity and participate in the sacraments. English settlers had very different ideas about color and religion and this was reflected in their abhorrence of intimate intercourse with the natives and the reluctance of many to see them as "brothers in Christ."[4]

In the early days of colonial rule, each community of settlers dealt with the Indians in its own way. Some tried to make treaties, others established trade relationships, and still others fought to maintain their holdings in Indian territory. In 1754 a general policy was established by the British Crown that took decision and jurisdiction away from local communities and from the various colonial administrations. The tribes were to be recognized as "independent nations under the protection of the Crown; Indian lands were inalienable except through voluntary surrender to the Crown; any attempt by an individual or group, subject to the Crown, or by a foreign state, to buy or seize lands from Indians, was illegal."[5] Attempts to implement this new policy met with strong resistance from many settlers. Some writers, reviewing the situation, have suggested that this conflict indirectly contributed to the American Revolution itself.[6]

As the frontier moved westward and homesteaders hungered for land for cultivation and grazing, the policies of the new American government vacillated between attempts at bilateral negotiations with the members of the so-called sovereign Indian nations and outright massacre and removal. What could not be accomplished by treaty—such as the Congressional Indian Removal Act of 1830, which specified that consent of the natives or their leaders was required by those to be moved to new territories—was accomplished by military force. In the first half of the nineteenth century, thousands of Indians from eastern states were transported, often under brutal conditions, to the territories of the West. It is reported that one-third of the Cherokees, who in 1838 were driven from their homes in North Carolina and Georgia, died en route to Oklahoma. Their route is still referred to as the "Trail of Tears."

Pierre van den Berghe reminds us that

The California gold rush was the final phase of the territorial expansion of the United States by a process of land encroachment and frontier wars between white settlers and a small number of Indian groups. It took several more decades to beat the last remnants of the indigenous population into total submission and to reduce the last Indian lands to the status of human zoos for the amusement of tourists and the delights of anthropologists.[7]

Van den Berghe's bitter reflection suggests that few were any longer interested in the fate of the original Americans, save for their own selfish motives. This is an exaggeration—but only a slight one.

After the Civil War attempts were made to resolve the "Indian problem" by means of government reservations established for the alleged purpose of assimilating the now subdued and severely depressed Indians. In 1871 Congress ruled that henceforth no Indian tribe would be recognized as an independent power. All Indians became wards of the federal government. Federal agents were to help the tribes adjust to reservation life and to farming. Yet, as should have been foreseen, adjustment proved difficult since both land ownership and agriculture were foreign ideas to a number of Indian peoples. Moreover, the programs to educate them to efficient land utilization were woefully inadequate. The provisions of the General Allotment Act of 1887 (also known as the Dawes Act) gave every male Indian the right to a tract of land (40 to 160 acres) to be kept in possession and not sold for 25 years. Because the property was to be divided equally among his heirs upon the death of the landholder, however, each succeeding generation necessarily would have less and less land to till. This situation provoked the comment: "Indians sometimes live a long time, and when Old Charlie Yellowtail dies at the age of ninety-nine, the number of heirs may be something little less than astronomical. Forty acres of land divided among, say 120 heirs, gives each just about enough room to pitch a tepee."[8]

The story of Wounded Knee was but one episode in a series of tragedies that ultimately spelled the complete subjugation and humiliation of proud Indian nations, in this case the Sioux of the Dakotas. Plainsmen and hunters, the Sioux had been steadily pushed onto reservations by government troops. In 1890, rumors of uprisings brought the wrath of the cavalry. It was described by Black Elk, an eyewitness, as follows:

Men and women and children were heaped and scattered all over the flat at the bottom of the little hill where the soldiers had their wagon-guns, and westward up the dry gulch all the way to the high-ridge, the dead women and children and babies were scattered. . . . It was a good winter day when all this happened. The sun was shining. But after the soldiers marched away from their dirty work, a heavy snow began to fall. . . . There was a big blizzard, and it grew very cold. The snow drifted deep in the crooked gulch, and it was one long grave of butchered women and children and babies, who had never done any harm and were only trying to run away.[9]

They couldn't, nor could many others. Reservation life created many problems of adjustment—and sheer survival—for the Indian residents. Moreover, their removal from the mainstream of life had other consequences. For those in areas where the competition of truly emancipated Indians would have constituted an economic threat (as in the northern plains states, the Pacific Northwest, or the desert areas of New Mexico and Arizona), the reservations provided places for finally putting to rest Indian claims on land and jobs. For missionaries and anthropologists they provided a locus for proselytizing and research. For most Americans the reservations began to be seen as living museums where part of our rich heritage was to be preserved in perpetuity.

Few Americans were aware of the true conditions of life in these places of perpetual internment, nor did they fathom the extent to which even the idea of preservation of traditional ways was disallowed by paradoxical "assimilationist" policies that demanded the sloughing off of Indian ways and the adopting of new ones—with rarely so much as a lick or a promise of where one might enjoy life in the new American mode. The farcical character of the whole charade was made clearly evident as more and more Hollywood film makers and Eastern commentators romanticized the life of the Indian. No longer solely objects of derogation, the "red men" came to be viewed as a heroic people, living reminders of a glorious past. In some circles it even became fashionable to boast of possessing "Indian blood."

On June 2, 1924, America's original residents were finally granted citizenship. Four years later the Institute for Government Research published a report on "The Problems of Indian Administration," pointing out the dismal failure of assimilationist policy and setting forth bold recommendations. At last somebody seemed to be caring.

When John Collier became Commissioner of Indian Affairs in 1933, a new program was instituted to permit the Indians to retain their traditions without the overwhelming imposition of "white" ways. The Indian Reorganization Act of 1934 also permitted Indians to sell their land to tribal members, to establish tribal councils to manage local affairs, and to incorporate into self-governing units. Since then progress has been very uneven. Some Indians have made significant gains. Here and there fallow lands have been irrigated and erosion halted. In some places education has been improved, especially with the long overdue demise of the assimilationist boarding schools. Birth rates have dramatically increased and death rates have declined as health and welfare problems are being dealt with more effectively through such government agencies as the Public Health Service, which took over health services from the Bureau of Indian Affairs in 1955.[10] Yet the same Bureau of Indian Affairs (a branch of the Department of the Interior) still maintains administrative control over most Native Americans, now numbering approximately one million, the large majority of whom live on reservations, two-thirds of them concentrated in the states of Oklahoma, Arizona, New Mexico, and the Dakotas.

The government's policies have vacillated significantly since the Reorganization Act more or less reversed the orientation of the Dawes Act. While the general thrust has been toward greater self-determination, this has been a mixed blessing. For example, in the 1950s, attempts were made to terminate all special arrangements and obligations. If implemented, such plans would have meant the severing of all ties to the Federal Government and the loss of lands as well. They were never put into effect. However, a more positive approach was institutionalized in the Self-Determination and Educational Assistance Act of 1975, the terms of which gave tribal leaders the rights to allocate federal funds to serve the special needs of their peoples.[11] Even with this new and seemingly enlightened policy, there are problems—problems of communication between local agents and the bureaucrats in Washington, between younger and older Indian spokespersons, between traditional leaders and more radical ones, often including those involved in pan-Indian activities such as those of AIM, the American Indian Movement.

Over the years many young Indians thought it best to leave the reservations and the villages to settle in the cities. Some were among the best trained and the most success-oriented and they took their skills and talents with them, leaving a vacuum behind. Most, however, were poor who, like other impoverished peoples, sought the opportunities they expected to be available in the urban centers. Yet in spite of the fact that some were integrated into the general community and found employment in specialized trades (for example, the high-steel workers among the Mohawks), most of those who relinquished their status as wards of the government suffered the plight of other "colored" minorities. Figures are difficult to obtain but estimates suggest that almost as many Indians are living in cities as on reservations. Most urban Indians are concentrated in metropolitan areas on the West Coast, in the Southwest, and the Midwest. There are, however, as many as 15,000 in New York City, mostly Mohawks but many from the West—"Hopi from Arizona, Navajo from New Mexico, Creek from Oklahoma, Blackfeet from Montana, and others. . . . "[12] Discriminatory practices in all of these places continue to limit severely opportunities for advancement and achievement.

For those who remain on the reservations life continues to be harsh.[13] In spite of the improvements that have taken place in recent decades, Indians remain members of a depressed minority situated in the bottom tenth of the economic hierarchy. As recently as 1970 the Census of Population showed that the average Indian had but five years of schooling, that the family income was only $1,500 per year, and that his rate of unemployment was a miserable 45 percent.

Some young Native Americans did not wait to see the 1970 census figures. They knew what was happening and many decided to fight. Following, and in many ways attempting to emulate, Black militants, representatives of different tribal groups have formed "Red Power" organizations as both cultural centers and bases for challenging the system that in their view does little of a positive nature and much that is destructive to Indian peoples.

In some areas the loose confederation of Indian militants gained notoriety and limited success. Perhaps the most dramatic cases were the invasion and occupation of the abandoned island of Alcatraz and its empty prison buildings in 1970, the takeover of the Bureau itself in Washington in 1972, the two-month siege of Wounded Knee in 1973, and the bloody skirmish at the Red Lake Reservation in Minnesota in 1979 in which two Chippewas were killed in the confrontation with federal authorities. Other attempts to dramatize their cause, to bring all Indians together, or to effect change have been less successful. One of the many reasons for this record is the important fact that Pan-Indianism is a new idea. Most Native Americans do not see themselves as brothers to members of distant (or sometimes even proximate) tribes. They are Navaho or Seminole or Cherokee or Sioux, not "Indians." And they often have very different notions of what they want and where they want to go. Still, there is a growing belief that all are owed reparations—of land, money, and respect.

In recent years legal suits have been filed to regain large tracts of land, especially in Maine and Massachusetts, several western states, and Alaska. In some instances, settlements out of court ended in "buying off" the Native American plaintiffs. This "buying off" is, of course, an old story, going back to colonial days.

The Colonists

For many years a debate has persisted over who first "discovered" America. Some have claimed that it was the Viking leader Leif Ericson who first set foot on these shores in 1004 A.D. Most people favor the view that it was Christopher Columbus, the Genoese sea captain whose several voyages were financed by King Ferdinand and Queen Isabella of Spain. A few people even argue that ancient Jews sailed across the Atlantic long before Ericson or Columbus; this claim is based on the shaky evidence of the discovery in Tennessee of several large rocks with seeming Hebrew inscriptions.

The debate is, at bottom, often not much more than a game of ethnic one-upmanship. (Rumor has it that one prominent Italian-American jurist sought to raise money to hire his own historian to descredit "Norsophiles" at Yale University who claimed to have discovered an old Viking chart of the eastern coast, the "Vinland Map.") The debate is also quite academic, for whichever European first set foot in America, he was not the original discoverer. There were people living on the North American continent for thousands of years, long before *any* European crossed the Atlantic Ocean. The irony is that the Indians do not even receive credit for getting here first.

The first nationals to lay claim to substantial portions of American soil were the Spanish *conquistadores* who penetrated the southwestern sector of what was to become part of the United States and who established settlements on the Florida peninsula. Unlike the British who were to follow, the Spaniards mingled extensively with the native populations and frequently cohabited with Indian women. They left an indelible impression upon southwestern and Floridian culture. Their descendants, the Hispanos of mixed Spanish and Indian ancestry, are still to be found in the Southwest, especially in New Mexico. Had the Spaniards remained in power, intergroup problems, attitudes toward minority populations, and patterns of discriminations would undoubtedly have assumed characteristics different from those that now exist. But this was not their destiny.

After the defeat of the Spanish Armada in 1588, rival nations began to establish and develop territories in the Western Hemisphere. Under the auspices of the West India Company the Dutch established trading posts in both North and South America—on the coast of Brazil, in the Antilles, at the estuary of the Hudson River (New York nee New Amsterdam), and northward along its banks (Fort Albany). Holland's control over these territories were short-lived, but the Dutch legacy lingers on, especially in the folklore and history of New York State and in the names of many famous families—Roosevelt, Vander Heuvel, Rensselaer, Vliet. (Moreover the Dutch left the English with a label—"Yankees"—an anglicized version of "Jan Kees," a sort of bumpkin.) In 1654 Holland lost her foothold in Brazil and, only a decade later, New Netherlands and Delaware[14] became British possessions.

France, too, had colonial ambitions in America and sent explorers and missionaries to stake out new lands. Eastern Canada and the huge Louisiana Territory came under French domination. Bitter warfare brought an end to French rule over Canada; the Louisiana Purchase (1803) ended French control over the Mississippi Valley and the Northwest territories. Yet, French nationalism powerfully persists in the Canadian province of Quebec where the majority of citizens are Roman Catholic, speak the French language, and retain many French customs. In the United States today, thousands of French-Canadians reside in New England, especially in Maine, Massachusetts, and New Hampshire, and many of their transplanted relatives variously called Acadians or "Cajuns" still live in Louisiana. There the imprint of France is seen in architecture and festivals such as the famed Mardi Gras. Moreover, the contributions of French intellectuals, including descendants of the Huguenots, is still apparent.

But it was England that become the supreme colonial power in North America. The English colonists consisted of tradesmen and fortune seekers, civil administrators and political refugees, religious dissenters and petty criminals. For the first time a large group of common folk crossed the Atlantic to settle here. Unlike the early explorers from Spain and France, they came in family groups, often with others from their home towns. In several cases entire communities moved from the British Isles to America.

The establishment of British America was a struggle from its inception. The death toll—from the hardships endured en route, from diseases that plagued the settlers after arrival, from marauding Indians who attacked their villages—was exceedingly high. And for those who survived these hazards there were other problems.

Religious prejudices were transplanted from the mother country to New England and the mid-Atlantic colonies. Colonists often were set against one another in their desire to maintain their particular brand of Christianity. Fighting the invisible ogres of blasphemy, heresy, and sin, colonists perpetrated persecutions as acts of faith, the victims often being members of minority sects—Quakers, Unitarians, Roman Catholics, and others.[15]

In addition to the former residents of England who constituted the largest portion of settlers, there were the Presbyterians from North Ireland, the Scotch-Irish, and the German refugees from the ravages of the Thirty Years' War. Small groups of Frenchmen, Welshmen, Irish-Catholics, and Sephardic Jews (of Spanish and Portuguese descent) were also numbered among the early colonists. Together, these North Europeans laid the cornerstone of modern American society and formed the basis of the "native" White majority.

Despite the immigration of millions of southern and eastern Europeans and thousands of Asians, Africans, and Latin Americans in the late years of the nineteenth century and the first quarter of the twentieth century, and of thousands more Asians and Latin Americans since 1965, White Anglo-Saxon Protestants still constitute the most powerful element in the population of the United States.

Americans from Africa

The first people of African descent to come to America arrived in 1619. Brought originally to Virginia and later to other colonies they were, like many Whites, indentured servants. Servitude was not uncommon in the middle colonies and these black-skinned newcomers did not occupy a unique status. Some gained their freedom after serving their masters for a specified period of time; others became free through conversion to Christianity. Most remained as "unfree" men and women, but even they were not considered to be slaves. In fact, neither Virginia nor any of the other colonies of British America had yet recognized the institution of chattel slavery.

By the 1660s the conditions of Blacks began to deteriorate. The expansion of agriculture and the growing demand for a large and cheap labor force brought slavery to American shores. Africans, wrenched from their native villages and sold into bondage by Spaniards and Englishmen, by Muslims and Christians, and, sometimes, by fellow Africans, were taken to coastal ports to be transported under the most brutal conditions imaginable to the islands of the Caribbean and to the port cities of the east coast of America. Many died of disease, hunger, and melancholia en route; many—some say the lucky ones—by throwing themselves overboard or by inviting execution by proving too intractable. Once in the New World, the survivors were sold at auction. One such slave, Olaudah Equiano, told his own story in a journal published in the 1770s. There he related how he had been captured, put aboard a slave ship, witnessed and experienced brutal treatment, was taken to Barbados, put on the auction block and sold.

> After a few days we were sold in the usual way, which is this: A signal is given, such as the beating of a drum. Buyers rush into the yard where the slaves are kept. They choose the group the like best. The general noise, and the eagerness of the buyers, increases the fears of the Africans. They regard the buyers as the people who have come to destroy them.
>
> With no feeling at all, people separate relations and friends. Most of them never see each other again. In the ship that brought me over, there were several brothers. In the sale, they were sold to different buyers. They cried when they were parted.[16]

Stories such as Equiano's have become better known in recent years through various popular accountings and television series such as that based on Alex Haley's *Roots*, a controversial historical novel.[17]

By the middle of the eighteenth century the practice of slavery was legalized in every English colony in America. In some places the new laws were soon rescinded. In fact, with the emergence of the United States as an independent nation, the slavery issue became the subject of congressional and local debate. The northern states began fairly early to abolish the practice by law, beginning with Pennsylvania where the Assembly, under the prodding of Thomas Paine, passed the first act for the emancipation of Negro slaves on March 1, 1780. Others followed suit.

In the South, however, the system was maintained intact. The "peculiar institution" had become a mainstay of the economic structure, and what some have called a "slavocracy" characterized a large section dominated by dependence on plantation labor.[18] There had been a brief period in the second half of the eighteenth century when declining profits in tobacco (the principal cash crop) seemed to portend a change in the social arrangements, but the invention of the cotton gin in 1793 and the rapid development of the British textile industry not only forestalled the anticipated change but made the southern planters even more intransigent.

The conditions under which the slaves lived and worked varied considerably not only from one region to another (the upper South as compared with the Piedmont or the Mississippi Delta) but also depended upon the size and character of the plantations themselves. Moreover, even within slave communities there was a definite stratification. Some Blacks worked in the house of their masters, benefited from special treatment, and found themselves trapped between the world toward which they often aspired and that which they knew just beyond the big yard. Others, the majority, were field hands who did the grueling work of planting the seeds and picking the cotton and chopping the stalks and clearing the fields and planting and picking and chopping again in a never-ending cycle of back-breaking toil. Women and children, as well as men, sweated their lives away in the fields.

Moreover, life in slave quarters was tempered and molded by events beyond the control of those forced to live there. Family life, for example, frequently meant the special bonds that existed between mothers and young children.[19] Social activities were narrowly circumscribed. Freedom in all phases of life was highly limited. Yet, as in any local community (even prison camps), a way of life did emerge which, significantly, included patterns of adaptation that permitted Blacks to cope with the system of enforced slavery. Thus, their customs often involved ways of playing the closed system to their (slight) advantage. Blacks learned to sabotage, to feign illness, and to clown. They also tried to shield their children from their inevitable fate (sometimes by actually taking their lives).[20] Rarely was the system attacked directly. It was simply too dangerous.

For a number of years a debate has been waged by scholars of the period—old-liners and revisionists, White and Black—over the question of how the slaves actually fared and how they survived. Some argue, for example, that even with the now widely conceded recognition that there was some sort of "slave culture," Blacks still internalized the low status in which they were held and came to see themselves as inferior to whites. Others have said they never fully succumbed. That debate continues.

What is undisputed is the fact that by the 1830s slavery was beginning to come under severe attack. Many southerners, in order to justify their continued subjugation of the Africans, invoked the doctrine of racial superiority. Earlier, few had argued that the Negro slaves were biologically inferior and a menace to white society, but they did so now. Moreover, they underscored the idea that, as "property," the slave had no rights that whites were bound to respect. Even the Supreme Court was to support this argument when it upheld the finding of a lower court in the famous Dred Scott decision of 1857. Dred Scott, a slave, having been taken into a territory that prohibited slavery, considered himself a free man under the rules of the Missouri Compromise. The Court claimed that the compromise was unconstitutional since "Congress has no right to enact a law which deprived persons of their property in the territories of the United States." Even so, there was great agitation to rid the nation of the institution of slavery and a powerful movement for abolition emerged in the North led by such white spokesmen as John Brown and such free Blacks as Frederick Douglass.

Ultimately the slavery issue was to be resolved in the midst of the bloody Civil War. While President Lincoln insisted in the beginning that the war had nothing to do with slavery as such (indeed, early in the war Union soldiers returned slaves to their masters under flags of truce), the matter became one of central concern. In terribly oversimplified terms, the South fought to defend its way of life, which depended significantly on the slave system; the North fought to keep the Union whole. In a short time the emancipation of slaves was regarded as necessary, first politically and then morally, to achieve the northern objective.

On January 1, 1863, by Executive Order, the President issued the Emancipation Proclamation. All slaves in the United States (referring to the rebellious Confederacy as well as the rest of the Union) were declared free—though not yet equal. Equality was to come with the Thirteenth Amendment to the Constitution. By the summer of 1863 the Union Army sought Black recruits to fight for their country, and it is estimated that close to 200,000 eventually donned uniforms, half of them to see action on the battlefield.

At the end of the war Black Codes were proposed. These were laws that would give Negroes legal rights to marry and bear witness in a court of law but not, for example, to own land or to work in particular trades. The codes were never put into effect. Other measures were.

During Reconstruction the African-Americans gained equal status in law and, in many places, they did so in fact. A civil rights bill was passed by Congress in 1866, but vetoed by Lincoln's successor, President Andrew Johnson. In 1868, a million Blacks were enfranchised. Yet, the surge toward equal rights in the decade after the war began to wane and Radical Reconstruction, maintained in large part by federal forces, proved to be but a temporary interlude between slavery and institutional segregation.

Although the Sumner Act of 1875 secured equal rights in public transportation, in hotels, and in theaters and other places of amusement, it was to be declared unconstitutional by an eight to one decision of the Supreme Court in 1883. Soon, what many diehard southerners saw as their redemption, the reinstitution of White power over Blacks, was to be fully under way. The era of segregation officially began with the Hayes-

Tilden Compromise of 1876. Hayes, an Ohio Republican, won the Presidency in an electoral college victory over the popularly elected New York Democrat. This event, and the compromise which brought it about, was to be a major turning point. Local autonomy was returned to the states of the South, the Freedmen's Bureaus, which had been set up to help Blacks adjust to the new conditions, were closed, and Federal troops were withdrawn. In their wake many northern businessmen called "carpet baggers" (a reference to the valises they carried) left, too. With "Redemption" came the chipping away of the newly won rights of Blacks. By the 1890s "Jim Crow" statutes divided southern society into a two-caste system with Whites occupying positions of power and Blacks reduced to second-class citizenship. The segregation laws prohibited the mixing of the races and barred "colored people" from virtually all White institutions.[21]

The states with the heaviest concentration of Blacks ignored or circumvented the Fourteenth Amendment (giving citizenship to Blacks) and the Fifteenth (specifying that the right to vote could not be denied because of race—though other tactics could be employed, like "grandfather clauses"). Most people in the North seemed no longer to be interested in rallying to the cause of freedom. Moreover, the system of segregation which had emerged after 1876 was legally sanctified in the famous *Plessy v. Ferguson* decision of the U.S. Supreme Court which, in 1896, proclaimed the principle of "separate but equal" to be the law of the land.

At the time of the Plessy case, nine out of ten Black Americans lived in the South, 80 percent in rural areas. While segregation existed in many states outside the old Confederacy, it was there that they suffered the most. With the curtailing of European immigration after World War I, many Blacks began their northward migration. Between 1910 and 1920 a half million moved to northern cities where they settled in tenement districts forming Black islands in a sea dominated by people more foreign and yet, in some ways, less alien and less alienated than they. And they stayed. The city became their new home and the ghetto their jail.

Ralph Ellison, the Black novelist, has poignantly described the problems they faced:

> In relation to their Southern background, the cultural history of Negroes in the North reads like the legend of some tragic people out of mythology, a people which aspired to escape from its own unhappy homeland to the apparent peace of a distant mountain; but which, in migrating, made some fatal error of judgment and fell into a great chasm of maze-like passages that promise ever to lead to the mountain but end ever against the wall.[22]

Although the opportunity to escape southern conditions led to the ever-growing trek northward, Blacks experienced residential, social, and economic discrimination wherever they went. Moreover, with World War I veterans returning and with nativist sentiment running at an all-time high, the new migrants frequently found themselves isolated, alone, and under attack whenever they dared to cross the color line. It was during this era that race rioting became a new feature of urban life. Thirty-three major interracial disturbances occurred between 1915 and 1949—eighteen of these between 1915 and 1919. With the exception of the Detroit riot of 1943 and the urban "burnings" of the 1960s, none of the more recent riots have been as fierce as those of the earlier period. The bloodiest of these were in East St. Louis and in Chicago, both cities in the northern state of Illinois.

The competition between Whites who sought to maintain their superordinate positions and Blacks who were hungry for work, housing, and respect continued. By and large, Blacks made slow progress. And even this progress—especially stimulated by the emergence of prideful new political and cultural movements in the 1920s (the era of the Harlem Renaissance)—was slowed, then stopped altogether, by the Great Depression of the following decade. And as might be expected, competition for increasingly scarce jobs served to intensify the prejudices of competitors. By 1940 a two to one Black-to-White unemployment ratio emerged—and it persists to this very day.

During Franklin Roosevelt's "New Deal" some changes began to bring the Black citizen closer to full equality before the law. Various groups, within and outside the Black community, tried and sometimes succeeded in gaining fairer treatment for America's largest racial minority. World War II accelerated the move.

Northward movement increased again and so now did the trek to the West where the defense industry served as the magnet. President Roosevelt's Executive Order 8802 sought to assure fair employment practices. By 1940 one in four Black Americans lived in the North or West and with the nation on wartime footing many found employment in factories earning higher wages than they had ever known. And at least a million Blacks entered the armed forces. But even during the war they found themselves in segregated units of the army and navy.

The military was not ordered integrated until 1948 (President Truman's Executive Order 9981), three years after the end of World War II. The order was not finally implemented until 1952 when, during the height of the Korean War, President Eisenhower made the changes in traditional policy.

In the early days of the postwar period, Blacks in the North and in the South did gain new status in law, though relatively few advantages in fact. They shared in the economic boom of the era, but while the absolute gains they made were sometimes considerable, the gap between the racial categories Black and White remained as wide as ever. Many thought that the independence movements in Africa might lead to the final and irrevocable emancipation of Black Americans. The African situation did not have that effect, but it served to provide a new reference to people who knew little of their origins or their heritage. Most important of all was the Supreme Court decision handed down on May 17, 1954, which unanimously struck down the constitutionality of the separate but equal doctrine and opened the door to widespread desegregation. As is well known, this decision proved difficult to enforce and prompted a variety of legal subterfuges that sought to reverse or at least to forestall a 1955 directive to move toward desegregation "with all deliberate speed."

The apparent failure of the people to honor the Court's decision, coupled with the seemingly unfulfilled promises that Black Americans had rejoiced in, accelerated a movement that had been growing from the turn of the century: the movement for civil rights. That movement and the changes that have taken place during the sixties and seventies are the subject of Chapter Seven. Several points concerning this period should be made here, however, before moving on to the histories of other American minority groups.

First, in the decade between 1954 and 1963 the principal thrust for desegregation and, in many cases, integration came from a coalition of Black and White reformers, most of whom tried to persuade their fellow citizens to honor the nation's highest ideals. Many became disillusioned; many lost faith in interracial organizations; many said that cooperation was a mask for White co-optation. Yet most of those who marched and picketed and boycotted and rode the "freedom buses" during those years saw integration as the primary goal. The National Association for the Advancement of Colored People (NAACP), Congress of Racial Equality (CORE), and other civil rights organizations were at the forefront of this movement. So, too, was the newly emergent Southern Christian Leadership Conference (SCLC) led by Dr. Martin Luther King, Jr.

The integration phase, if one can call it that, reached its height with the grand march on Washington in August of 1963 when 250,000 Black and White Americans joined hands to sing "We Shall Overcome" and Reverend Martin Luther King spoke of his dream.[23]

Within a year King's dream seemed shattered. What happened is a complicated story, better saved for a later chapter. But it is important to note that whatever progress had been made up to that centennial celebration of the Emancipation Proclamation had been much less the product of good-will than of hard work and political pressure.

In succeeding years integration was largely to be replaced by new, more strident, and far more Black-oriented ideology—Black Power. New and young leaders began to tire of promises of things to come. They felt that the civil rights movement was failing to reach those who needed help most, especially those in the northern ghettos. While acknowledging certain successes—the Civil Rights Acts of 1964, 1965, 1968, for example—many of these leaders felt that the victories were, in reality, rather hollow. They had been won at too great a cost and the net result, it was often argued, was that white guilt had been assuaged but few Blacks had really been helped.

Whatever the reality, and doubtless there was more than a kernel of truth in their portrayal, the new leaders shifted the focus and concentrated on the issue of "getting it together," that is, the coalescence of community among Black people throughout the nation. In many ways the wildest dreams of Stokely Carmichael and H. Rap Brown and other new-breed leaders were to be realized.[24] At least some of them.

Within a few years Black people began to walk taller and to express publicly the rage boiling up inside. Within a few years Black Power had become a household slogan. Within a few years universities and other particularly vulnerable institutions conceded that they had been guilty of racism or, at least, had failed to cast a wide enough net. These institutions began actively to recruit Black students who, in turn, demanded and often won special programs in Black Studies. But during those same years the average wages of Black unskilled laborers fell further behind their White counterparts, the average reading level of Black children fell further behind that of White children, and the average contribution of White supporters of Black liberation movements (no small factor) fell dramatically.

The period of the mid- and late 1970s was one of both consolidation and hesitation. There was consolidation on the part of certain segments of the Black community, particularly those in the growing middle class. However, in making considerable progress, as sociologist William J. Wilson points out, they made even more apparent the widening gap in Black America.[25] The hesitation came from various sources: a government rededicated to move toward desegregation but beset by contradictory directives emanating from its own various agencies; a wary White community, especially in working-class areas, concerned about the consequences of school busing and forced integration; confused Blacks—and other minorities—uncertain as to whether it was better to continue pressing for "class action," that is, categorical treatment via affirmative action programs or to work toward more strictly meritocratic principles. The situation was not helped by vacillations in official policy, cutbacks in support for reform programs and urban rehabilitation, or court rulings regarding such celebrated cases as that of Allen Bakke, the White California medical school applicant who claimed he was reportedly denied admittance to a state institution solely on the basis of "reverse discrimination." Bakke's claim was eventually supported by the Supreme Court, which still urged then some affirmative action measures be employed. That decision, to be discussed in detail later, was symbolic of the confusion that existed at the end of the decade. It was variously interpreted as a victory for egalitarians and as a cop-out.

European Immigrants

The first census to include the "nationalities" of Americans was that of 1820 when all those who had entered the United States along the eastern seaboard and the Gulf Coast were listed by country of origin. According to that census there were 9,638,000 Americans, 20 percent of whom were Negroes and the rest mainly persons of Anglo-Saxon stock. Between 1820 and 1980 over 50 million immigrants came to the United States, the overwhelming majority from Europe and Canada.

Between 1820 and the beginning of the Civil War over 3,500,000 European immigrants arrived in America. Many were from England, many from Scandinavia, but the two largest groups came from Ireland and Germany. Severe economic and social conditions led many Irish citizens to seek a new life in the United States. Between 1847 and 1854 about 1,200,000 men, women, and children left the "Emerald Isle" for this country, and by the end of the Civil War period the Irish constituted seven percent of the white population.

As many writers have pointed out, the Irish were in the vanguard of a new period of immigration—those who, despite their origins in the rural counties of Eire, forsook the soil (or were too poor to push on) and settled in the growing cities along the eastern seaboard. As the late President Kennedy described them,

In speech and dress they seemed foreign; they were poor and unskilled; and they were arriving in overwhelming numbers. The Irish are perhaps the only people in our history with the distinction of having a political party, the Know-Nothings, formed against them in 1849.[26]

The Irish suffered severe discrimination in the new land and most often found employment only in the lowest-paying and most physically demanding jobs: as ditchdiggers, or dockers, or "terriers" working on the railroads and in the canal beds. Yet, despite their own heritage of exploitation, few Irish immigrants saw a connection between their plight and that of American Blacks. In fact, many Irish newcomers became "Negrophobes," opposing to abolitionist activities and siding with some of the most reactionary forces in the north.[27] Some argue that the Irish proletariat feared the potential competition of Blacks (as other "White ethnics" would a century later); others claim anti-Black sentiment was more a form of displaced aggression, blaming Blacks for what they could not blame on White Protestant bosses and landlords. In some respects (clearly, not in all), the urban experience for Blacks in the twentieth century—in terms of attitudes of others and in terms of occupations—has its parallel in the Irish experience in the middle of the previous century.

In time, as they became acculturated to American ways and as others became even more visible targets for the animus of America Firsters, the Irish began the slow climb. It took many in and out of politics, including ward politics, and many more into public service, especially in the police force of New York, which used to be the Irish city, and Boston, which became and, in many ways, remains the political stronghold of the Irish clans so sharply portrayed in the novels of Edwin O'Connor.

The Irish also were to dominate the hierarchy of the Catholic Church in America. Even today the percentage of Irish-American compared with Italian- or German-American bishops and archbishops (to say nothing of parish priests) far exceeds their proportion of the population. (It should be noted that, while for the Irish, parish and precinct were frequently one and the same, priests frequently spoke out on nonecclesiastical subjects, and the range of opinions grew wider with each passing year until 1980 when the new Pope, John Paul II, forbade such practice.)

Many German Catholics came to America, too. But they rarely linked politics and parochialism so neatly as did the Irish. They were more German than Catholic and, like thousands of their Protestant countrymen who came to America before the Civil War, often moved out from the port cities of the East, dispersed themselves widely across the land and entered a myriad of occupations. Many became homesteaders in the Middle West and others settled in such cities as Baltimore, Buffalo, St. Louis, Minneapolis, and, especially, Milwaukee. In these cities German-Americans began various businesses, including such to-be-famous breweries as Anheuser-Busch, the makers of Budweiser, and Schlitz, "The Beer that made Milwaukee famous."

Germans—Protestants as well as Catholics—came in the beginning of the nineteenth century, in the middle (especially as political refugees after the failures of reform in 1948), and throughout the rest of the century. In time, they were to become the largest immigrant group to come to America. Yet, oddly enough, few people think of German-Americans as "immigrants" or as members of "an ethnic group." Why not?

For one thing, they did not arrive in a single wave that lasted but a decade or two like so many others. For another, they shared many of the values and cultural traits of the Scandinavians and Anglo-Americans among whom they often settled, including the Protestant work ethic. While they retained some of their cultural baggage, they also shared it (the Sunday picnic, the kindergarten, New Year's parties, and the frankfurter or "hot dog"). Moreover, they were themselves a rather heterogeneous group, which made stereotyping far more difficult. The Milwaukee brewers were a far cry from the St. Louis intellectuals such as the illustrious Carl Schurz, the "Forty-eighter," historian and newspaper publisher, who became an advisor to Presidents (beginning with Lincoln), Ambassador to Spain, U.S. Senator, and Secretary of the Interior. And both were quite different from the stalwart and religious farmers known a the "Pennsylvania Dutch" (the word a corruption of *Deutsch*).

In the second decade of the twentieth century some German-Americans underwent a difficult period when their original "fatherland" became their new country's enemy. During World War I many Germans suffered from discrimination by fellow Americans; to avoid identification and ostracism, some anglicized their names: Stein to Stone, Schmidt to Smith, Battenberg to Mountbatten, and Feldmann to Mansfield.

A similar attitude did not emerge during World War II, and few German-Americans were singled out, officially or unofficially, as dangers to American security. Unlike their Japanese-American counterparts, they were never evacuated from any centers of population or placed in concentration camps.

On the other hand, some groups of German-Americans had been sympathetic to the aims of Nazism in the 1930s (including anti-Semitic policies), but most of the "Bunds" folded with the onset of American involvement. Of course the overwhelming majority of Americans of German origin supported and defended the United States and applauded its victory in Europe under the leadership of their *landsmann*, Dwight David Eisenhower.

Almost one hundred years earlier, in the realization that immigration was going to continue to grow, the Castle Garden immigration depot was opened in New York in 1855. The depot was put to the test in the years following the Civil War (a war in which many immigrants fought side by side with citizens). After the war immigration began to flow more freely; the flow became a stream, and the stream, a torrent. By the middle of the 1880s hundreds of ships were sailing toward the eastern seaboard carrying human cargo. Between 1880 and 1914 about 7,500,000 eastern and central Europeans—Hungarians, Bohemians, Slovaks, Czechs, Poles, and Russians (almost one-half of whom were Jewish)—immigrated to the United States. Here they established or joined specific ethnic communities and helped to create and maintain what some saw as spiritual and cultural homes away from home. Polonia, the name given by Polish immigrants to their "place" in America was one such borderless land.[28]

During this same period four million Italians, mainly from *Il Mezzogiorno* (literally "mid-day" but popularly referring to the south) and from Sicily, came to this country. The Italians, like many of those from eastern Europe, came from farming areas but they were not farmers in the popular conception of the term. They were laborers whose place of work was the field instead of the factory. Called *contadini*, the Italian peasants eschewed agricultural toil upon emigration. According to various estimates well over 90 percent settled in cities, usually in urban neighborhoods called "Little Italies," which were further often subdivided into a "Little Sicily," a "Little Calabria," a "Little Naples."[29] There, in the overcrowded tenements of an already worn-out slum, they bedded down, sought work, dreamed of success—or of home, and there they rubbed elbows with others who were equally poor, bewildered, and bedraggled. The novelist Pietro DiDonato describes the conditions in a vivid passage from his classic work, *Christ in Concrete*.

Table 1 Total Number of Immigrants to the United States by Continent of Birth, 1820–1986.
Four periods of immigration, showing the shift of immigrants by their continent of birth (figures in thousands).

Continent	1820–1960*		1961–1970†		1971–1980†		1981–1986†	
	Total	% of Total	Total	% of Total	Total	% of Total	Total	% of Total
Europe	34,574.0	82.63	1,238.6	37.29	801.3	17.83	384.3	11.09
North America	5,753.2	13.75	1,351.1	40.67	1,645.0	36.61	1,093.4	31.40
South America	1,119.1	2.68	228.3	6.87	284.4	6.33	225.9	6.52
Asia	1,119.1	2.68	445.3	13.41	1,633.8	36.36	1,644.5	47.44
Africa	47.5	0.11	39.3	1.18	91.5	2.04	94.5	2.73
Australasia	79.8	0.19	13.6	0.42	19.6	0.44	11.8	0.34
All other	266.7	0.64	5.5	0.16	17.7	0.39	11.7	0.34
Totals:	41,840.9	100	3,321.7	100	4,493.3	100	3,466.1	100

Sources: *Statistical Abstract of the United States, 1961, 82nd ed. Washington, D.C.: U.S. Department of Commerce, Bureau of the Census, 1961, p. 93, Table 113.
†*Statistical Abstract of the United States, 1988, 108th ed. Washington, D.C.: U.S. Department of Commerce, Bureau of the Census, 1988, p. 10, Table 8.

The tenement was a twelve-family house. There were two families on each floor with the flats running in box-car fashion from front to rear and with one toilet between them. Each flat had its distinctive powerful odor. There was the particular individual bouquet that aroused a repulsion followed by sympathetic human kinship; the great organ of Tenement fuguing forth its rhapsody with pounding identification to each sense. The Donovans' tunnel caught the mouth and nostrils with a broad gangrenous gray that overwhelmed the throat, but on acquaintance nourished into a mousey buffet. Missus Donovan, an honest Catholic woman, was old, cataplasmic, and sat for hours in the closet-small hallway toilet breathing in private heavy content, or at the front-room window munching her toothless gums. . . . The large Farabutti family in one of the upper flats had an oily pleasing aroma—the Maestro carrying with him a mixture of barbershop and strong di Nobili tobacco—and the children savoring of the big potato-fried-egg sandwiches which they chewed while shouting at cat-stick. The Hoopers had a colorless moldy emanation that hung and clung anemically but drily definite. The gaunt woman on the top floor who wore the gaudy old-fashioned dresses and brought men home with her talcumed herself stark flat white and left an insistent trail of old bathrooms littered with cheap perfumes. The top floor right—Lobans'—gave off a pasty fleshiness as though the bowels were excreting through the pores. Their breaths were revolting, and everyone in the family had snarling lips ready to let go profanities.[30]

The immigrants from the south, central, and eastern Europe represented economically some of the more impoverished peoples of the continent. Many had come to work in the expanding industries of this country, intending to return to their homelands. Some "birds of passage" went back and forth (as do southern Italians, Spaniards, Turks, Yugoslavs, and Greeks—the *Gastarbeiterin* [guest workers] who work in Germany and Scandinavia today).

Some, like the Jews, had no homelands to which to return. It was such immigrants about whom Emma Lazarus wrote:

Give me your tired, your poor,
Your huddled masses yearning to breathe free,
The wretched refuse of your teeming shore,
Send these, the homeless, tempest-tost, to me:
I lift my lamp beside the golden door.[31]

The new arrivals to Ellis Island (which replaced Castle Garden as the portal of entry in 1892) were not the adventurers, explorers, traders, or conquerors of an earlier era. Yet they were also pioneers. As the historian Max Lerner put it, "the experience of the immigrants recapitulated the early American pioneer hardships, in many ways on harder terms, since the difficulties they encountered were those of a jungle society rather than a jungle wilderness."[32] Oscar Handlin called them "the uprooted."[33]

Because of their limited resources few immigrants ventured far beyond the ports of debarkation or the inland cities along the main railroad lines. They found employment as laborers and miners, workers in heavy industry and in the needle trades. Jobs were obtained through old-country connections, employment agencies, or through newly found friends and neighbors. The tasks they performed were arduous, the hours long, the conditions frequently intolerable, and the paychecks often inadequate to provide for growing families. For the first generation there was little time for recreation. What little leisure they had was spent within the confines of neighborhoods where attempts were made to keep Old World traditions alive.

Members of each immigrant group tended to gather together, and ethnic islands became a natural feature of the urban topography. Somewhat like the local communities of medieval Jews, these modern ghettos emerged in the older sections of the cities. But, as individuals improved their economic and social positions, they moved "uptown," leaving their older neighborhoods to those who followed. In the metropolitan centers of the North the pattern was often repeated: The areas of original settlement successfully became the ghetto communities of the older settlers, then the Irish and Germans, East Europeans, Jews, Italians, and more recently blacks from the South, Puerto Ricans and other Hispanics.

The children of European immigrants found themselves torn between the customs of their parents and the world into which they sought admission. For many the past was to be forgotten, the future lay ahead. Theirs was the generation of acculturation, and they were often caught between two conflicting value systems. As they learned the norms of American life and tried to adhere to them, they frequently evoked the antagonism, even the wrath, of those who had already "arrived." Fear of the stranger had greeted their parents; now hostility toward those eager to compete added fuel to the smoldering embers of anti-foreign prejudice. Restrictive practices became commonplace, and increasing numbers of jobs, schools, fraternities, restaurants, and clubs became forbidden territory. The signposts were clear: "Americans Only," "Irish Need Not Apply," "No Jews Allowed."

The first restrictive legislation directed against European immigrants was passed in 1891. The language of the Immigration Act seemed indiscriminately to link the mentally incompetent with the indigent. An excerpt clearly illustrates the point.

. . . all idiots, insane persons, paupers or persons likely to become a public charge, persons suffering from a loathsome or a dangerous contagious disease, persons who have been convicted of a felony or other infamous crime or misdemeanor involving moral turpitude, polygamists, and also any person whose ticket or passage is paid for with the money of another or who is assisted by others to come, unless it is affirmatively and satisfactorily shown on special inquiry that such person does not belong to one of the foregoing excluded classes, or to the class of contract laborers excluded by the act of February twenty-sixth, eighteen hundred and eighty-five, but this section shall not be held to exclude persons living in the United States from sending for a relative or a friend who is not of the excluded classes under such regulations as the Secretary of the Treasury may prescribe. . . . [34]

Table 2 Total Number of Immigrants, by Country of Birth, 1820–1986.
Four periods of immigration, showing the shift of immigrants from their country of birth, in descending order of numbers (figures in thousands).

1820–1960*		1961–1970†	
Germany	6,726.3	Mexico	443.3
Italy	4,962.4	Canada	286.7
Ireland	4,676.4	Cuba	256.8
Austria-Hungary	4,275.8	Great Britain	230.8
Great Britain	3,784.6	Italy	206.7
Canada	3,555.4	Germany	200.0
U.S.S.R.	3,344.5	Philippines	101.5
Sweden	1,249.8	China and Taiwan	96.7
Mexico	1,158.7	Dominican Republic	94.1
Norway	837.9	Greece	90.2
France	684.9	Portugal	79.3
WEST INDIES	619.8	Poland	73.3
Greece	487.2	Jamaica	71.0
Poland	432.3	Colombia	70.3
China	408.5	Yugoslavia	46.2
Turkey	365.5	Ireland	42.2
Denmark	351.4	Argentina	42.1
Japan	325.4	AFRICA	39.3
Switzerland	323.9	Japan	38.5
Netherlands	320.9	Haiti	37.5
Portugal	283.9	Ecuador	37.0
SOUTH AMERICA	234.8	Korea	35.8
Belgium	189.0	France	34.3
Spain	180.9	India	31.2
Rumania	159.0	Spain	30.5
Czechoslovakia	129.3	Netherlands	27.8
CENTRAL AMERICA	115.6	Hong Kong	25.6
AUSTRALASIA	79.8	Trinidad and Tobago	24.6
AFRICA	47.5	Czechoslovakia	21.4
		Brazil	20.5

In 1894 the Immigration Restriction League began. It was to be the strongest force against unrestricted acceptance of immigrants for the next quarter of a century and was largely responsible for congressional action in 1917, which added further limits to earlier legislation by stating that every immigrant had to demonstrate an ability to read. As Joseph Hraba and others have pointed out, such a literacy test was clearly an attempt to cut down the flow of Slavic and Italian immigrants.[35]

Following World War I mounting isolationism and anti-foreign feelings reached their peak. In 1921 and again in 1924 further restrictive legislation was passed, sharply curtailing the immigration of "undesirable" national

Table 2 *Continued*

1971–1980†		1981–1986†	
Mexico	637.2	Mexico	401.7
Philippines	360.2	Philippines	273.8
Cuba	276.8	Vietnam	264.8
Korea	272.0	China and Taiwan	219.4
China and Taiwan	202.5	Korea	201.8
Vietnam	179.7	India	145.9
India	176.8	Dominican Republic	130.8
Dominican Republic	148.0	Jamaica	120.1
Jamaica	142.0	Laos	105.2
Italy	130.1	AFRICA	94.5
Great Britain	123.5	Cuba	92.0
Canada	114.8	Great Britain	85.4
Portugal	104.5	Cambodia	83.6
Greece	93.7	Iran	79.0
AFRICA	91.5	Canada	66.6
Colombia	77.6	Colombia	63.0
Germany	66.0	Haiti	56.6
Trinidad and Tobago	61.8	El Salvador	53.8
Haiti	58.7	Guyana	53.1
Ecuador	50.2	Poland	44.0
Japan	47.9	U.S.S.R.	42.1
Hong Kong	47.5	Germany	41.6
Guyana	47.5	Thailand	32.5
Iran	46.2	Pakistan	31.8
Thailand	44.1	Hong Kong	30.7
Poland	43.6	Peru	26.7
U.S.S.R.	43.2	Portugal	25.2
Yugoslavia	42.1	Guatemala	25.1
El Salvador	34.4	Japan	24.0
Lebanon	33.8	Rumania	22.0

Note: Citations in capital letters refer to regions rather than countries.
Sources: *Statistical Abstract of the United States, 1961*, 82nd ed. Washington, D.C.; U.S. Department of Commerce, Bureau of the Census, 1961, p. 93, Table 113.
†*Statistical Abstract of the United States, 1988*, 108th ed. Washington, D.C.; U.S. Department of Commerce, Bureau of the Census, 1988, p. 10, Table 8.

groups and setting forth rigid quotas favoring north Europeans and all but excluding others. In 1921 the Immigration Quota Act, signed by President Harding, provided that the annual number of aliens permitted to enter the United States from any nation was not to exceed three percent of the total number of foreign-born members of that particular nationality residing in this country in 1910. The Johnson Act of 1924 (sometimes known as the National Origins Act) limited immigration even more severely. The formula provided for the admission of 150,000 persons each year, with national quotas fixed at two percent of the total of foreign-born members of any given nationality group residing in the United States in 1890. These enactments served to close the "Golden Door."[36]

The Immigration and Nationality Act of 1952 (also known as the McCarran-Walter Act) recodified the national immigration laws, slightly improved the opportunities for some, such as those from Asian countries, but, in general, reduced the flow and increased the categories of restriction. Reflecting concerns about "communist subversives" at the height of the Cold War, the bill required very careful screening of "security risks."

The following year President Truman, over whose veto the McCarran-Walter Act had been passed, was able to enact the Refugee Relief Act of 1953, admitting slightly more than 200,000 refugees over the quota limits in a three year period. Most of the newcomers were expellees and escapees from communist-controlled Eastern Europe. Not long after 32,000 Hungarian refugees were permitted to enter the U.S. as "parolees." (Parolees were those given temporary visas but who were later able to apply for permanent residence. In succeeding years parolee status was used to give asylum to other refugees, especially Cubans, Soviet Jews, and various people from Southeast Asia.)

During his brief period in office John F. Kennedy initiated new legislation, which was to significantly alter general immigration policies in the United States. He did not live to see it pass, but, in 1965, his successor, Lyndon Johnson, signed a bill that allowed people to apply for immigration to the United States not on the basis of strict national ratios but on hemispheric quotas. The government said it would now accept up to 170,000 people from Europe and an equal number from Asia up to a maximum of 20,000 individuals from any single country (regardless of how many had come from that place in the past) and as many as 120,000 from this hemisphere without any national limitation. There was one caveat in all instances: preferences were to be given to relatives of citizens, resident aliens, and those with special skills and talents. Moreover, special provisions were included to continue to consider the admission of certain people deemed as refugees. (A decade later the Indochina Immigration and Resettlement Act of 1975 was passed to further assist "sponsored" refugees. In many ways, the '75 Act was a forerunner of the Refugee Act of 1980, the most comprehensive piece of refugee legislation in U.S. history.)[37]

A policy as flexible as this one might have saved thousands upon thousands of victims of Nazism in the years before and during World War II, but, for a variety of reasons, few exceptions were then permitted. Until the post-war period the general sentiment that prompted the restrictive legislation of the 1920s remained reflected in the laws of the land. Certain peoples were favored; certain others were considered undesirable and severely limited in their opportunities to enter the country.

Jews

Included among the potential immigrants who had been effectively barred from entry into the United States were hundreds of thousands of European Jews, the vast majority of whose coreligionists had come to America after 1880. Jews were not, however, newcomers to this country. As early as 1654, 23 Jewish refugees from Brazil settled in New Amsterdam. By the time of the Revolution almost three thousand Jews—mainly of Spanish and Portuguese descent (called Sephardim)—were living in the seaboard colonies.

The first Jewish settlers, generally traders and merchants, found little opposition to their presence in most of the cities and towns where they worked and lived. There were scattered instances of discrimination in the areas of Dutch control and some Jews suffered religious persecutions in certain English colonies, where they were sometimes forbidden to hold public office or to bear arms. More often, these barriers were absent, ignored, or offset by the fact that many Protestants looked with favor upon the "Israelites" in their midst—the descendants of the ancient Hebrews whose testaments had so markedly influenced Christian thought. By 1700 freedom of worship was widely recognized and in 1740, when the Jews of British America were granted full citizenship, they achieved a degree of freedom probably unmatched anywhere in the world.

The Sephardim were joined by Ashkenazic Jews (from eastern and central Europe) who began coming to America during the late Colonial Period. Shortly after the turn of the nineteenth century, economic conditions and political unrest prompted the migration of German Jews. In 1836 the first communal migration of Jews—large families and even whole communities—moved to America. Throughout the nineteenth century the number of Jews emigrating from Germany rose steadily. It is estimated that the American Jewish population was 15,000 in 1840, 50,000 in 1850, 150,000 in 1860, and 250,000 in 1880.

Many of the German Jews left the seaboard cities and moved to smaller communities to the south and west. In many instances they went as peddlers and stayed to build the retail emporia that are now found scattered in towns and cities across the nation. (It is frequently noted that the Jewish-owned store is as commonplace in a southern town as the Confederate monument that stands in the square.) While the Jews often had to live down the "curse of Shylock," the images and portraits of Jewish peddlers and merchants as being dishonest, blatant discrimination was rarely found. Like their more cosmopolitan countrymen from the upper strata of German-Jewish society, these Jews had little difficulty in establishing themselves economically, in forming religious congregations, and in adapting themselves to local patterns. It was not until the wave of east European immigration began rolling toward the United States that anti-Jewish discrimination gained a significant foothold in this country.

In 1880, 250,000 Jews were living in the United States; by 1924 the number exceeded three million. Beginning in the 1880s, Jews from Poland, Russia, Romania, and other east European lands migrated to America. Included were many who fled from pogroms (organized massacres) and other insufferable conditions in their lands of original domicile—which few would call homelands.

There, squeezed between a growing middle class and a rapidly proletarianizing peasantry, the members of once independent Jewish communities found themselves increasingly threatened by forces beyond their control. The *shtetl* (village) became vulnerable to attacks from outside and many decided to leave. For most, America was the city of hope, "the Golden Medina." And so they left, most entering this country as wide-eyed, hopeful, and frightened refugees.

The vast majority of the east European Jews were economically impoverished and traditional in their religious beliefs. The largest percentage of these immigrants remained in the larger cities where they could find work (especially in the expanding garment industry) and where they could continue their religious practices. Like other ethnically distinct groups, east European Jews began to develop their own communities.

The conspicuousness of their dress, uniqueness of their customs, strangeness of their everyday language (Yiddish), and their Orthodox faith, all combined to reinforce traditional images of Jews as a clannish and mysterious people. Along with other recent immigrant groups they became the targets of anti-foreign sentiments.

In spite of their old-country ways the Jewish immigrants possessed several cultural traits that enhanced their adjustment and rapid mobility in American society. Years of relegation to marginal occupational roles, traditions that placed high value on education and the learned professions, and emphasis on familial responsibility, all served to aid many Jews in their struggle to find acceptance and, in time, prosperity in competitive America.

Yet the very fact that a substantial number of Jews began to surpass others in the rapidity of their ascent increased animosity and fanned the embers of anti-Semitism (an old phenomenon distinct from general anti-foreign attitudes). Because some Jews were extremely successful financially, they were referred to as the quintessential "unscrupulous money changers" and "crass capitalists" (combining traditional stereotypes with more modern images such as that evoked by Karl Marx and others). Because some Jews were deeply engaged in radical politics and labor organizations, others tried to paint all Jews "red." And some, like the members of the Ku Klux Klan and even as notable and powerful a figure as Henry Ford, ignoring the ridiculous contradictions in their allegations, called the Jews both "parvenu" and "pinko." Moreover, the search for scapegoats during the Great Depression often found the Jews, including such advisors to President Roosevelt as Bernard Baruch, targets for the bitter frustrations felt by many Americans. (As mentioned previously, the rise of Nazism evoked some sympathy here as well, and several new "hate" organizations sprang up to defame the Jews.)

It was during this era (the late 1930s) that about two hundred thousand European Jews—mostly from Germany and Austria—managed to migrate to the United States. Many more refugees from Nazi-dominated countries would have come had it not been for America's restrictive immigration laws.

Reactions against the horrors practiced by the Nazi regime greatly served to reduce anti-Jewish sentiments. In the two decades following World War II virulent anti-Semitism showed a marked decline, although restricted neighborhoods and social discrimination continued to exist in many of our cities and suburbs. The epidemic of swastika daubing in 1960, the temple bombings in 1962, the rise of George Lincoln Rockwell's American Nazi party (later called the American National White Workers' Socialist party) and other neo-Nazi organizations, the emergence of certain reactionary patriotic movements of the radical right in the early 1960s, and the occurrence of "Black anti-Semitism" and Third World anti-Zionism on the part of the radical left in the late 1960s indicated the continued existence of anti-Semitic feelings in certain segments of the population. Some have thought it a portent of more serious difficulties. Indeed, in late 1969, it seemed reasonable to say:

American Jews, delighted at Israeli victory in the Six-Day War, have evinced much less enthusiasm for their own country's protracted conflict in Southeast Asia and its stalemated war against poverty at home. Other groups in American life share the sense of frustration. In the search for scapegoats that may soon ensue, Jews may find themselves most vulnerable to attack from right, left, and below. By seeking reform and compromise on most issues instead of radical change they may come increasingly to appear too white for the black militants, too red for the white conservatives, and too yellow for their own children.

Jews are not unaware of such possibilities. They know that latent anti-Semitism can be revived in America as it has been in the past. But they do not seem worried. They feel they can ride out the coming storms. Like their forebears who came to settle on the Lower East Side, the majority of Jews still believe in America and in the American people.[38]

The predictions were, in fact, quite accurate. Certain Black leaders did begin to separate themselves from too strong identification with Jews. Some Jews did grow increasingly less enthusiastic about particular aspects of the civil rights struggle when Blacks pressed for quota systems as ways of ensuring affirmative action. With memories of how numerus *clausus* had been used against Jews still fresh in their minds, they feared that quotas set to percentages in the population regardless of the good intentions of the advocates of equal opportunity would greatly reduce their opportunities for achievement based on merit.

At the same time, a number of non-Jewish white people began to echo Archie Bunker's concerns about Jewish "lib-er-als" and "eggheads." And some Jewish children (like many non-Jewish youngsters) did seek to distance themselves—physically and socially—from parents they thought were too bourgeois.

The Yom Kippur War of 1973 exacerbated the situation as increasing numbers of non-Jews blamed Israelis and, indirectly, all Jews, for the oil crisis. In the following seven year period popular support for Israel among non-Jewish Americans waned considerably as sympathy for the Palestinian refugees and their cause gained favor in various circles, including a number of church groups once publicly pro-Israel.

By 1980, many Jews and Blacks seemed to recognize the need to reform old coalitions, many white conservatives began to have second (or third) thoughts about Israel (seeing it once again as a bastion of democracy and military power in a turbulent Middle East), and many young Jews were found in the vanguard of new religious movements, some of which also involved resurging ethnic pride. Still, tensions continued. Some of these were all too familiar reminders of earlier periods. Jewish institutions— synagogues, community centers, even graveyards—once again became targets for anti-Semites; attacks on identifiable Jews, especially those who were Orthodox and dressed in the traditional manner increased; and on many campuses, rallies on behalf of supporters of Palestinians sometimes turned their anger on Jewish counterdemonstrators. Ironically, the plight of the Palestinians also led to significant soul searching—and action— within the general American Jewish community.

For years, the majority of American Jews had given unqualified support to Israeli policies. While most applauded the accord with Egypt engineered by President Jimmy Carter, they remained wary of the intentions of those in other Arab states and of the Palestinian Liberation Organization which had vowed to recapture what was claimed as Arab land. Yet the hard measures used to suppress the uprising of the Palestinians living within the occupied West Bank and Gaza Strip in the late 1980s raised troubling questions for increasing numbers of American Jews about both the morality and efficacy of Israeli actions. By the end of the decade many broke ranks with those who continued to support the Israeli hardliners, favoring a new policy that would give genuine autonomy to the Palestinians.

Asian Americans

The Lower East Side of New York, where the Russian-Jewish immigrants first congregated, was sometimes referred to as an "Oriental Enclave," for to some people the Jews were "Orientals". In the years to come many observers would notice that members of each cohort appeared to have certain common traits, not least attitudes toward family, work, and education. But the true Orientals (or Asians, as they now prefer to be called) who came to America in the nineteenth century were very different from the Jews and other European immigrants. They had racial characteristics that set them apart and certain misunderstood cultural traits which made them special targets for racist attacks.

The first Chinese came to America during Gold Rush days in the late 1840s. Over the years their immigration increased sharply and by 1882 there were about 320,000 Chinese people living in America, mostly on the West Coast. Most of them had come from a single province in Southeast China where economic conditions forced many men to leave home as contract laborers or "coolies" to work in this country as miners or railroad workers during the early days of westward expansion. Many intended to return to China to attain new status based on the wages of their toil. As a result of this hope and because of strong filial ties, few made much effort to adapt to western institutions. Some did return, but most stayed in the United States. Many suffered from vicious attacks. There were outright murders in Los Angeles in 1871 and a massacre of 29 persons took place in Rock Spring, Wyoming, in 1885.[39]

When the railroads were finished and the mines were shut down, many Chinese moved back to the West Coast cities, where they turned to occupations that had nothing especially Oriental about them—running hand laundries, cigar shops, curio shops, and restaurants—and a few remained in outdoor labor. Moreover, since "merchants" had higher status in the eyes of immigration officials than "workers," many called themselves merchants, thus giving an exaggerated statistical sense of the size of the Chinese-American middle class.

Immigration officials were an important factor in the lives of the Chinese. California, the state with the largest Chinese population, had long looked with disfavor upon these (and, it turned out, other) "Orientals." They repeatedly passed discriminatory legislation—deemed essential in the face of the "yellow peril"—to curtail the activities of Chinese residents. In 1882 the Chinese became the first group singled out by the federal government for separate treatment, when the Chinese Exclusion Act was passed. It was renewed in 1892, and in 1902 all Chinese immigration was made illegal. The ban was not lifted until 1943 when China was our military ally and then only a crack: 105 persons were to be admitted each year. The Act of 1965 changed things considerably and hundreds of thousands of Chinese (and other East Asians) were able to come to America.

The restriction against immigration did not reduce anti-Chinese sentiments. "Chinatowns," inhabited mainly by single men, were considered by many Americans to be centers of licentiousness, narcotic addiction, corruption, and mystery. Traditional ties and loyalties, clan connections and "company" allegiances, gave these areas local community control years before that phrase was to become a part of everyday rhetoric. Ever-present prejudice and blatant discrimination increased the pressure for ingroup solidarity in Chinese neighborhoods. On their turf and in their own way, economic and welfare and educational institutions were established as were places of recreation and amusement. Today, many Chinese-Americans still find solace in their own communities and want to maintain their own bicultural patterns.

Chinese-Americans suffer much less prejudice and discrimination than in earlier years; still Chinatowns remain—especially in San Francisco, Los Angeles, and New York—and so do many problems. Most of these have to do with internal conflicts in the communities, as between citizens and recent immigrants from Hong Kong, or between shop owners and those who work in the ubiquitous sweatshops, or between the old guard and the "red" guard, sometimes composed of the children of middle-class Chinese-Americans. Also, as might be expected, the shift of American foreign policy toward Peking and ultimate recognition of the People's Republic of China as the sole legitimate government after almost a quarter of a century of support for Nationalistic China and the Chiang regime confused and angered many Chinese-Americans who felt a sense of kinship with Taiwan. It has also delighted many others who see China the country, not the political entity, as their homeland.

Whatever the sentiments of the Chinese-Americans regarding detente with Peking, the opening of the People's Republic has served to interest millions of other Americans in Chinese culture and society. If anything, America entered the 1980s in a positive mood toward China, a sentiment that continued during much of the following decade.

There is one additional group of Chinese who have been emigrating to the United States in increasing numbers—the "ethnic Chinese" of southeast Asia, mostly refugees from Indochina. In the immediate wake of the war in Vietnam, Vietnamese who had worked for the U.S. government fled their country and the new regime. In the years that followed, others, including Chinese businessmen and professionals and their families, sought to escape from both communism and ethnic discrimination. In fact, a large percentage of the "boat people," those who obtained passage on everything from sampans to freighters, were of Chinese descent.

The Japanese were a half step behind the Chinese at each phase of their early settlement—in America. The first Japanese settlers came in 1869, 21 years after the first Chinese; and the large migration took place a decade after the major Chinese immigration and *after* the Chinese Exclusion Act had been invoked. The latter point is important, for it shows that while the two groups were frequently lumped together, significant distinctions were also made between them.

Save for the few members of the Wakamatsu Colony of pioneers who came here in the late 1860s under very special circumstances, no Japanese migrated to this country again until 1885; until then almost no one could leave Japan. With a shift in the policy of the new Mejii regime, however, many departed their native land to find work in Hawaii and in the United States itself. When they arrived here some sought work in the cities, but it was hard to obtain and so they turned to mining and logging and, particularly, farm labor. The latter proved to be advantageous to employers and newcomers alike—for a large number of immigrants had worked the soil before and took pride in what they could do with it. But they proved too good for some Californians to tolerate.

As they saved and began to buy land for their own farms or, as in the case of quite a few members of the second generation, left their jobs as laborers or domestics and sought to enter competitive vocations, prejudices began to mount. They also came to feel the brunt of racism used as "a mask for privilege," to use Carey McWilliam's phrase. The Japanese and Korean Exclusion League was formed to protest against "unfair competition."

Immigration was greatly reduced in 1907 as a result of President Theodore Roosevelt's "Gentlemen's Agreement with the Japanese Government" to stop the issuance of passports to potential farm workers. (Others, including some merchants and many students, continued to come.) But this was not enough to satisfy the Californians. They sought and got their own Alien Land Law in 1913; it prevented the Japanese ("aliens ineligible for citizenship") from purchasing their own farms. Owing to World War I and the need for produce, the threat of denial—and or removal—was stayed. In fact, immigration restrictions themselves were lifted and about seventy-five thousand Japanese entered the country to become mostly farm laborers. One student of the period writes that "farm income reached a peak in 1920 when the Japanese in California produced land crops valued at 67 million dollars.[40] He also points out that

... after the war, the release of war workers from city factories, the return of soldiers, and the "increasing danger" from a rising nationalistic Japan reignited agitation against the Japanese. Although they had developed much of the marginal land of California, they were accused of having secured the richest and most desirable farm land.[41]

The land law was soon amended and ultimately served to curtail sharply Japanese agricultural activities—though it did not stop them entirely.

The Japanese reaction to discrimination was quite different from that of many other ethnic groups, including the Chinese. For the most part they eschewed a "ghetto" existence but they did tend to help one another. This became especially important in the cities to which many farm workers and former owners had to move. While feeling pressure from the Issei (first generation) they found solace among their kinfolk—and from people from the same home district. Yet the *Nisei* (the second generation) were more inclined to be attracted to the world beyond the "Little Tokyos" of Seattle, San Francisco, and Los Angeles.

Following the attack on Pearl Harbor almost the entire Japanese-American population—citizens and aliens alike—was removed by military decree from the cities of the West Coast and placed in "security" camps in the desert, the Rocky Mountains, and as far way as Arkansas. Japanese-Americans living in other parts of the country were placed under surveillance, but were not interned. This unprecedented action of the government was prompted by fear of disloyalty from the Japanese-American minority, the seeds of suspicion often having been sown by those for whom the Japanese had long been an economic threat. Eventually the order was rescinded, and a year after the evacuation, the Japanese began to resettle. Many established new homes in the Midwest, some in the mountain states and in the East, and others finally returned to the West. It is estimated that the Japanese-Americans suffered a financial loss of over 350 million dollars through the forced evacuation. Although Congress appropriated some money for restitution to these displaced persons, few were able to recoup their losses, many could not offer sufficient proof of their claims, and no government, of course, could compensate them for the disruption of their lives.[42]

More often than not, the Japanese had to begin again in different occupations from those they had engaged in prior to the war. Without sufficient funds only a small number could return to their prewar activities. Nonetheless, in the main the status of Japanese-Americans has improved considerably since 1945. Being more widely dispersed throughout the country, they now occupy a minority-group position somewhat analogous to that of American Jews.[43]

In addition to the half million Chinese and almost as many Japanese who crossed the Pacific to the United States, many thousands of Filipinos also made this journey. Their emigration came about as a result of the special circumstances whereby the Philippines became a territory of the United States in 1898 at the end of the Spanish-American War. Most of those who came were laborers or domestics and some have remained in such positions over the years. The United States Navy, for example, still uses Filipinos as mess stewards on shore and shipboard. Some resent this automatic treatment. Others are pleased to have their "niche" even in the context of a sort of uniformed domestic service. In recent years, an increasing number of well-educated Filipinos, including many doctors, have come to continue their studies or to find work in the United States.

Another large cohort of Asian immigrants, and one that is gaining recognition in the United States today, is Korean. Long subjected to the same restrictions as the Japanese (whose government controlled Korea throughout most of the first half of this century), those Koreans who came in the early years were, like the Japanese, mostly farm laborers. A second wave appeared in the 1950s: the wives of the servicemen who had fought in the Korean War. Since 1965 increasing numbers have come to the United States as regular immigrants. Like others before them, the recent arrivals have carved their own economic niches in this society. Most prominent are the groceries operated by newcomers from Korea in many of our major cities. Because of their strong commitment to family and education, it is said that few children of Korean greengrocers will remain in the produce business. The assumption is corroborated by the high and climbing rates of enrollments of Korean-American youngsters in American colleges and universities.

The war in Vietnam and its complicated aftermath brought a new cohort of people to America: the "Indochinese," a generic name for those who had lived in Vietnam, Laos, or Cambodia—the three countries of what, for a time, was French Indochina. The first to come were government officials and military leaders who were airlifted out of Vietnam after the fall of Saigon in April 1975. Aided by public and private agencies, they were moved to Pacific island bases, then to camps in various parts of the United States, and then helped to resettle in many communities where they often began to form new ethnic enclaves.

In late 1970s the world was alarmed by reports of "boat people" who had escaped from Vietnam but were having difficulty finding places of asylum on the shores of neighboring countries. (Many of the escapees were, as noted previously, ethnic Chinese.) An international agreement set up an elaborate system by which the new refugees could find temporary havens in camps established under the authority of the United Nations High Commissioner for Refugees (UNHCR) in Thailand, Malaysia, Singapore, Indonesia, Hong Kong, Macao, and the Philippines. Camps were established where they would be cared for and where American and other immigration authorities from western nations would interview and process the refugees for "third country resettlement." The vast majority of Vietnamese and Laotians who applied to come to the United States were eventually accepted and brought to this country.

The Cambodians were not as fortunate. Victims not only of the international war but also of the terrible reign of Pol Pot and his Khmer Rouge, which took power in 1975, many escaped into Thailand. There additional border camps, operated by the UNHCR, were also set up. However, unlike most of the other camps, these were essentially holding centers. Save for those who had fought with the Lon Nol forces during the Vietnam War, a relatively small percentage of those seeking resettlement in the United States were considered and accepted.

Today there are approximately 750,000 refugees from Vietnam and Laos and around 130,000 former Cambodians in the United States. In general, the Indochinese refugees have been well accepted into American communities and many have already made their marks, excelling in a variety of spheres. Some have resented their presence, including some members of old non-White minority groups who argue that the public seemed more concerned with the refugees' plight than with their needs. (These issues are discussed more fully in Chapter Nine.)

Hispanic Americans

Because of their particular history many of the Filipinos are often classified not only with other Asian-Americans but also with those now listed under the rubric "Spanish-surnamed," or Hispanics. However, relative to other people with Spanish names, the Filipinos comprise a tiny minority. While receiving their names from the same source—if at a considerably earlier time—the Hispanics are in fact, a multigroup minority that includes descendants of very early settlers living in areas taken over from Mexico after the Treaty of Guadalupe Hidalgo at the end of the Mexican-American War, recent immigrants from Mexico and other Latin-American countries, and Puerto Ricans, who have been citizens since 1917.

Oldest are the Hispaños of mixed racial parentage—Spanish and Indian—whose history dates back to the days of the Spanish conquest. The Southwest has been their traditional home for over four centuries. They became American citizens by default when New Mexico, California, and other southwestern territories were ceded to the United States after the Mexican-American War in 1948. Prior to their annexation, the social patterns of Mexican society prevailed in these territories, and the lifeways of many Hispaños still mirror those of their countrymen south of the Rio Grande.

Shortly after the turn of the twentieth century, increasing numbers of Mexican laborers crossed the border to work in the United States. Restrictions on overseas immigration during World War I gave impetus to the migration from Mexico; almost a million Mexicans entered the country between 1910 and 1930. Most of these found employment in southwestern states—Texas, Arizona, and California; some became migratory workers moving northward and eastward with the seasons. Over half of these newcomers took up residence in the United States and, while few sought to obtain citizenship, their offspring became Americans by birth.

Characteristically, the second generation sought access to what was denied their parents, and some gained entry to "Anglo" society. The majority, however, found the paths to American-style success blocked by barriers of prejudice and discrimination and especially by a particular form of racism that implied that Mexicans were ideally suited for "stoop labor" and therefore should be restricted to what they "did best." This widespread attitude served to keep many influential people in the Southwest from making the necessary changes in the educational system and in social welfare to assist the Mexican workers in moving off the fields and up the ladder of social mobility. The slum *barrios* in El Paso and San Antonio, in Trinidad, Colorado, in Tuscon, Arizona, and in Los Angeles and San Diego are living reminders of these facts of social life for our Mexican-American citizens; so, too, are the labor camps and rural settlements that pockmark the fertile valleys of California. In these places (and similar ones throughout the Southwest) two types of migrants from Mexico are to be found: the "wetbacks," who cross the border illegally in search of employment, and the "*braceros*," legal entrants with permits to work as contract laborers. Over the years the *bracero* program was sharply curtailed, then phased out. At its height in 1960, 427,000 entered. Few were admitted under the special provisions of the Mexican Laborer Acts after 1965 and none by 1970. By law, all Mexicans must now enter legally, under the revised Immigration and Nationality Act. The fact is that many continued to enter the country illegally. Some estimate that the figures reached one million in 1978 alone.

In the recent past Mexican laborers served to heighten anti-Mexican prejudice of white citizens (or "Anglos" as they are referred to in that part of the country). Willing to work for lower wages or contracted in large groups for agricultural and industrial employment, they constitute a perceived economic threat of several sorts. In addition to depressing the value of local labor, they were often seen as a part of the Mexican-American community and everyone named Ramirez or Gonzalez or Diego got tainted with the same stigma.

Of late, instead of resenting this grouping of contract laborers and others with themselves, Mexican-Americans have joined with them to fight for union representation and collective bargaining in the vineyards, lettuce fields, and orange groves where they toil. And not only is there a growing sense of cohesiveness beginning to assert itself among the disparate members of *La Raza*, but a demand for both political power and recognition of cultural pride is being voiced by an increasing segment of this minority of as many as eight million people.

"Chicano" used to be a term of derogation (a corruption of "Mexicano") but, for many so labeled, in the 1960s it became a term of pride and solidarity. As one well-known Mexican-American has said, "Call us whatever you like, *we* know what we are and are proud of it."[44]

Increasingly the voices of Mexican-Americans—Cesar Chavez in California, Corky Gonzalez in Colorado, Ries Tijerina in New Mexico, and a variety of new leaders in Texas—were raised, and many, Anglos and Mexican-Americans, started to listen closely. They saw changes that altered both the public stereotypes ("Frito Bandito") and the substance of life for Mexican-Americans. In the late 1970s one factor, perhaps more than any other, boosted the self-esteem of Mexican-Americans as well as their brothers, sisters, and cousins south of the border. This was the discovery of enormous reserves of fossil fuel in Mexico, a deposit reportedly as large as that in Saudi Arabia. For the first time, the giant to the north was put on the defensive, and Mexicans possessed an important bargaining chip as they negotiated various matters of significance to them, not least immigration policies.[45]

Like other peoples so often categorized as "non-White" minorities, Mexican-Americans are seeking a legitimate and equal place in a pluralistic America. They are determined to be recognized for something far more important than the ubiquitous taco stands that dot the byways of the Southwest.

Tens of thousands of migrants other than Mexicans cross the Rio Grande to enter the United States. Many of them, like a large percentage of the Mexicans, have no papers. Illegal aliens, they are often known as "the undocumented." While a significant number are traditional economic migrants eager for employment and opportunities for a better life, many others enter this country hoping to find a safe haven from political persecution.

Unfortunately, unlike the refugees from Indochina, Cuba, and the Soviet Union, the Central American asylum-seekers are frequently viewed with suspicion by the agents of the Naturalization and Immigration Service (INS). There are many explanations for this. One of the most plausible is that, despite changes in American immigration laws which no longer define refugees as "individuals fleeing communism" (as they did from 1952–1980), the fact remains that government officials seem to continue to favor those fleeing left-wing regimens (like those in Vietnam or Cuba) over those leaving countries the United States supports (such as El Salvador).

To aid the Central Americans, a new form of the old "underground railroad" (devised by abolitionists to spirit slaves out of the south) has been established. Called "the Sanctuary Movement," American citizens have provided aid and comfort to the undocumented exiles and fought to have their status altered to permit legal recognition. One compromise that is still being debated is to give certain certain border-crossers visas that are labeled "Extended Voluntary Departure," allowing them to stay in this country as long as the crisis which creates "a well-founded fear of persecution" in their home countries persists.

Often grouped with Mexican-Americans and so-called Latinos are the Puerto Ricans. Although they too are of mixed racial origins and are Spanish-speaking, they are a distinct—and distinctive—people.

Puerto Rico, an island in the Caribbean, has been an American possession since the Spanish-American War. By their own choice Puerto Ricans became United States citizens in 1917. (Until recently, few Americans knew this, nor much else about these fellow citizens. In fact, until the mid-1950s many mapmakers misspelled the name of their home island, calling it "Porto Rico.")

Migration from the island to the mainland began early in this century; it has fluctuated with economic conditions in the states. Since World War II, Puerto Rican migration has risen sharply, in large part because of increasing job opportunities, the appeal of the popular culture of large cities, and dramatically improved transportation facilities, which have brought Puerto Rico closer to the mainland.

As in earlier days, New York is the gateway for new arrivals, and as in the past, many who first arrive in New York remain there. Puerto Ricans—like their predecessors from southern and eastern Europe and southern Blacks whose migration to New York has paralleled their own—have found employment in the garment industry and as service workers in this great commercial and tourist center. While Puerto Ricans are to be found in all parts of the country—including Alaska and Hawaii—over three-fourths of their total number live in New York City. In 1980, nearly two million Puerto Ricans were living in the mainland and close to half of that number in New York City.[46]

Like other newcomers to the city, many Puerto Ricans have found themselves relegated to the worst and most overpriced neighborhoods. Their children attend crowded schools; they often hold the lowest-status jobs; they frequently suffer "winter temperatures and more chilling social contacts."[47] Despite the fact that in many ways they have come better prepared for life in the United States than many other ethnic minorities, they are still having difficulty climbing the ladder.[48]

Census Bureau data provides graphic evidence of the difficulties Puerto Ricans have in succeeding, despite the fact that they are far more likely to have come from urban areas and have a much higher proportion of skilled and semiskilled workers than the native population. Furthermore, in contradiction to the assertion that "primarily Puerto Rico's unemployed come to New York," it has been found that the migrants are more regularly employed at home than the rest of the population and received a slightly higher income than the Puerto Rican average. They come not to seek work, but to seek *better* work. Finding it for many is still a problem and nearly a third of Puerto Rican families continue to live below the poverty level.[49]

There is little question that Puerto Ricans have faced considerable racial discrimination in the United States. Some specialists feel it has been especially hard for members of this particular cohort to cope with the "racially dichotomous" (White versus non-White) character of mainland thinking, a rather sharp contrast to the "racially continuous" (from White to Black) situation on their home island. Puerto Ricans are the first major group to migrate to the urban centers of the United States, bringing with them a tradition of widespread racial mixing. While it is true that lighter-skinned Puerto Ricans generally have higher status in San Juan than New York, there are many exceptions. Indeed, it is said that "on the mainland, the color of a person determines what class he will belong to; in Puerto Rico, the class a person belongs to determines his color." Another popular expression for the same phenomenon is that "money whitens!"

A small number of Puerto Ricans, reacting to others' perceptions of them in the United States, tried a new ploy in the 1960s and 1970s. They called themselves "Cubans." They recognized that, for many Americans in the dominant group, Cubans were then seen as desirable rather than undesirable Hispanics.

Until the Castro Revolution, there were relatively few Cubans in the United States. Some were in business; most were laborers. But with the fall of Juan Batista, hundreds of thousands of Cubans sought and gained admittance to this country as exiles from the new, socialist regime. Between 1959 and 1970 some 700,000 refugees entered the United States, most arriving and staying in the Miami area. While some were exceedingly wealthy, the majority were of modest means and had to start their lives anew. That these "refugees from communism" were successful accounted for the favorable press they began to receive across the country. In south Florida, however, things were different. The Cubans—and their tightknit community organization—were envied by other recent immigrants. They were also resented by "indigenous" minorities, especially Blacks, who sometimes claimed the Cubans were elbowing their ways into the system and taking jobs away from members of their community. As the Cubans began to move into the political arena, the tensions rose even higher.

In 1980, a second large wave (approximately 150,000) of Cuban exiles made the 90 mile trip to Florida coast. These "boat people" were quite different from their compatriots: They were generally poorer and less well educated. And many more were black. Still, being *Cuban*, the larger ethnic community felt obligated to offer assistance—more, argued many embittered American Blacks, than *they* were able to receive. The increasing influx of other Hispanics did little to dampen the sense of outrage.

As noted above, in the late 1980s, thousands of Guatemalans, Salvadorans, and Nicaraguans crossed the Mexican border, often illegally, seeking asylum in the United States. While the authorities were highly selective in their willingness to consider such undocumented aliens as refugees—being somewhat more kindly disposed to those fleeing Nicaragua, a Marxist state, than El Salvador, an ally of the United States heavily supported by American aid, they finally did allow large numbers to stay in the country, at least temporarily. In January 1989, a large contingent of Nicaraguans moved from the border areas in Texas to Miami and Dade County, Florida, where they were assisted by various social service and employment agencies, many of them run by sympathetic Cuban-Americans. The presence of the Central Americans greatly exacerbated an already strained relationship between the city's Black and Hispanic populations and resulted in several days of violent confrontation.

Conclusion

Many of those who migrated to America left their countries of origin seeking freedom and a new life in the New World. Some came to make their fortunes; some to escape religious persecution, political tyranny, or economic deprivation; and some were unwillingly brought in the chains of bondage. For most, immigration was the beginning of a new and exciting adventure, but for others the journey to America was a bitter and harrowing experience.

In this brief sketch of America's principal immigrant groups we have only touched upon the reception of newcomers by those already in the United States. In Chapter Three we turn to a discussion of various proposals for coping with "strangers" in the land, an interpretation of these, an examination of the patterns of ethnic separation that emerged, and a consideration of a statistical breakdown of America's racial, religious, and ethnic composition.

NOTES

1. There are many general texts that describe the history of and reaction to America's minorities. Among the most useful are Nathan Glazer (ed), *Clamor at the Gates* (San Francisco: Institute for Contemporary Studies, 1985); Leonard Dinnerstein and David Reimers, *Ethnic Americans* (New York: Harper & Row, 1975); Oscar Handlin, *The Uprooted* (Boston: Little, Brown, 1951); Marcus Lee Hansen, *The Atlantic Migration 1607–1860* (New York: Harper Torchbook, 1961); Marcus Lee Hansen, *The Immigrant in American History* (Cambridge: Harvard University Press, 1940); John Higham, *Strangers in the Land: Patterns of American Nativism, 1860–1925* (New Brunswick, N.J.: Rutgers University Press, 1955). See also Charles F. Marden and Gladys Meyer, *Minorities in American Society*, 3rd ed. (New York: American Book Company, 1968); David Reimers, *Still the Golden Door: The Third World Comes to America*, (New York: Columbia University Press, 1985); Richard A. Schermerhorn, *These Our People: Minorities in American Culture* (Boston: D. C. Heath, 1949); and Maxine Seller, *To Seek America* (Englewood, N.J.: Jerome Ozer, 1977).
2. John Collier, "The United States Indian," in J. B. Gittler (ed.), *Understanding Minority Groups* (New York: Wiley, 1956), pp. 34–36. See also Frank Lorimer, "Observations on the Trends of Indian Populations in the United States," in Oliver La Farge (ed.), *The Changing Indian* (Norman, Okla.: University of Oklahoma Press, 1942). Lorimer cites estimates of the number of the Western Hemisphere at the time of the first white settlement as 8 and 13 million.
3. See, for example, Ruth Benedict, *Patterns of Culture* (Boston: Houghton Mif-

flin, 1934); Paul Radin, *The Story of the American Indian* (New York: Liveright, 1944); and Peter Farb, *Man's Rise to Civilization* (New York: Dutton, 1968).

4. For a discussion of the "somatic norm image" see Harry Hoetink, *The Two Variants in Caribbean Race Relations* (New York: Oxford University Press, 1967).

5. John Collier, *Indians of the Americas* (New York: Mentor Books, 1947), pp. 116–117.

6. Marden and Meyer, *op. cit.*, pp. 361–362.

7. Pierre van den Berghe, *Race and Racism* (New York: Wiley, 1967), p. 86.

8. Alden Stevens, "Whither the American Indian?" in Milton L. Barron (ed.), *American Minorities* (New York: Knopf, 1958), p. 148.

9. John Neihardt (ed.), *Black Elk Speaks* (Lincoln, Neb.: University of Nebraska Press, 1961), p. 258.

10. Marden and Meyer, *op. cit.*, pp. 362–371. See also William and Sophie Brophy, *The Indian: America's Unfinished Business* (Norman, Okla.: University of Oklahoma Press, 1966).

11. For fuller discussion see Joseph Hraba, *American Ethnicity* (Ithaca, Ill.: F. E. Peacock, 1979), esp. pp. 229–236.

12. Patrick Huyghe and David Konigsberg, "Bury My Heart at New York City," *New York*, (February 19, 1979), p. 54.

13. See Murray Wax, *Indian-Americans: Unity and Diversity* (Englewood Cliffs, N.J.: Prentice-Hall, 1971).

14. Delaware had been a Swedish possession. It was surrendered to the Dutch in 1655.

15. See Arnold and Caroline Rose, *America Divided* (New York: Knopf, 1953), pp. 28–31.

16. "The Interesting Narrative of the Life of Olaudah Equiano, or Gustavas Vassa, the African," as cited in Peter I. Rose (ed.) *Many Peoples, One Nation* (New York: Random House, 1973), p. 77.

17. See Alex Haley, *Roots* (New York: Dell, 1979).

18. See Kenneth M. Stampp, *The Peculiar Institution* (New York: Vintage Books, 1956).

19. See, for example, Herbert Gutman, *The Black Family in Slavery and Freedom, 1750–1925* (New York: Random House, 1976).

20. There is considerable controversy over these issues. See Stanley Elkins, *Slavery* (Chicago: University of Chicago, 1959); and Ann J. Lane, *The Debate over Slavery: Stanley Elkins and His Critics* (Urbana, Ill: University of Illinois Press, 1971). See also Peter I. Rose (ed.), *Slavery and its Aftermath* (Vol. I of *Americans from Africa*) (New York: Atherton Press, 1970); esp. pp. 103–194.

21. See C. Vann Woodward, *The Strange Career of Jim Crow* (New York: Oxford University Press, 1957), p. 8.

22. Ralph Ellison, *Invisible Man* (New York: Random House, 1962).

23. Martin Luther King, Jr., "I Have a Dream," *SCLC Newsletter*, 12 (September 1963).

24. See Peter I. Rose (ed.), *Old Memories, New Moods* (Vol. II of *Americans from Africa*) (New York: Atherton Press, 1970), esp. pp. 237–320.

25. See William J. Wilson, *The Declining Significance of Race* (Chicago: University of Chicago Press, 1978).

26. John F. Kennedy, *A Nation of Immigrants*, rev. ed. (New York: Harper & Row, 1964), p. 18.
27. See, for example, John B. Duff, *The Irish in the United States* (Belmont, Calif.: Wadsworth, 1971), pp. 31–36.
28. Helen Znaniecki Lopata, *Polish Americans* (Englewood Cliffs, N.J.: Prentice-Hall, 1976), pp. 12–32.
29. Joseph Lopreato, *Italian Americans* (New York: Random House, 1970), pp. 36–44.
30. Pietro DiDonato, *Christ in Concrete* (Indianapolis: Bobbs-Merrill, 1937), pp. 137–138.
31. Emma Lazarus, "The New Colossus," *Poems* (Boston: Houghton Mifflin, 1889), pp. 202–203.
32. Max Lerner, *America as a Civilization* (New York: Simon and Schuster, 1958), p. 88.
33. Handlin, *op. cit.*
34. As cited in Hraba, *op. cit.*, pp. 16–17.
35. *Ibid.*, p. 17.
36. See, for example, William S. Bernard, *American Immigration Policy—A Reappraisal* (New York: Harper & Row, 1950), pp. 23–24. Also see Benjamin M. Ziegler (ed.), *Immigration: An American Dilemma* (Boston: D. C. Heath, 1953).
37. Gail Paradise Kelly, *From Vietnam to America* (Boulder, Colo.: Westview Press, 1979). See also Norman and Naomi Zucker, *The Guarded Gate* (New York: Harcourt Brace Jovanovich, 1987).
38. Peter I. Rose, "The Ghetto and Beyond," In Peter I. Rose (ed.), *The Ghetto and Beyond* (New York: Random House, 1969), p. 17.
39. See, for example, Rose Hum Lee, *The Chinese in the United States of America* (New York: Oxford University Press, 1960); Francis L. K. Hsu, *Challenge of the American Dream: The Chinese in the U.S.* (Belmont, Calif.: Wadsworth, 1971); and Stanford M. Lyman, *Chinese-Americans* (New York: Random House, 1973).
40. Harry H. L. Kitano, *Japanese-Americans* (Englewood Cliffs, N.J.: Prentice-Hall, 1969), p. 17.
41. *Ibid.*; see also William Petersen, *Japanese-Americans: Oppression and Success* (New York: Random House, 1971).
42. Leonard Bloom and Ruth Riemer, *Removal and Return* (Berkeley: University of California Press, 1949), pp. 202–204. See also Maisie and Richard Conrat, *Executive Order 9066: The Internment of 110,000 Japanese-Americans* (Sacramento, Calif.: California Historical Society, 1976).
43. Stanford M. Lyman, "Japanese-American Generation Gap," *Society*, 10 (January-February 1973), 55–63.
44. See John H. Burma (ed.), *Mexican-Americans in the United States* (New York: Schenkman, 1970); Ellwyn Stoddard, *Mexican-Americans* (New York: Random House, 1973); and Joan Moore, *Mexican Americans*, 2d ed. (Englewood Cliffs, N.J.: Prentice-Hall, 1976).
45. See, for example, *The New York Times* (February 15, 1979), p. 1.
46. See Joseph P. Fitzpatrick, *The Puerto Rican New Yorkers*, 2d ed. (Englewood Cliffs, N.J.: Prentice Hall, 1987), p. 15.
47. Clarence Senior, *Strangers—Then Neighbors* (New York: Freedom Books, 1961), p. 22. See also Elena Padilla, *Up from Puerto Rico* (New York: Columbia

University Press, 1958); Christopher Rand, *The Puerto-Ricans* (New York: Oxford University Press, 1958); and Patricia Cayo Sexton, *Spanish Harlem* (New York: Harper, 1965).

48. See report by Edward C. Burks, "Affluence Eludes Blacks, Puerto-Ricans," *The New York Times* (August 17, 1972), p. 33.

49. Vincent N. Parrillo, *Strangers to These Shores* (Boston: Houghton Mifflin, 1980), p. 417.

3

ONE AMERICAN OR MANY?

Coming Full Circle

Sometime in the spring of 1970 the "American saga" seemed to come full circle. An attempt was made by a dozen Mohawks to establish a beachhead on Ellis Island, the place where thousands upon thousands of European immigrants had first touched American shores. The motorboat failed and the plot to seize the island on the East Coast as others had seized the island of Alcatraz in San Francisco Bay was foiled.

When someone suggested that the Indians were stupid for attempting the occupation of the island, a member of the raiding party retorted, "We're stupid? It was your ancestors who landed on these shores, thought they were somewhere else, and called us Indians. Indians live on the other side of the world!"

That bit of repartee is more profound than it seems on the surface. In a few words it expresses the frustration of many American minority group members who know that they are seen as ignorant, sneaky, sullen, argumentative, or aggressive while the members of the dominant group fancy themselves as paragons of virtue and intelligence. In the United States this majority is preeminently white, Protestant, and of European background. Its standards are those set, by and large, by its legacy; and so, in a way, are its prejudices.

Ko Lum Bo

But suppose, as George Stewart once suggested, that the English and other north Europeans had not settled our eastern shores first. Suppose that the approach had been from the west and that Asians, rather than Europeans, had landed and established political control and, for all intents and purposes, political and cultural hegemony over the new territories. Stewart put it this way:

... during one of the vigorous and expansive periods of the Chinese Empire, one of their navigators (who might have been named Ko Lum Bo) conceived the idea of sailing eastward from China and thus arriving at Ireland, which was known to be the farthest outpost of Europe. The Chinese wished to reach Ireland it may be believed, because they had heard tales that those barbarous islanders made a certain drink called Wis Ki.

Ko Lum Bo made his voyage, and discovered a country that he supposed to be part of Ireland, although he was disappointed in not finding any Wis Ki being manufactured by the natives.

During the course of the next two centuries the Chinese colonized this country, eventually discovering it to be not Ireland, but a wholly new continent. Nevertheless they continued to call the natives Irish, or sometimes Red Irish.

The Chinese colonists introduced their own well-established ways of life. They continued to speak Chinese, and to practice their own religion. Being accustomed to eat rice, they still ate it, as far as possible. Vast areas of the country were terraced and irrigated as rice paddies. The colonists continued to use their comfortable flowing garments, and pagodas dotted the landscape. In short, the civilization was Asiatic and not European.[1]

Dropping Stewart's delightful and pointed bit of social science fiction, we remind ourselves that it was the English, Scotch-Irish, and north Europeans who did come, bringing with them much of their own cultural baggage, which, from the start, they thought superior to that of the natives. Manners of speaking and dressing, organizing communities, regulating commerce, teaching and preaching were transplanted from the British Isles to America. Of course, the New World (and especially, the hinterlands of North America) was of a scale that was hard to comprehend. As the new society developed, adjustments were constantly necessary. Innovations were commonplace. Even so, many aspects of the core culture were retained. And so, like the Chinese who never came (at least not in the manner imagined), the English—and others who did—developed a new or, better stated, modified version of their old societies. And all who were here (meaning the diverse tribes of Indians) or were to come (including thousands of slaves and millions of immigrants) were to be affected by the laws and lifeways of the Anglo-American Establishment.

Immigrants and the American Dream

For four centuries America served as a magnet—first for the rich and venturesome and later for the tired and poor and "tempest-tost." The majority of immigrants—English, Irish, German, Scandinavian, Italian, Jewish, and Slav—came of their own free will, ready and willing to share in the wealth and bounty of America. Many were disillusioned; many suffered from discrimination by those who had so recently been newcomers themselves; many found it difficult to reconcile their Old World ways with the new. And yet, in time, one group after another began the slow climb and, for many, the American dream (of equal opportunity) proved more than a catch phrase.

In spite of the divisions and conflicts among the varied groups that are so much a part of American history and American folklore, for those who were white, almost all things were considered possible. As Raymond Aron, the French sociologist, accurately observed:

As far as I am concerned, the greatest achievement of American society is to have drawn millions of people from the lower classes of Europe and made them into good American citizens. That is an extraordinary performance, an unprecedented marvel of acculturation.

But you didn't do it without paying a heavy price. Poverty in America is aggravated by ethnic heterogeneity, by the unfinished acculturation of certain fragments of the American population. You have a permanently unintegrated fringe, consisting chiefly of blacks and Puerto-Ricans. You did very well in assimilating national minorities, but not nearly as well with racial minorities.[2]

There are various explanations of these facts of American life. One that is the simplest is quite persuasive. Those who proposed programs for the best way of integrating disparate peoples into a single nation did so generally without regard to color and yet rarely were "Colored people" ever seriously considered on a par with white immigrants. The theorists and policy makers dealt with those they saw as *ethnic* minorities, not racial ones—at least not until recently.

Theories of Integration

The nature of adjustment of increasing numbers of immigrants to life in America has been of concern to both scholars and politicians since the early days of the colonial period. In the deliberations and debates over the problem of integrating ethnically heterogeneous peoples into a unified, English-speaking national group, various courses of action with explicit goals in mind have been promulgated. The three principal theories of adjustment—offered by the Founding Fathers, by the newcomers themselves, or by their spokesmen—have been popularly referred to as "Anglo conformity" (a term coined by George Stewart and Mildred Cole), "the melting pot," and "cultural pluralism."[3] Sociologists, ever wont to give more precise designations to social processes, came to call these *assimilation, amalgamation,* and *accommodation,* respectively.

Assimilation

During the eighteenth century the majority of those who had come to America—White, Protestant, Anglo-Saxon—saw themselves standing on the threshold of a new world. The United States itself was conceived in the spirit of liberty and dedicated to the belief "that all men are created equal . . . endowed by their Creator with certain inalienable Rights." However, the authors of these phrases shared the belief of many others that American social norms and values of the future lay within the framework of traditionally British social, religious, and cultural institutions; and, while America was envisaged as an asylum for Europe's refugees, some of the leading figures of the day had strong reservations about what the effects of unrestricted immigration might be. In a letter to John Adams, George Washington wrote:

> My opinion, with respect to immigration, is that except of useful mechanics and some particular descriptions of men or professions, there is no need of encouragement, while the policy or advantage of its taking place in a body (I mean the settling of them in a body) may be much questioned; for, by so doing, they retain the language, habits and principles (good or bad) which they bring with them.[4]

Most of those who were of the opinion that an open-door policy should prevail emphatically maintained that the immigrant should take off his foreign mantle and quickly adapt himself to *American* ways. John Adams made this position quite clear when he wrote:

> They come to a life of independence, but to a life of labor—and, if they cannot accommodate themselves to the character, moral, political, and physical, of this country with all its compensating balances of good and evil, the Atlantic is always open to them to return to the land of their nativity and their fathers. . . . They must cast off the European skin, never to resume it.[5]

If the Founding Fathers had their ideas about the best course of national integration, so, too, did many of the newcomers.[6] The immigrants often envisioned America as a vast land affording unlimited economic and social opportunities in an atmosphere free from harassment and interference. By the mid-nineteenth century many came to this country with clear intentions of maintaining their separate cultural identities. The Germans, for example, who settled in Wisconsin, Missouri, and Texas, succeeded in establishing a number of settlements where the German language was the vernacular and where German nationalism persisted, even though they had to modify many behavior patterns to adjust to the new frontier they faced.

According to historian Frederick Jackson Turner, assimilation itself was enhanced by the opportunities that abounded on the frontier. Writing especially about the settlement and acculturation of German immigrants, Turner stated:

> Our early history is the study of European germs developing in an American environment. Too exclusive attention has been paid by institutional students to

the Germanic origins, too little to the American factors. The frontier is the line of most rapid and effective Americanization. The wilderness masters the colonist. It finds him a European in dress, industries, tools, modes of travel, and thought. It takes him from the railroad car and puts him in the birch canoe. It strips off the garments of civilization and arrays him in the hunting shirt and the moccasin. It puts him in the log cabin of the Cherokee and Iroquois and runs an Indian palisade around him. Before long he has gone to planting Indian corn and plowing with a sharp stick; he shouts the war cry and takes the scalp in orthodox fashion. In short, at the frontier the environment is at first too strong for the man. He must accept the conditions which it furnishes, or perish, and so he fits himself into the Indian clearings and follows the Indian trails. Little by little he transforms the wilderness but the outcome is not the old Europe, not simply the development of Germanic germs, any more than the first phenomenon was a case of reversion to the Germanic mark. The fact is, there here is a new product that is American.[7]

Turner continued, making a second point. The farther west people traveled, the greater the influence of the frontier and the less the counterpull of the Old Country. "Thus," he wrote, "the advance of the frontier has meant a steady movement away from the influence of Europe, a steady growth of independence on American lines."[8]

Many westerners, especially Californians, argue the same point today saying, in effect, that ethnicity is much more an "eastern phenomenon." Thus, it is said that if you ask a New Yorker or Philadelphian or even a Chicagoan where he or she comes from, the answer will be "Ireland," "Russia," "Italy," or perhaps, "England." But if you ask white persons from Los Angeles or San Jose, they will often reply, "Kansas," "Oklahoma," or "the East." Still, more careful probing reveals the existence and persistence of ethnic ties and the maintenance of many ethnic neighborhoods among the White population of western and southwestern cities as well as the ghettos and barrios and suburban clusters of non-White minority group members.

Such enclaves have long existed even on the frontier itself. One thinks of those of the Scandinavians, rugged farmers and fisherfolk idealized in Willa Cather's O Pioneers, Ole Rolvaag's Giants in the Earth, and in Vilhelm Moberg's trilogy, The Emigrants, Unto a Good Land, and The Last Letter Home. While some settled in the Delaware Basin most did not dally long on the east coast but moved on to the prairies and woodlands of the northern midwest, areas that became strongholds of Swedish and Norwegian culture and religion.[9] Their trek to the wilderness, first by wagon train, later by rail, was a lesson in adaptation but also in resistance to change as well. They attacked the frontier and shaped it; perhaps, some might say, more than it shaped them—reversing the variables in the Turner hypothesis. Isolation from the dominant drift of American social patterns permitted the widespread and long-lived retention of indigenous lifeways, many of which continue to this day.

As indicated in the preceding chapter, the Irish—and most of the other immigrants who came later—tended to concentrate in urban areas where it was more difficult to maintain a separate existence. Yet, the presence of these new immigrants in the same communities as the older Americans brought about a reevaluation of sentiments about assimilation. The new-comers—whose backgrounds differed even more radically than those of the Germans or Scandinavians from those of the early settlers—were often viewed as constituting a substantial threat to the established majority. "Could *these* aliens ever become real Americans?"

Labor unrest and agitation attributed largely to the foreign elements in the population, the specter of Catholicism in Protestant America, and the growth of overcrowded urban slums inhabited by groups of oddly dressed people who seemed to speak in various forms of gibberish revived and reinforced anti-foreign attitudes. As a result of those developments, new movements arose to keep the United States "American."

First there was the anti-Irish Know Nothing party of the pre-Civil War period. In the 1890s the American Protective Association was created to "save the country from the papacy." Later anti-Semitic organizations arose, including the Ku Klux Klan (which was also violently anti-Negro) and other hate groups mirroring earlier nativistic sentiment. Among them were the Coughlinites, the John Birch Society, and the American Nazi party.[10]

In 1882 the first restrictive legislation was passed to limit the flow of immigrants (in this case, Chinese laborers) to the United States. In the years that followed, resentment grew as increasing numbers of European nationals established ethnic communities where Old World ties were perpetuated. No longer could the dominant group avoid coming to grips with the problem of immigrants who arrived at the rate of a million a year and whose political strength alone was very great. A new kind of assimilationist policy emerged to enforce more directly the adoption of American ways. This was the "Americanization Movement," which, through propaganda and education, sought to break down the immigrants' ties to the past.

Here is how Henry Pratt Fairchild described the situation in 1926:

It was perhaps in keeping with the interest and faith in education, which has been called the outstanding feature of the American nationality, that the task of Americanization should have presented itself to the pioneers in the movement primarily as an educational matter. Recognizing that the process of assimilation consists in the elimination of unlikeness, it was natural that in considering the unlikeness of the foreigner they should have been impressed with the difference in what he knew. It was perfectly clear that one of the great barriers that separated the native from the foreigner was the fact that the native knew certain things that the foreigner did not know. Prominent among these were the English language and United States civics and history. The first and most obvious step in Ameri-canization, therefore, seemed to be to teach these things to the foreigner.

Thereupon there was launched upon the country one of the most remarkable campaigns of intensive specialized education that the world has ever known. Every conceivable educational device was utilized. The land was flooded with lessons, lectures, and literature. Night schools and shop classes were organized. Rallies, pageants, and conferences were held. A special magazine was established and issued for a few numbers. An elaborate training course for workers among immigrants was planned and offered for adoption among colleges and universities. As the movement grew, and the needs of the immigrant woman as well as the immigrant man were recognized, classes were set up in millinery, dressmaking, diet, and the American care of babies. To these enterprises time, money, and personal service were contributed by men and women, professionals and volunteers, with a devotion and enthusiasm which could be enlisted only by loyalty to the nation in a time of stress and danger. Coming at any other time, when we were not accustomed to displays of self-sacrifice and public spirit, the Americanization movement would have been a striking exhibition of the operation of altruistic sentiments.[11]

Fairchild went on to describe the failure of the movement which, in his eyes, was never clearly understood for it confused means with ends and its advocates never really appreciated the difficulties of altering character along with language instruction and history lessons. There was more to divesting oneself of "alien" ways than the protagonists, many of them vehemently xenophobic, could understand or effectively deal with.

To be sure, many advocates of Americanization were not anti-foreign but were troubled by what they saw as the slowness of integration and the growing potential for conflicts, especially during the World War I period. They felt the need for a device to unite the people. Yet, whether anti-foreign or integrationist, there was often the common view that every effort should be made to get newcomers to rid themselves of their old ways. The sentiment was summarized by one American, who not so long ago explained:

I am sure foreign people make a mistake in keeping customs of their own land alive and featured in this country. If this country meets their expectations they should forget the folklore of Europe, St. Patrick's Day Parades, German Days, and get behind American things. If they can't do this they should be returned to the land they love. This country is supposed to be the world's melting pot. If they won't melt, they should not belong.[12]

This is, to be sure, a rather odd rendering of the melting pot idea which, as we shall see, referred to combining with rather than accepting the ways of others. But it is typical of the sentiment of those who saw their country being threatened and changed by outsiders.

Amalgamation

While the idea of assimilation—or "Anglo conformity"—has been most prevalent through much of our history, there have been other views about the best way to achieve an integrated society. Some hoped to develop a society where the "best" traditions of the various nations would be blended into a dynamic unity. This conception of amalgamation was already established in the years immediately following the American Revolution and is illustrated in comments of the French-born, naturalized American J. Hector St. John de Crevecoeur. In his 1782 *Letters from an American Farmer,* he described the new American as he saw him:

> He is either a European or the descendant of a European; hence, that strange mixture of blood, which you will find in no other country. . . . He is an American, who, leaving behind him all his ancient prejudices and manners, receives new ones from the new mode of life he has embraced, the new government he obeys, and the new rank he holds. . . . Here individuals of all nations are melted into a new race of men, whose labours and posterity will one day cause great changes in the world. Americans are the western pilgrims, who are carrying along with them the great mass of arts, sciences, vigor, and industry, which began long since in the east. They will finish the circle.[13]

Over the years others would also argue that the problems of diverse peoples would best be resolved through the gradual fusion of cultural traits into a new and unique system. Even at the height of the period of new immigration, long after the great influx of groups from northern Europe had ended, imagery of amalgamation was still used to explain the best policy for the United States. Thus, the English writer Israel Zangwill expanded the notion to include persons from every corner of the globe. In a play, "The Melting Pot," he portrayed America as a crucible:

> There she lies, the great melting pot—listen! Can't you hear the roaring and the bubbling? There gapes her mouth—the harbour where a thousand mammoth feeders come from the ends of the world to pour in their human freight. Ah, what a stirring and a seething—Celt and Latin, Slav and Teuton, Greek and Syrian, black and yellow— . . . Jew and Gentile. . . .[14]

The politician William Jennings Bryan echoed the sentiments of Zangwill: "Great has been the Greek, the Latin, the Slav, the Celt, the Teuton, and the Saxon; but greater than any of these is the American, who combines the virtues of them all."[15]

Summarizing the views of various writers, sociologists Donald Light and Suzanne Keller indicate that assimilation *and* amalgamation are more likely to be possible when "(1) the immigrants' appearance and customs resemble those of the dominant group, (2) they arrive in small numbers, (3) they are too far from their homeland to return for visits, and (4) they possess skills that the dominant group admire and need."[16] But, while far from home, those who came to America in the floodtide of immigration from 1880 to 1924 were, often as not, different in manners and mores, members of fairly large groups and relatively unskilled.

The problem of immigrant adjustment was often presented as an either/ or proposition. Thus, the assimilationists argued that newcomers must become apostates from their old and established ways, "get behind American things," and reconcile themselves to the new and strange way of life of the host society. Others, who supported the melting-pot view, felt that people should merge themselves through cultural fusion. The former position presumed that by forcibly assimilating immigrants to a single, already established pattern, in time, they would benefit from a way of life superior to that which they brought to America. Many newcomers, however eager they were to become Americans, were understandably reluctant to abandon their familiar ways, and many resisted the more draconic aspects of Americanization. The melting-pot philosophy, while far more democratic in intent, was also unrealistic. People were not about to simply mix together in the great crucible to form one new American type, the result of a blend of the cultural ingredients of Europe, Africa, and Asia. Recognition of this fact encouraged the emergence of the idea of cultural pluralism.

Accommodation

As Milton Gordon has suggested, "Cultural pluralism was a fact in American society before it became a theory—a theory with explicit relevance for the nation as a whole.[17] This theory developed into an image of the United States as a country enhanced by its diversity. Against absorption or fusion, advocates of pluralism saw America as "a multiplicity in a unity."[18] Jane Addams, John Dewey, and Randolph Bourne were among those who spoke out against the policy of "Americanization" and the destruction of traditional cultural values of immigrants. But no one more eloquently presented the case for cultural pluralism than the philosopher Horace Kallen, who likened the new society to a symphony orchestra:

As in an orchestra, every type of instrument has its special timbre and tonality, found in its substances and form; as every type has its appropriate theme and melody in the whole symphony, so in society each ethnic group is the natural instrument, its spirit and culture are its theme and melody, and the harmony and disonances and discords of them all make the symphony of civilization, with this difference: a musical symphony is written before it is played; in the symphony of civilization the playing is the writing, so that there is nothing so fixed and inevitable about its progressions as in music, so that within the limits set by nature they may vary at will, and the range and variety of the harmonies may become wider and richer and more beautiful.[19]

The theory of cultural pluralism was thus based on the assumption that there is strength in variety, that the nation as a whole benefits from the contributions of different groups. Cultural pluralism involves giving and taking and, most importantly, the sharing of and mutual respect for other ideas, customs, and values. In such terms America can be seen as a mosaic of ethnic groups, a "nation of nations," each retaining its unique qualities while contributing to the overall pattern.

All who spoke for cultural pluralism emphasized the fact that ethnic groups ("nationalities," as they were called) should have the right to remain separated, and Kallen, in an oft-quoted sentence, suggested that individuals who were born into such groups were inextricably bound to them. He said that "Men may change their clothes, their politics, their wives, their religions, their philosophies, to a greater or lesser extent, [but] they cannot change their grandfathers."[20]

The fact is that despite a considerable degree of adaptation to dominant lifeways and to the invention of new forms based on the fusion of ideas and practices, America remains in many ways what it has always been, a structurally pluralistic country, a nation of ethnic blocs whose members are joined by the labels they have inherited, by the tribal ties of kinship, social organization, and economic interests; and by the prides and prejudices of others. (Other variables—religion, class, region—are important too and, as we shall see, need to be factored in along with ethnic ties.)

Those minority individuals who tend to be found enjoying a truly high degree of social integration are likely to be members of the academic community, or artists, writers, journalists, or entertainers. But these are the exceptional cases, those "in which persons from different ethnic backgrounds interact in primary group relations with considerable frequency and with relative comfort and ease."[21] For most Americans close social relations occur within what Gordon calls the *ethclass*, defined as "that subsociety created by the interaction of the vertical stratification of ethnicity with the horizontal stratification of social class."[22] In simple terms this means, for example, that, by and large, upper-class "WASPs" associate at an intimate level with those who share their ethnicity and their social-class position; while middle-class Jews, middle-class Italian-Americans, working-class Polish-Americans, or poor White Southerners generally socialize with their own kind.

White Immigrants and Non-White Minorities

In the many discussions and debates about assimilation, amalgamation, and, especially, pluralism in American life, all sorts of racial, religious, and nationality groups are included in both the explanations of what has happened and in blueprints for the future. Yet proponents of each view often have tended to deny or to overlook fundamental differences among the voluntary immigrants, the various Indian nations whose lands were overrun, and, especially, the African-Americans who were forced to come and who now comprise close to 15 percent of the population.[23]

Many have argued—and, perhaps, wanted to believe—that Blacks would take their place, all other factors being equal, in the manner of the other "newcomers." While it is patently naïve to refer to people whose ancestors came when only Indians and Pilgrims populated the land as "newcomers," it is true that their urban experience is relatively recent and that the northward trek, made by so many Black men and women in the hundred years, does represent an important internal migration. And there are certain parallels. But even in such terms the analogy does not hold completely.

During the late nineteenth and early twentieth centuries, hope, a belief in the American Dream, and definite opportunities were important incentives for poor people from many lands. Overcoming various obstacles, many Irish-, Italian-, Polish-, and Jewish-Americans managed to make it, and they found successful accommodation in the new environment. But it is also true that opportunities for Europe's immigrants—even the desperately poor—were far greater than those afforded non-White people and, especially, Blacks. As economist John Kenneth Galbraith is reported to have quipped: "If you have to be poor, at least have the good sense to be born at a time when everybody is poor."[24]

There was yet another problem. Not only did Black people enter the urban economy at the wrong time according to the Galbraith dictum but also, unlike the members of most other American minority groups, they did not have the same choices to inspire them nor did they have the same sorts of communal resources to fall back upon (as had many of the European immigrants). They were different.

Recognition of this fact opens a Pandora's box, one with practical, political, emotional, and theoretical implications. The argument that Blacks could resolve their dilemma in the manner of other cases of "immigrant adjustment" assumed that their dilemma was the same. It is not, and, in many ways, it never was.

Sociologist Robert Blauner, one of the leading opponents of the "Negro-as-immigrant" school, has written that

... the entrance of the European into the American order involved a degree of choice and self-direction that was for the most part denied people of color. Voluntary immigration made it more likely that individual Europeans and entire ethnic groups would identify with America and see the host culture as a positive opportunity rather than an alien and dominating value system. It is my assessment that this element of choice, though it can be overestimated and romanticized, must have been crucial in influencing the different careers and perspectives of immigrants [the] colonized in America, because choice is a necessary condition for commitment to any group, from social club to national society.

Sociologists interpreting race relations in the United States have rarely faced the full implications of these differences. The *immigrant model* became the main focus of analysis, and the experiences of all groups were viewed through its lens. It suited the cultural mythology to see everyone in America as an original immigrant, a later immigrant, a quasi-immigrant or a potential immigrant. Though the black situation long posed problems for this framework, recent developments have made it possible for scholars and ordinary citizens alike to force Afro-African realities into this comfortable schema. Migration from rural South to urban North became an analog of European immigration, blacks became the latest newcomers to the cities, facing parallel problems of assimilation. In the no-nonsense language of Irving Kristol, "The Negro Today Is Like the Immigrant of Yesterday."[25]

Unique Americans

The Blacks' experience in America is unique—it has no real parallel. And Black Americans are unique. Paradoxically, Blacks may well be at once the most alienated and the least foreign of all the citizens: most alienated because of their special history, which began in subjugation, continued in separation, and persists to this day under various forms of segregation; least foreign because, ironically, having been cut off from their native roots, they had few guides but those of the master and his agents. This is not to say that no "Africanisms" survived. Of course they did. Still, most Black Americans, for good or ill, were imbued with many of the same goals and aspirations of those of the dominant group. Many of their cultural traits were similar too.

What they said and what they ate, what they believed and, in some ways, the way they worshiped, were heavily southern Americana. And so with their names. And in these names one finds the true paradox of being both a part of and apart from society. Names are labels by which others know you. Black people's names are those of Whites, usually white masters. It is little wonder that one of the symbolic gestures in the search to assert both self-hood and people-hood by young Blacks in the 1960s was to cast off their "slave names" and to adopt African ones—or simply to call themselves "X."

By and large this assertion did not come about until quite recently. For years, Black people—named Smith and Jones and Brown and Washington—quested after the American Dream and sought to take their place with Whites. For many, the venture proved quixotic. Some succeeded, however, and became Black equivalents of the white *nouveaux riches*, with all the material trappings to indicate having arrived. Others eschewed such life styles but sought other benefits in the dominant society, especially through higher education and work in the professions. They often found that barriers remained, and rejection often heightened smoldering bitterness and exacerbated doubts about the rightness of seeking to integrate in the first place.

The bourgeois Blacks sometimes proved more akin to the Arabs in French Algeria than the Italians or Jews or Irish-Americans with whom they were so often compared. As Raymond Aron points out:

The French never established an integrated society in Algeria. Ironically, the young Algerians who came closest to being French, by education and training, were usually the most hostile. But this is understandable, because they were the most sensitive to their rejection by the French ruling class.[26]

Persistent relegation to inferior status and the internalization of values regarded as most typically American (such as the idea of individual achievement through hard work) led to a different sort of response on the part of many Blacks compared to members of most other American ethnic groups. Some began to argue that the more they learned about the wider society and its members' unwillingness to honor its own lofty ideals, the less they should encourage their "brothers" and "sisters" to accept its basic tenets. Since Whites appeared eager to maintain their position of preeminence, some Blacks began saying that integration was, in fact, highly dysfunctional for them—just as it was for the indigenous people of Algeria.

These observations are not to suggest that all social scientists or policy makers who saw Blacks as the latest immigrants were or are white supremacists. But they may have been quite naïve in assuming that admitting Black children to "white" schools, opening neighborhoods, and saying, in effect, "You're as good as I am" would solve the problem. Assimilation may have been the goal at one time but it has been severely challenged (see Chapter Seven).

Many observers simply failed to accept the uniqueness of the Blacks' experiences and offered what in an earlier reference to immigrants was called an either/or response. In the context of the 1960s the argument often went like this: If Black people are not to be segregated, they must be integrated. But "integration," as used in such a context, turned out to be little more than a liberalized and modernized version of "Anglo conformity." Ironically, the pluralism that many wanted for others (and sometimes for themselves) was rarely even considered as a model for Blacks, the people who by all counts would benefit most by accepting their uniqueness.

Until recently many liberal integrationists—in the universities, in the government, and even in the civil rights movement itself—saw but one side of the problem. They recognized but failed to understand the subculture that had grown out of reactions to barriers erected by whites during and after slavery. To those who wanted a fairer deal at the hands of the society, they were invariably told, "Throw off your unacceptable ways and become like me." James Farmer, the founder of the Congress of Racial Equality (CORE), once put this point of view in very clear perspective. Writing on integration, he said:

... we [Blacks] learned that America simply couldn't be color-blind. It would have to become color-blind and it would only become color-blind when we gave up our color. The white man, who presumably has no color, would have to give up only his prejudices. We would have to give up our identities. Thus, we would usher in the Great Day with an act of complete self-denial and self-abasement. We would achieve equality by conceding racism's charge: that our skins were afflicted; that our history is one long humiliation; that we are empty of distinctive traditions and any legitimate source of pride . . . .[27]

This interpretation was very difficult for many integration-minded people to accept for they saw little advantage in encouraging Blacks to retain behavior patterns that they frequently defined as pathological deviations from White standards. Blauner called the stance a part of the "dogma of liberal social science" which reflects in large measure general liberal sentiments.

The argument is evident in many places and sources. It is clearly articulated in the monumental study *An American Dilemma*, in which Gunnar Myrdal and his colleagues assert that "the Negro is an exaggerated American" and that his principal values are "pathological elaborations" of those commonly shared.[28] Historian Kenneth Stampp referred to those who were "white men with black skins."[29] Nathan Glazer and Daniel Patrick Moynihan, in the first edition of *Beyond the Melting Pot*, a study of New York City's ethnic groups, asserted that "the Negro is only an American and nothing else. He has no values and culture to guard and protect."[30] (Glazer and Moynihan modified their view in a later edition.[31])

These ideas were put forth by others, too, relying in no small measure on the work of the late E. Franklin Frazier, one of American's best-known black sociologists. For example, here is what Frazier wrote in his 1957 revision of *The Negro in the United States:*

Although the Negro is distinguished from other minorities by his physical characteristics, unlike other racial or cultural minorities the Negro is not distinguished by culture from the dominant group. Having completely lost his ancestral culture, he speaks the same language, practices the same religion, and accepts the same values and political ideals as the dominant group. Consequently, when one speaks of Negro culture in the United States, one can only refer to the folk culture of the rural Southern Negro or the traditional forms of behavior and values which have grown out of the Negro's social and mental isolation. . . .[32]

Frazier went on to say that "Since the institutions, the social stratification, and the culture of the Negro minority are essentially the same as those of the larger community, it is not strange that the Negro minority belongs among assimilationist rather than the pluralist, secessionist, or militant minorities."[33]

Frazier, it turns out, may well have been both correct and highly misleading. He assumed, along with many commentators on the Black experience (both Black and White), that to have a culture, a unique culture, one must possess a distinctive language, a unique religion, and a national homeland. As Robert Blauner has suggested, this view may be appropriate for what anthropologists would call a holistic culture, complete with the institutions of an integrated social system. Black Americans did not possess this kind of culture. But they developed their own life styles and sensitivities, often combinations of African remnants and southern Protestant characteristics, characteristics developed through encounters with racist America.

Black writers such as Richard Wright, LeRoi Jones, and Ralph Ellison—in quite different ways, to be sure—have portrayed the extent to which Blacks have had to respond to the "either/or" interpretation. In his brilliant novel *Invisible Man*, Ellison wrote:

I am an invisible man. No, I am not a spook like those who haunted Edgar Allan Poe; nor am I one of your Hollywood ectoplasms. I am a man of substance, of flesh and bone, fiber and liquids, and I might even be said to possess a mind. I am invisible, understand, simply because people refuse to see me. Like the bodiless heads you see sometimes in circus sideshows, it is as though I have been surrounded by mirrors of hard distorting glass. When they approach me they see only my surroundings, themselves, or figments of their imagination—indeed, everything and anything except me. Nor is my invisibility exactly a matter of biochemical accident to my epidermis. That invisibility to which I refer occurs because of a peculiar disposition of the eyes of those with whom I come into contact. A matter of construction of their inner eyes, those eyes with which they look through their physical eyes upon reality.[34]

In contrast to most Whites, most Blacks have long found themselves in a perpetual state of cultural schizophrenia. They have had to deal with what W. E. B. Du Bois called a sense of "twoness." "One ever feels his twoness," he wrote, "an American, a Negro; two souls, two thoughts, two unreconciled strivings; two warring ideals in one dark body."[35]

Vernon Dixon has argued that "the application of the 'either/or' conceptual approach to race relations produces racial harmony [only] when the Blacks and Whites embody total sameness."[36] And this is an impossibility. Therefore, he proposed a new and different approach, called by the rather cumbersome term "di-unitalism," in which one simultaneously recognizes the similarities *and* differences between Blacks and Whites. Above all the analyst (and, presumably, the policy maker) would have to learn to understand the ambiguity that marks the social position and often helps shape the personalities of Black Americans.

Pluralism and Discrimination

In an ironic sense, demands by Blacks arguing that they too belong to an ethnic group, a special one at that, have strengthened the general ideology of pluralism. What is sauce for the goose is sauce for the gander, and, responding to Black pressures, many "old ethnics" have become ethnophilic ganders (see Chapter Eight). In principle at least, the doctrine of pluralism is once again coming to pervade the conventional wisdom concerning intergroup relations in the United States. In recent years, the "Nation-of-Nations" motif has been extolled by public officials, educators, and religious leaders. School children are told that every group member has the right voluntarily—not by will of the majority—to retain (or to give up) his or her separate identity, and that while people should be judged as individuals, one must recognize the significance of membership in an ethnic, racial, or religious group. "Affirmative Action" is one expression that signals the official recognition of pluralist policy. As we shall see in a later chapter, such recognition stirred considerable debate among many thoughtful and troubled Americans.

At the end of that decade, especially in the late 1980s social cleavages between various groups in American society—reflected not only in voluntary or "positive" pluralism, but in institutionalized patterns of discrimination that denied the very rights implied in the idea of pluralism itself—still persisted. These patterns were most noticeable in the areas of housing, education, employment, and, especially, social interaction.

Careful examination of majority-minority relationships reveals an even more complex situation than this contradiction between principle and practice suggests. Moreover, the oversimplified notion of pluralism itself often obscures the nature of the adjustment of diverse groups to American life, for it lumps together socially and sociologically distinctive processes.[37]

Behavioral Assimilation—and Social Separation

In the United States the dominant group has sometimes adopted the traits of minorities. Well-known examples include such linguistic adaptations as "moccasin," "faux pas," "kibbitz," and "Gesundheit," and such ethnic dishes as pizza, "Danish" pastry (known in Denmark as *Wiener Brot*), and "sacramental" wine, as well as such social activities as Latin-American dances, "soul" music, the games of mah-jongg and chess, the sports of judo, lacrosse, soccer, and jai alai.

Generally, however, the cultural patterns of the dominant groups have been impressed upon and adopted by members of racial and ethnic minorities. They have accepted, as their own, patterns of living, dress, and speech—much in the way that Washington, Jefferson, and, John Adams had hoped would be the case. Constantly exposed to the dominating modes of life of the majority group, it is not surprising that minority-group members accommodate themselves to expected behavior patterns. Milton Gordon calls this "behavioral assimilation." Taking over dominant-group behavior patterns does not necessarily lead to a substantial amount of social interaction on a close, personal basis between members of the established majority- and minority-group members. Instead, behavioral assimilation is limited to such general norms as a common respect for law and order, acceptance of modes of employer-employee relationships, conformity to styles and fashion touted by the mass media, and widespread use of the symbols of success as nurtured by advertisers. It is less apt to be found in intimate personal relations.

The more personal the nature of a potential situation for social interaction, the greater are the barriers to primary and intimate intergroup participation. Here, once again, Gordon's notion of the *ethclass* is important. Since, as he points out, most close social interaction takes place where social class and ethnicity intersect, it is not surprising that movement in either direction—vertically (up and down the social ladder) and horizontally (from one ethnic category to another) presents difficulties. Some of the problems are related to normative patterns of what is appropriate behavior with whom; some are related to manners of dress, speech, and other attributes that are classbound and, often, culturally-specific. In the latter cases one thinks of the wearing of certain outfits like black leather jackets, sateen shirts, and engineer boots as opposed to down parkas, button-down collars and penny loafers, or speaking in the argot of the street (Brooklynese, say, or Black English) as opposed to middle-class speech. Of course it is always possible to change one's clothes, learn new speech patterns, and take on the characteristics of the trend-setters or upper classes. Such adaptation is not unlike the "Anglo-conformity" referred to earlier as a form of behavioral assimilation. But it is not the whole story.

First, it is probably true that imitation of those one wants to emulate becomes easier the higher up the ladder one goes. Imitation is facilitated because one's ability to master the rules and to pick up the nuances have improved with practice. Not surprisingly, those who are the poorest—and lowest in the hierarchy—have the hardest time assimilating.

But there is another matter. Being able to dress and talk like a middle-class white Ivy Leaguer (or whatever the modal type is that is being modeled) does not necessarily carry over into social interaction. Social distances are frequently maintained even as cultural barriers fall.

Thus, despite the outward manifestations of acceptance and a high degree of behavioral assimilation, various minorities have been—and are—excluded from social cliques, informal groups, and even such communal activities as religious services and leisure-time pursuits. The late John Dean reported that field staffs who investigated Jewish-Gentile relations in a number of American cities found that there was very limited informal social mixing between Jews and Christians.[38] Not long ago Andrew Greeley noted a similar phenomenon occurring between Protestants and Catholics living in a middle-class Chicago suburb.[39]

It is evident that the structural definitions of social situations—as formal or informal, secondary or primary—are relevant cues to the levels at which behavioral assimilation breaks down and social separation is required and maintained. It should be noted, once again, that the actual levels of acceptance or tolerance vary markedly; that the behavior of those in "dominant groups" is far from uniform; and that within all minorities differential modes of reaction to rejection and discrimination prevail.

Not all members of minority groups wish to have close relationships with others who differ from them culturally. The desire to maintain social distance is most clearly evident among members of certain religious groups—such as Mennonites and Hasidic Jews—who, in order to retain their systems of belief intact without threat of exposure to or enticement from the members of other faiths, avoid almost all intergroup activities. Similarly, certain cultural traditions may be thought to be threatened by the overpowering influence of a cordial host society. Solomon Poll's description of the Hasidim of Williamsburg, Brooklyn, provides an illustration of social separation:

Resistance to Americanization is such that although there is no physical wall to isolate them, a strong "sociological wall" separates this group from activities that might encroach on its cultural stability. All the institutions, including the economic activities of the group, are such that they are conducive to a Hasidic "way of life."[40]

Yet, such intensive resistance to general Americanization and to opportunities to develop and maintain relationships on the basis of personal considerations rather than ethnic status is not the prevailing mode. In fact, most members of minority groups welcome opportunities for acceptance as individuals rather than as labeled "minorities"—and this still includes many Blacks despite the growing pride in self and community referred to previously. Many would be pleased not to always be judged as ambassadors or exemplars of whatever group they happened to belong to.

Studies of social distance have shown that such individual recognition is more possible in certain realms of social life than in others. Even within these spheres, minority groups and their members are ranked according to various criteria of acceptability. In certain occupations that stress performance standards, Jews, Blacks, and other American minority-group members have found acceptance without becoming apostates—their minority status being considered irrelevant. As suggested earlier, notable cases include those in the academic world, the arts, entertainment, sports, the "demiworld," and the underworld.

Nevertheless, away from the academy, the ball park, the arena, or the theater, where people are patrons or spectators or engage in a certain amount of risk-taking, many are unable to be exempted and unable to bridge the status gap. They turn instead to traditional occupations, select friends from within their own groups, withdraw into the minority community, and resign themselves to lives in which their status as members of minority groups becomes of utmost importance, whether they wish it or not. And where the gap between the dominant and minority group is great, social inbreeding within the minority community heightens group cohesion and simultaneously reinforces the image of clannishness. There are variations, but the general and pervasive pattern is one of behavioral assimilation and social separation, or what Milton Gordon calls "structural pluralism."

America's People Today

The United States remains a nation of identifiable and often separable racial, religious, and ethnic groupings. Information regarding the racial and religious composition and national origin of the population is readily available in the periodic reports of the U.S. Bureau of the Census and other sources. This kind of information, however, should be understood in the context of the methods used for data-gathering; the meanings of "race," "creed," and "ethnicity," each present different problems for both enumerators and analysts. "Race," for example, has been assessed on the basis of information that "cannot be hidden from the enumerator, about which [he] can make assumptions without serious error, and about which people will be willing to furnish information.[41] Until 1960 this meant that the census-taker was the ultimate judge of the racial designation of a given respondent and, as a result, statistics often reflect the biases of enumerators rather than the racial identity of respondents. (Since 1960 self-classification has been the method of defining both race and ethnic affiliation, probably resulting in greater accuracy than in earlier censuses.)

Racial Groups in the United States

The extent to which the social definition of "race" (referred to in Chapter One) has long affected the ultimate percentages given for the population is indicated in the description of the category of "Negroes" or "Blacks." As noted, for many decades the U.S. Bureau of the Census claimed that besides persons of mixed Negro and white descent, the category includes those of mixed American-Indian and Negro descent, unless the Indian ancestry very definitely predominates or unless the individual is regarded as an Indian in the community.[42]

To the present day, while "White" and "Black" (however loosely the terms may be defined) are set aside as separate and distinct groupings, others are categorized by a combination of color and place of ancestral origin. In the 1970 Census, included among the "Other Races" were American Indians, Japanese, Chinese, and Filipinos; under the heading "All Others" were grouped Aleuts, Asian Indians, Eskimos, Hawaiians, Koreans, Indonesians, Polynesians, and "other races not shown separately."[43]

The 1980 Census indicates that approximately 84 percent of the American population is White, 12 percent is Black, 2 percent Asians, and the rest "others." Census Bureau studies show that, compared with the last decennial enumeration, there has been only a slight change in the proportional representation of racial groups in the United States. Moreover, five of every ten Blacks in the country still reside in the South. For the first time in many years, the number of Blacks moving out of the South was surpassed by the number moving into the South.[44] Even more dramatic is the increase of Blacks in the overall percentage of city residents. An increase in the percentage of Whites moving from these same inner-city areas to the suburbs has also been noted, thereby increasing the ratio of Blacks rather markedly, especially in certain centers. In addition to Washington, a city that was 71 percent Black by 1970,[45] Newark, Gary, Atlanta, Cleveland, and Detroit all had Black majorities by the end of the decade.

In contrast to the situation of Blacks, members of other non-White groups are most heavily concentrated west of the Mississippi; seven of every ten members of this category live in the West, eight of ten in the coastal area. The only states with a substantial proportion of non-Negro non-Whites are Alaska (20 percent—mainly Aleuts, Eskimos, and Indians) and Hawaii (67 percent—mainly Japanese and Chinese).

Table 3 presents a breakdown of all racial groups enumerated in the 1980 Census. (Note that at that time, because of self designations, Hispanics were grouped under both "White" and "Black" rubrics.)

Table 3   Racial Groups in the United States in 1980.

Race	Total, in thousands	% of Total
White	189,035	83.46
Black	26,482	11.69
Indian*	1,534	0.68
Asian†	3,726	1.64
Totals:	226,546	100

Note: In the 1970 Census, most Hispanics in the United States were grouped as "White."
   In the 1980 Census, persons of Spanish origin might have been of any race.
Source: U.S. Bureau of the Census, 1980, Census of Population, Vol. 1, Chap. D, Part 1, Section A, Table 253; 1981.
*Includes American Indian, Eskimo, Innuit, and Aleut
†Includes Pacific Islanders

Religious Groups in the United States

In American society the freedom to worship in one's own way is a fundamental guarantee of the Bill of Rights. There is a proliferation of religious organizations, ranging in structure from the highly bureaucratized Roman Catholic Church to transitory and loosely organized storefront Protestant churches. Some religious groups are basically fundamentalist; others are more liberal in their interpretations of sacred writings and theology.

Despite this diversity in organization and religious perspective (and despite the proclivity of Americans to search for new avenues to express religious feelings, as in the recent appeal of Hare Krishna and Zen, which do not follow orthodox Western religious traditions), Americans remain a church-going people. The United States, as Will Herberg once suggested, is a nation ever caught in a paradox of "pervasive secularism and mounting religiosity."[46] Sociologists of religion have suggested that, while the old "melting pot" idea was not ever going to accurately characterize American society, the notion of a "triple melting pot" might. This means that Americans might increasingly be seen and, presumably see themselves, as Protestants or Catholic or Jewish, rather than as members of particular nationality groups.[47] Many have accepted the idea, observing a tendency of third- and fourth-generation "ethnics" to act more and more like members of the social classes in which they find themselves or toward which they aspire while still retaining nominal affiliations with the churches in which they were raised. However, the trend suggested by Herberg might have been prematurely predicted. First of all, as Gerhard Lenski has pointed out in *The Religious Factor*, a study of Detroit, there are at least four groups: Catholics, Jews, white Protestants, and black Protestants.[48] Lenski's work has been followed by a series of studies reported by Andrew Greeley, which suggest that Catholics have not been so ready to slough off their ethnic identities and cease being Irish-Catholics, Polish-Catholics, or Italian-Catholics.[49]

To complicate matters, the commitment of many Americans to the basic tenets of their faiths became increasingly vague in the 1960s, a period of considerable upheaval in this country and abroad. In the early days of the decade, religious principles underscored many of the activities of activists who challenged the status quo, especially in the area of civil rights. Most of the leaders came from clerical backgrounds, and many of their organizations were explicitly identified with religious bodies such as the Southern Christian Leadership Congress. Yet, the rising tide of Black Consciousness led simultaneously to a sense of failure on the part of many traditional religious liberals and a resurgence of ideas of separatism. The "Roots phenomenon," as we shall see, slowed the trend toward integration in certain circles while bringing about a revival of ethnic pride, including a pride in older traditions and beliefs.

Table 4 Religious Bodies—Membership 1985.

	Membership, in thousands	% of total
Protestants*	79,096	55.34
Roman Catholics	52,655	36.84
Jews†	5,835	4.08
Eastern Churches	4,026	2.82
Old Catholic, Polish National Catholic, and Armenian Churches	1,024	0.72
Buddhist Churches of America	100	0.07
Miscellaneous‡	191	0.13
Totals	142,926	100

*Includes non-Protestant bodies such as Latter Day Saints and Jehovah's Witnesses.
†Estimates of the Jewish community, including those identified with Orthodox, Conservative and Reform synagogues or temples.
‡Includes non-Christian bodies such as spiritualists, Ethical Culture Movement members and Unitarian-Universalists.
Source: Statistical Abstract of the United States, 1988, 108th ed. Washington, D.C.; U.S. Department of Commerce, Bureau of the Census, 1988, p. 52, Table 76.

Late in the decade a second disillusionment, this one over the failure to effect marked changes in the general social system, resulted in a new quest, a quest for meaning. Many young people left the radical political movement for new religious organizations, including the "Campus Crusade for Christ," the Unified Christian Church ("Moonies"), "Jews for Jesus," and similar bodies. Within the traditional churches a new spiritualism was also evident, and new practices involving much more active participation of congregants (as in "charismatic Christianity") attracted many who came to observe and stayed on to enjoy the warmth that they felt now pervaded the sanctuaries.

A study conducted by the National Council of Churches of Christ in the United States indicated that by 1988, approximately 142,926,000 belonged to churches and synagogues.[50] And the Council's report took into account only those religious bodies with memberships of 50,000 or more. (See Table 4).

Breaking the country down according to denominational affiliation of the adult church members, the council estimated that in 1988, approximately 55 percent belonged to one of the Protestant denominations. The largest number was Baptist (Black and White, Northern and Southern), followed by Methodist (including the predominantly White United Methodist Church and the predominantly Black African Methodist Episcopal Church, the African Methodist Episcopal Zion Church, and the Christian Methodist Episcopal Church), Lutheran, Presbyterian, Protestant Episcopalian, and a variety of smaller denominations and sects. Roman Catholics comprised 36 percent of the total; 4 percent was Jewish, and 3 percent belonged to one of the Eastern Orthodox Churches. The remainder were members of other religious groups, including Seventh Day Adventists, Mormons (members of the Church of the Latter Day Saints), Quakers, (members of the Society of Friends), Unitarians, Christian Scientists, Buddhists, and several other non-Western religions.

Ethnic Groups in the United States

The distinctions between the major religious denominations in America are fairly well defined, and membership statistics are not difficult to obtain. Racial breakdowns, while open to many questions about what are the precise definitions of particular racial aggregates, are likewise available, but accurate data on ethnic-group membership and identification are far more elusive. As noted in Chapter One, ethnic divisions include various kinds of groupings: those with common national backgrounds, those whose racial designation places them in a special category with which they identify and are so identified by others, and those whose group identity may transcend both racial and national boundaries. The complexity of the problem of ethnic classification is illustrated by such facts as the following: Jews are both a religious and cultural minority; the descendants of Irish, Italian, and Polish immigrants are predominantly Roman Catholic, but they also are members of particular national groups; Puerto Ricans, mainly Catholic, sometimes considered to be Blacks, bring distinctive cultural and linguistic patterns from Puerto Rico to the mainland; Southern-born Black Americans, at least to some degree, are culturally as well as racially identifiable, when compared with other Blacks, such as West Indians or Africans, who may share their looks but not necessarily their outlooks.

Overlapping of this kind prevents the clear-cut enumeration of ethnic-group membership. Moreover, there are few reliable statistics on the national origins of the native-born. Estimates are most frequently based on projections of statistics on immigration to the United States, as indicated in Table 2, Chapter Two. Although census enumerators continue to request information about country of birth from both the respondent and his or her parents, such data do not provide a valid basis for ascertaining the true size or constituency of nationality groupings in America today. Most people now living in this country were born here, as were most of their parents, and projections of immigration statistics alone do not, and cannot, indicate the degree to which individuals have retained their identity with the land or cultural traditions of their forebears.

The problem of estimating the size of ethnic groups is further complicated by the increasing incidence of intermarriage between individuals.

of different national and religious backgrounds. (Despite sharp rises, members of racial categories have remained relatively endogamous.) Several recent studies indicate that class affiliation and residential propinquity remain, in large measure, the main determinants of marital choice for those of differing national but similar religious backgrounds, especially among Roman Catholics.

Even the growing trend toward more intermarriage does not mean that enclaves of national-ethnic groups no longer exist. There are still communities where traditional schisms—between English and Irish, between French- and English-Canadians, between Chinese and Japanese—remain little changed. Moreover, even in those places where "international" marriage is fairly commonplace, many third- and fourth-generation Americans continue to retain a strong sense of identification with the country from which grandparents or great-grandparents migrated. Survey researchers still find that residents often make a single selection when asked to indicate with which of the larger-known ethnic groups in the community they most strongly identify.

Thus, while in some instances the traditional barriers between certain ethnic divisions are becoming increasingly blurred, national-ethnic groupings, as well as those based upon racial or religious factors, persist in the United States.

The Continuation of Intergroup Tensions

Almost all of America's immigrants and many of their descendants at one time or another have been the targets of discrimination, and many have been its perpetrators: categorical discrimination is not confined to the majority. One might expect that this historical experience, especially within the context of an open (or semi-open) society with a strong democratic ethos, would work to eliminate group barriers and intergroup tensions. In the long run, this may indeed be the case, but, as we know, group antipathy and friction continue. Why do these patterns persist?

This question cannot easily be answered. One clue is offered, however, by the fact that each new group, in seeking its place among those already in the United States, sought to integrate but was often thwarted by others engaged in the same struggle for acceptance. What Max Lerner wrote a quarter century ago still pertains:

From the beginning there were stereotypes imposed upon the more marginal immigrants. As was perhaps natural, the members of each new wave of immigration were assigned the lowliest tasks, the longest hours of work, the poorest and dirtiest living quarters. The basic pattern was, however, for the immigrants of each new influx to be in time absorbed by the rest, yielding the role of strangeness in turn to the still later comers. Most of them moved up the hierarchical ladder while those who followed grasped eagerly to the lowly places that had been relinquished.[51]

This pattern of group mobility, which shows a rough correlation between time of arrival and social status (with the notable exceptions of low-status Native Americans on the one hand and relatively high-status Jews on the other), may help to account for the fact that "there has never been any real alliance of minority groups to withstand the prejudice and discrimination from the majority."[52] The rationale for this bold statement will be developed in succeeding chapters on the nature of prejudice and discrimination and the reactions of minority groups to their status.

NOTES

1. George Stewart, *American Ways of Life* (Garden City, N.Y.: Doubleday, 1954), pp. 11–12.
2. As quoted in Milton Vorst, "Talk with 'A Reasonable Man'," *New York Times Magazine* (April 19, 1970), p. 96. See also Candace Nelson and Marta Tienda, "The Structuring of the Hispanic Ethnicity," in Richard D. Alba (ed), *Ethnicity and Race in the USA* (New York: Routledge, 1988), pp. 49–74.
3. See, for example, Milton M. Gordon, "Assimilation in America: Theory and Reality," *Daedalus*, 90 (Spring 1961), 263–285.
4. W. C. Ford (collector and ed.), *The Writings of George Washington* (New York: Putnam, 1889), Vol. XII, p. 489. This quotation is discussed in greater detail by Milton M. Gordon, *op cit.*, pp. 266–267.
5. This letter was published in *Nile's Weekly Register*, 18 (1820), 157–158. See the discussion in Marcus L. Hansen, *The Atlantic Migration, 1607–1860* (Cambridge: Harvard University Press, 1940), pp. 96–97.
6. See Nathan Glazer, "Ethnic Groups in America: From National Culture to Ideology," in M. Berger, T. Abel, and C. H. Page (eds.), *Freedom and Control in Modern Society* (Princeton, N.J.: Van Nostrand, 1954), p. 163.
7. Frederick Jackson Turner, *The Frontier in American History* (New York: Henry Holt, 1920), pp. 3–4.
8. *Idem.*
9. See Dorothy Burton Skårdal, *The Divided Heart: Scandinavian Experience Through Literary Sources* (Oslo: Universitetsforlaget, 1974).
10. For a detailed discussion of nativism, see S. M. Lipset and Earl Raab, *The Politics of Unreason* (New York: Harper & Row, 1970).
11. Henry Pratt Fairchild, *The Melting Pot Mistake* (Boston: Little, Brown, 1926), pp. 158–159.
12. This is the comment of a lifelong resident of a small town in upstate New York. See Peter I. Rose, "Small-Town Jews and Their Neighbours in the United States," *Jewish Journal of Sociology* (England), 3 (December 1961), 187.
13. J. Hector St. John de Crèvecoeur, *Letters from an American Farmer* (New York:

Albert and Charles Boni, 1925), pp. 54–55; originally published in London, 1782. For a critical commentary, see Marcus Cunliffe, "Crèvecoeur Revisited," *Journal of American Studies*, 9 (August 1975), 129–144.

14. Israel Zangwill, *The Melting Pot* (New York: The Jewish Publication Society of America, 1909), pp. 198–199.

15. As quoted in Robert E. Park and Ernest W. Burgess, *Introduction to the Science of Sociology* (Chicago: University of Chicago Press, 1924), p. 734.

16. Donald Light, Jr., and Suzanne Keller, *Sociology* (New York: Knopf, 1975), p. 241. See also W. Lloyd Warner and Leo Srole, *The Social Systems of American Ethnic Groups* (New Haven: Yale University Press, 1945); and Ronald J. Silver, "Structure and Values in the Explanation of Acculturation Rates," *British Journal of Sociology*, 126 (March 1965), 68–79.

17. Gordon, *op. cit.*, pp. 274–275.

18. Horace M. Kallen, "Democracy versus the Melting-Pot," *The Nation*, 100 (February 18, 1915), 190–194, and (February 25, 1915), 217–220; see also Horace M. Kallen, *Cultural Pluralism and the American Idea* (Philadelphia: University of Pennsylvania Press, 1956).

19. Kallen, "Democracy versus the Melting-Pot," (February 25, 1915), *op. cit.*, p. 220.

20. *Ibid.*

21. Gordon, *op. cit.*, pp. 279–285. See also Gordon, "Social Structure and Group Relations," *Freedom and Control in Modern Society*, *op. cit.*, pp. 141–157.

22. Milton M. Gordon, *Assimilation in American Life* (New York: Oxford University Press, 1964)), pp. 51 ff.

23. See L. Paul Metzger, "American Sociology and Black Assimilation: Conflicting Perspectives," *American Journal of Sociology*, 76 (1971), 627–647. See also Harry H. Bash, *Sociology, Race, and Ethnicity* (New York: Gordon and Breach, 1979); and Stanford M. Lyman, *The Black American in Sociological Thought* (New York: Capricorn Books, 1972).

24. As quoted in Charles Silberman, *Crisis in Black and White* (New York: Random House, 1964), p. 41. See also James Weldon Johnson, *Black Manhattan* (New York: Knopf, 1930); Claude McKay, *Harlem: Negro Metropolis* (New York: Dutton, 1940); and Oscar Handli, *The Newcomers* (Cambridge: Harvard University Press, 1959).

25. Robert Blauner, *Racial Oppression in America* (New York: Harper & Row, 1972), pp. 56–57. Irving Kristol's article (referred to by Blauner) and several others dealing with the question of "The Negro as Immigrant" appear in Peter I. Rose (ed.), *Nation of Nations* (New York: Random House, 1972), pp. 197–275 passim.

26. As quoted in Milton Vorst, *op. cit.*, pp. 96–97.

27. James Farmer, *Freedom—When?* (New York: Random House, 1965), p. 87.

28. Gunnar Myrdal, et al., *An American Dilemma* (New York: Harper & Row, 1944).

29. Kenneth Stampp, *The Peculiar Institution* (New York: Vintage Books, 1956).

30. Nathan Glazer and Daniel Patrick Moynihan, *Beyond the Melting Pot* (Cambridge: M.I.T. Press, 1963), p. 53.

31. See 1971 edition.

32. E. Franklin Frazier, *The Negro in the United States* (New York: Macmillan, 1957), p. 680.

33. *Ibid.*
34. Ralph Ellison, *Invisible Man* (New York: Random House, 1947), p. 3.
35. W. E. B. Du Bois, *The Souls of Black Folk*, 1903. (As published in New York: Fawcett Publications, Premier Americana Editions, 1961), pp. 15–16.
36. See Vernon J. Dixon, "Two Approaches to Black-White Relations," in Vernon J. Dixon and Badi Foster (eds.), *Beyond Black or White* (Boston: Little, Brown, 1971), pp. 22–66ff.
37. Gordon, *op. cit.*, pp. 279–285. See also Gordon, "Social Structure in Group Relations," *Freedom and Control in Modern Society, op. cit.*, pp. 141–157.
38. John P. Dean, "Patterns of Socialization and Association Between Jews and Non-Jews," *Jewish Social Studies* 17 (July 1955), 249–251. Dean's hypothesis was substantiated in the author's study of isolated Jews. The majority of small-town Jews interviewed indicated that they enjoyed a degree of intimate interfaith socializing unparalleled in the urban community; see Rose, *op. cit.*, p. 182.
39. Andrew Greeley, *Why Can't They Be Like Us?* (New York: Dutton, 1971).
40. Solomon Poll, *The Hasidic Community of Williamsburg* (New York: Free Press, 1962), p. 3.
41. Donald Bogue, *The Population of the United States* (New York: Free Press, 1959), p. 122.
42. U.S. Bureau of the Census. *1960 Census of Population Supplementary Reports*, PC (S1)-10, Washington, D.C., p. 2.
43. *Ibid.*
44. U.S. Bureau of the Census. *The Social and Economic Status of the Black Population in the U.S.*, Current Population Reports, Special Studies Series, P-23, No. 80 (Washington, D.C.: U.S. Department of Commerce, 1979), pp. 7, 168.
45. *Statistical Abstract, 1972*, pp. 21–23.
46. Will Herberg, *Protestant-Catholic-Jew* (New York: Doubleday, 1955), p. 14.
47. *Ibid.*, Chaps. 2 and 3: see also Ruby Jo Kennedy, "Single or Triple Melting Pot? Intermarriage Trends in New Haven: 1870–1940," *American Journal of Sociology*, 58 (January 1952), 56–59.
48. Gerhard Lenski, *The Religious Factor* (New York: Doubleday, 1961); see also Gerhard Lenski, "The Religious Factor in Detroit, Revisited," *American Sociological Review* (February 1971), p. 50.
49. Andrew Greeley (ed.), *Ethnicity in the United States: A Preliminary Reconnaissance* (New York: Wiley, 1974).
50. U.S. Bureau of the Census, *Statistical Abstract*, 1989.
51. Max Lerner, *America as a Civilization* (New York: Simon and Schuster, 1957), p. 503.
52. Arnold and Caroline Rose, *America Divided* (New York: Knopf, 1953), p. 65.

4

PREJUDICE

On Being Culture-Bound

All good people agree,
   And all good people say,
All nice people like Us, are We
   And everyone else is They.[1]

In a few short lines, Rudyard Kipling captured the essence of what sociologists and anthropologists call *ethnocentric thinking*. Members of all societies tend to believe that "All nice people like Us, are We ... " They find comfort in the familiar and often denigrate or distrust others. Of course, with training and experience in other climes, they may learn to transcend their provincialism, placing themselves in others' shoes. Or, as Kipling put it,

... if you cross over the sea,
   Instead of over the way,
You may end by (think of it!) looking on We
   As only a sort of They.[2]

In a real sense, a main lesson of the sociology of intergroup relations is to begin to "cross over the sea," to learn to understand why other people think and act as they do and to be able to empathize with their perspectives even if one still does not accept them. But this is no easy task. Many barriers—political, economic, social, and personal—stand in the way of such international (and intergroup) understanding. According to William Graham Sumner, ethnocentrism, "leads a people to exaggerate and intensify everything in their own folkways which is peculiar and which differentiates them from others."[3] Intensive socialization to particular points of view and notions of what is right and wrong and good and bad has a long-lasting effect.

Sometimes the teaching is very explicit regarding the superior quality of one's own culture; sometimes it is more subtle. Consider the following poem written by Robert Louis Stevenson and taught to many English and American children.

> Little Indian, Sioux or Crow,
> Little frosty Eskimo,
> Little Turk or Japanee,
> O! don't you wish that you were me?
>
> You have seen the scarlet trees
> And the lions over seas;
> You have eaten ostrich eggs,
> And turned the turtles off their legs.
>
> Such a life is very fine,
> But it's not so nice as mine:
> You must often, as you trod,
> Have wearied, not to be abroad.
>
> You have curious things to eat,
> I am fed on proper meat;
> You must dwell beyond the foam
> But I am safe to live at home.
>
> Little Indian, Sioux or Crow,
> Little frosty Eskimo,
> Little Turk or Japanee,
> O! don't you wish that you were me?[4]

Raised on such literary fare it should not be surprising that children develop negative ideas about the ways of others. Undoubtedly many young people in this society still find it hard to understand how those in other lands can become vegetarians, worship ancestors, practice infanticide, or engage in polygamy. They are confused by the fact that many Moslem women wear the *chador* (the veil to cover their faces), that Balinese women go bare-breasted, and that some people wear no clothes at all. They are troubled when they learn that many nations emerging from colonial status favor one-party states or communism over our political system.

Sometimes the ethnocentrism is manifest in writings by those who are viewed as experts on the comparative study of culture. Consider the following remarks of the famous anthropologist Margaret Mead. In a book on American character published in 1942, she wrote:

> If I were writing about the way in which the Germans or the Japanese, the Burmese or the Javanese would have to act if they were to win the war, I would not need to use so many moral terms. For none of these peoples think of life in as habitually moral terms as do Americans.[5]

American ethnocentricity, while manifest in general attitudes toward others is, of course, tempered somewhat by the very heterogeneity of the population that we have been examining. Thus, while there are broad standards—expressed in the ways most Americans set goals for their children, organize their political lives, and think about their society in contrast to others, living in our racial and ethnic mosaic makes us more inclined to think in terms of layers or circles of familiarity. Blacks from Chicago feel and think very "American" in Lagos or Nairobi as do Italians from Brooklyn when visiting relatives in Calabria or Sicily. But when they get home, they will generally revert to feeling "Black" in contrast to "White" and Italian or Italian-American in comparison to others in their own communities, respectively.

Ethnocentrism is found in political as well as in ethnic contexts. Much of the discussion of patriotism and loyalty is couched in language that reflects rather narrow culture-bound thinking. At various periods in our history this phenomenon has been particularly marked—we remind ourselves of the nativistic movements of the pre-Civil War period, of the anti-foreign organizations during the time of greatest immigration, and the McCarthyism of the early 1950s. During the McCarthy era there was a widespread attempt to impose the notion that anyone who had ever joined a Marxist study group, supported the Loyalists in the Spanish Civil War, or belonged to any one of a number of liberal organizations was "un-American."

It is clear that not only those "over the sea" are viewed (and view others) ethnocentrically. These distinctions between "they" and "we" exist within societies as well. In modern industrial societies most individuals belong to a wide array of social groups that differentiate them from others—familial, religious, occupational, recreational, and so on. Individuals are frequently caught in a web of conflicting allegiances. This situation is often surmounted by a hierarchical ranking of groups as referents for behavior. In most societies, including our own, the family is the primary reference group. As we have seen in the United States, ethnic or racial identity and religious affiliation are also relevant referents. Members of other ethnic, racial, and religious groups are often judged on the basis of how closely they conform to the standards of the group passing judgment.

Thus, several studies have shown that in American society many Whites holding Christian beliefs, who constitute both the statistical majority and the dominant group, rank minorities along a continuum of social acceptability. They rate members of minority groups in descending order in terms of how closely the latter approximate their image of "real Americans." Early studies of "social distance" indicated that most ranked groups in the following manner: Protestants from Europe at the top, then Irish Catholics, Iberians, Italians, Jews, Spanish-Americans, American-born Chinese and Japanese, Blacks, and foreign-born Asians.[6] A 1966 study suggested the following rank order: English, French, Swedes, Italians, Scots, Germans, Spaniards, Jews, Chinese, Russians, and Blacks.[7] (In late 1979 Iranian-Americans became scapegoats for many other Americans frustrated by the takeover of the United States Embassy in Teheran by supporters of the Ayatollah Khomeini. Were a social distance scale constructed at the time, Iranians—and Muslims in general—probably would have ranked very low.) While, over the years, most Americans generally have considered those of English or Canadian ancestry to be acceptable citizens, good neighbors, social equals, and desirable marriage partners, relatively few feel the same way about those who rank low in scales of social distance.

There is an interesting correlate to this finding. Investigators have found that minority-group members themselves tend to accept the dominant group's ranking system—with one exception: each tends to put his or her own group at the top of the scale.[8]

Ranking is one characteristic of ethnocentric thinking; generalizing is another. The more another group differs from one's own, the more one is likely to generalize about its social characteristics and to hold oversimplified attitudes toward its members. When asked to describe our close friends, we were able to cite their idiosyncratic traits: we may distinguish among subtle differences of physiognomy, demeanor, intelligence, and interests. It becomes increasingly difficult to make the same careful evaluation of casual neighbors; it is almost impossible when we think of people we do not know at first-hand. Understandably, the general tendency is to assign strangers to available group categories that seem to be appropriate. Such labeling is evident in generalized images of "lazy" Indians, "passionate" Latins, and "penny-pinching" Scots.

Ranking others according to one's own standards and categorizing them into generalized stereotypes together serve to widen the gap between "they" and "we." Freud has written that "in the undisguised antipathies and aversions which people feel toward strangers with whom they have to do we may recognize the expression of self-love—of narcissism."[9] In sociological terms, a function of ethnocentric thinking is the enhancement of group cohesion. There is a close relationship between a high degree of ethnocentrism on the part of one group and an increase of antipathy toward others. This relationship tends to hold for ethnocentrism of both dominant and minority groups.[10]

Many writers refer to such antipathetic attitudes as bases for group prejudice. For example:

It is this very group consciousness, or ethnocentrism, which lays the foundation of group prejudice. If there were no strong feelings for one's own group, there would not be strong consciousness of other groups. An awareness of one's own group as an in-group and of the others as out-groups is fundamental in group relationships.[11]

Defining Prejudice

Prejudice may be defined as "a system of negative beliefs, feelings, and action-orientations regarding a group of people."[12] This definition characteristically emphasizes the negative side of prejudice. Literally, of course, "prejudice" refers to positive as well as negative attitudes. Yet, because of the detrimental psychic and social consequences that often result from hostile attitudes, sociologists usually concern themselves with "negative prejudice."

The definition of group prejudice stated above incorporates the three major dimensions of all attitude systems: the *cognitive* (beliefs), the *affective* (feelings), and the *conative* (predispositions to act in particular ways, or policy orientations).[13]

The cognitive component pertains to the "intellectual" side of prejudice, for it involves knowledge, however faulty. This is expressed in stereotypical conceptions and misconceptions of various social groups, for example: Whites who believe that Blacks are shiftless, ignorant, and oversexed; Gentiles who imagine that Jews are avaricious, brash, clannish, and "too intelligent for their own good"; Englishmen who think of the Irish as argumentative, heavy drinkers; Irishmen who imagine Englishmen to be stuffy bores. By analogy, cognition refers to "cranial" reactions, that is, pictures in the mind's eye. While the ethnocentric individual frequently generalizes about groups he knows little or nothing about, the prejudiced person generalizes about groups he *thinks* he knows well.

The affective dimension refers to the way one *feels* about the group he perceives. The emotions evoked are "visceral" in that they are often manifest in feelings of revulsion, fear, hate, or indignation, as illustrated by the following expressions:

> It makes me sick just thinking about my kids going to school with those Puerto-Ricans.

> Every time I see a black man on the street at night I get scared stiff.

> Don't you just hate the way Arabs are moving in? I simply can't stand them.

> I know it's wrong, but I really shiver at the thought of rooming with an Iranian student next year.

Often emotions aroused in the prejudiced person are based upon the stereotypes he or she holds of certain people. If one thinks that Greeks are underhanded or sharp businessmen, this tends to elicit apprehension in dealing with them. Similarly, if one believes that Mexicans typically carry knives, one may well feel frightened when confronted by a member of this group.

Group prejudices involve both thoughts and feelings about people. "However false as to fact, prejudice has a certain logic, a logic not of reason but of the emotions. . . . Prejudice is more than false belief; it is a structure of false belief *with a purpose*, however unconscious."[14] This is why prejudice as an attitude represents a predisposition to act (the conative dimension) in a particular way toward a social group. It is a state of readiness for action but not in itself overt behavior or discrimination.

Prejudice and Discrimination

Discrimination may be defined as the differential treatment of individuals considered to belong to particular groups or social categories.[15] Although frequently they are opposite sides of the same coin, prejudice and discrimination, as both analytical and concrete concepts, should not be confused. The difference between prejudice as an attitude and discrimination as overt behavior was summed up by an English judge in his comments to nine youths convicted of race rioting in the Notting Hill section of London:

> Everyone, irrespective of the color of his skin, is entitled to walk through our streets in peace with their heads held erect and free from fear. . . . These courts will uphold (these rights) . . . *think what you like.* . . . *But once you translate your dark thoughts into savage acts, the law will punish you, and protect your victim.*[16]

American civil rights workers have also recognized the significance of the distinction. The late Dr. Martin Luther King, Jr., in his first address to the Atlanta, Georgia, "Jaycees" put it bluntly: "The law may not make a man love me, but it can restrain him from lynching me, and I think that's pretty important."[17]

The prejudiced person may not actually behave outwardly the way he or she thinks or says he or she will act. Attitudes do not always lead to hostile or aggressive actions. Furthermore, many individuals discriminate against others without harboring negative feelings toward the groups to which they belong. In one of several books on intergroup relations published in the mid-1950s, Dean and Rosen reported that "conformity with the practices of segregation and discrimination is often quite unrelated to the intensity of prejudice in the individuals who conform."[18] Others have continued to corroborate the generalization, adding the following corollary: social contact itself and the conventions characteristic of the particular circumstances in which contact takes place often help to determine how an individual will act at a given time. Sometimes people may even behave toward others in direct opposition to their own predispositions. The situation itself frequently provides the cues for "appropriate" behavior. For example, for years many liberals conformed to practices of segregation when vacationing in the South; and southerners who held moderate views about the desegregation issue often remained silent on the matter in their home communities.

By comparing the presence or absence of prejudicial attitudes on the part of individuals with their willingness or reluctance to engage in discriminatory activity, Robert K. Merton described the relationship between prejudice and discrimination. The paradigm that he devised includes four types of persons and their characteristic response patterns.[19]

The Unprejudiced Nondiscriminators

These "all-weather liberals," as Merton called them, sincerely believe in the American creed of freedom and equality for all, and practice it to the fullest extent. They are the vigorous champions of the underdog, take the Golden Rule literally, and cherish American egalitarian values. It would appear that liberal individuals such as these would be most able to influence others in the realm of intergroup hostility and discrimination. Yet, as Merton indicates, their effectiveness is limited by certain "fallacies."

First there is the "fallacy of group soliloquies." Liberals tend to expend their energies in seeking out one another and talking chiefly to others who share their point of view. The feeling of agreement that logically ensues by interacting mainly with those who agree leads to the second fallacy, that of "unanimity." Through discussions with likeminded individuals the liberal may feel that many more people agree with his attitudes regarding ethnic relations than do in fact. Finally, there is the "fallacy of privatized solutions," depicted by Merton as follows:

> The ethnic liberal, precisely because he is at one with the American creed, may rest content with his own individual behavior and thus see no need to do anything about the problem at large. Since his own spiritual house is in order, he is not motivated by guilt or shame to work on a collective problem.[20]

The problem of the unprejudiced nondiscriminator is not one of ambivalence between attitude and action—as in the case of the two types described below—but rather it is a lack of awareness of the enormity of the problem and a clear-cut approach to those who are not so liberally inclined.

Unprejudiced Discriminators

The many homeowners throughout the urban North who deny having any personal feelings against Black people and yet steadfastly try to keep them out of their neighborhoods for fear of altering the character of those neighborhoods illustrate the case of the unprejudiced discriminator who is, at best, a "fair-weather liberal." More pragmatic than "all-weather liberals," they discriminate when such behavior is called for, seems to be appropriate, or is in their own self-interest. Expediency is the motto, and the creed is to "live and let live; a man's got to get along."[21] Merton suggests that the "fair-weather liberal" is frequently the victim of guilt because of the discrepancy between conduct and personal beliefs and is thus especially amenable to the persuasion of the liberal.

Prejudiced Nondiscriminators

This third type might be called "timid bigots." Like so many of the gentle people of prejudice, they are not activists. They feel definite hostility toward many groups and subscribe to the conventional stereotypes of others. Yet, like the "fair-weather liberals," they too reach to the exigencies of the situation. If the situation—as defined by law or custom—precludes open discrimination, they conform. They serve Black customers, sit next to them on buses or trains, send their children to school with Black children. "What can I do," they say, "fight the system, fight city hall?"

Although both the "fair-weather liberal" and the "fair-weather illiberal" share the theme of expedience, Merton states:

Superficial similarity in behavior of the two in the same situation should not be permitted to cloak a basic difference in the meaning of this outwardly similar behavior, a difference which is as important for social policy as it is for social science. Whereas the timid bigot is under strain when he conforms to the creed, the timid liberal is under strain when he deviates. . . . He does not accept the moral legitimacy of the creed; he conforms because he must, and will cease to conform when the pressure is removed.[22]

Prejudiced Discriminators

These are the people who embody the commonly held assumption that prejudice and discrimination are mutually dependent. Such "active bigots" neither believe in the American creed nor act in accordance with its precepts. Like the "all-weather liberal," the prejudiced discriminator conforms to a set of standards; but in this case "his ideals proclaim the right, even the duty, of discrimination."[23] He or she does not hesitate to express the basic attitude—"all Whites are superior to Colored people"—or to convert it into overt behavior. He or she is willing to defy law, if necessary, to protect beliefs and vested interests.

Each of these categories is, of course, an *ideal* type, a model against which reality is to be measured. While it is rare that one finds a single individual who is all saint or all sinner, "fair weather liberals" and "timid bigots" do exist. Several caveats should be borne in mind: while many people prejudiced against one minority, say Italians, often tend to dislike others, such as Jews and Blacks,[24] prejudice toward one minority does not necessarily mean prejudice toward all. Those who are anti-Black are not, *ipso facto*, anti-Semites—and vice versa.[25]

Nor do dominant groups have a monopoly on prejudice. Many minority-group members subscribe to images of other minorities that coincide with those held by members of the dominant groups. Examples include the anti-Semitism manifested by some Blacks, as well as anti-Black sentiments expressed by some Jews, both of which came to light during the crisis over the community control of schools in New York City in 1968-1969,[26] a decade later, over the resignation of Andrew Young, a Black minister and former Congressman, who was U.S. representative to the United Nations from 1976 to 1979, and in the presidential primaries of 1988 when Jesse Jackson was a Democrat contender. Furthermore, for many racial, religious, and ethnic minorities the dominant group represents "the enemy camp." Thus there are many anti-White Blacks and anti-Gentile Jews who seek to avoid social relations with their "adversaries."[27] Brewton Berry and Henry L. Tischler indicate that such hostility is often a by-product of socialization. They cite a story told by the late editor of the *Carolina Israelite*, Harry Golden, to illustrate the point—focusing on how prejudice is learned.

My first impression of Christianity came in the home, of course. My parents brought with them the burden of the Middle Ages from the blood-soaked continent of Europe. They had come from the villages of Eastern Europe where Christians were feared with legitimate reason.

When occasionally a Jewish drunk was seen in our neighborhood, our parents would say, "He's behaving like a Gentile."

For in truth, our parents had often witnessed the Polish, Romanian, Hungarian, and Russian peasants gather around a barrel of whiskey on Saturday night, drink themselves into oblivion, "and beat their wives." Once in a while the rumor would spread through the tenements that a fellow had struck his wife, and on all sides we heard the inevitable, "Just like a Gentile."

Oddly enough, too, our parents had us convinced that the Gentiles were noisy, boisterous, and loud—unlike the Jews. . . . If we raised our voices, we were told, "Jewish boys don't shout." And this admonition covered every activity in and out of the home: "Jewish boys don't fight." "Jewish boys don't get dirty." "Jewish boys study hard."[28]

Explaining Prejudice

There are many explanations for the causes of prejudice and the sources of discrimination.[29] Until the first quarter of the twentieth century, most theories of prejudice focused primarily on physical traits and group differences. Some writers attempted to prove that certain groups are innately superior to others; others speculated that there is an instinctive aversion of people to the unfamiliar that accounts for antipathy toward aliens and strangers.

Biology and Behavior

In spite of the influence of Voltaire, Rousseau, and others who argued that there is a universal oneness in human nature, the eighteenth and nineteenth centuries saw the birth of a doctrinaire theory of group prejudice. Taxonomical classifications of human "races" paved the way for elaborate schemes that "proved" that some varieties of humankind were superior to others and that, inevitably, sought to justify the maltreatment of non-White people by Europeans.[30]

For example, the eighteenth century scientist, Carl von Linne (also known as Linnaeus) divided Homo sapiens into four racial groupings, each of which was purported to instill a distinctive "mentality" in its members. The African (*Afer niger*) was said to be slow and negligent, cunning and capricious. The American Indian (*Americanus rufus*) was described as tenacious, free, and easily contented. The Asiatic (*Asiaticus luridus*) was viewed as a haughty, stern, and opinionated fellow. The European (*Europaeus albus*) was envisaged as possessing the traits of liveliness and creativity and was considered to be superior to the other racial types. While Linnaeus based his typology on color—black, red, yellow, white—and region, others (such as J. F. Blumenbach, Anders Retzius, Samuel G. Morton, and Josiah C. Nott) divided human beings into categories according to other physical attributes, and each series of measurements led to a different kind of classification of "races."

These classifications, devised by Europeans or White Americans, for the most part seemed to come to the same conclusion: "Non-Whites are innately inferior." The equation of somatic differences with culture traits gave birth to the theory of racial superiority or racism. Throughout the Western world it was asserted that Colored people were degenerate, simple-minded, untamed, uncivilized. Racism was used by several writers to justify the slave system in the United States and to sanction exploitation by American, British, and other colonialists, many of whom viewed conquest and subjugation as the "White man's burden." Darwin's theory of evolution and the possibility of "separate creation" gave added legitimacy to the doctrine. The superordinate status of Whites was taken to be evidence that the fittest survive and that the aggressive, not the meek, inherit the earth.

Since its inception, the dogma of racism has persisted in various forms. Nietzsche, Gobineau, H. S. Chamberlain, and Adolf Hitler, among others, argued that certain "racial" groups possess the traits of leadership, greatness, and nobility, while others are born to follow, to serve, or to be exterminated as useless parasites.

Early in the twentieth century many social scientists rejected the doctrine of racial superiority and the supposition that racial origins determine culture patterns. Yet, some held to the view that people instinctively dislike the strange and different. The saw *xenophobia* (the dislike of foreigners) as an inborn trait passed from one generation to the next. This was an element in the social thought of the early American sociologist F. H. Giddings, who argued that people identified with the members of their own social groups and excluded outsiders, owing to a "consciousness of kind." It was "natural" he claimed, for people to like what they know and to fear the unknown. Sociologists E. B. Reuter and G. W. Hart, in one of the early introductory textbooks in sociology, stated that prejudice was to be attributed to "the universal fear of things new and strange."[31] For a time even Robert E. Park, the scholar who was to become one of the major guiding forces behind the empirical study of intergroup relations, subscribed to the view. In 1924 Park wrote, "It is evident that there is in race prejudice as distinguished from class and caste prejudice, an *instinctive* factor based on the fear of the unfamiliar and uncomprehended."[32]

The I.Q. Controversy

Those who assume biological superiority (and inferiority) and innate or natural group aversion imply that there is something inherent in racial and ethnic bodies largely determining the thoughts, abilities, and group-focused loves and hates of their members. To most modern social scientists such a view is unacceptable. Looks may be transmitted through the genes but not outlooks. The perspectives people have are thought to be the result of nurture, not nature. Even within groups similarly socialized idiosyncratic differences are very great. Some people are strong and others weak, some are intelligent and some are feeble-minded. But the strong and the intelligent are to be found in all racial and cultural groups. The manner in which given individuals are able to optimize whatever innate potentialities they may possess are dependent, in part at least, upon the opportunities afforded in the social milieu into which they are born and in which they are raised. Indeed, according to the members of the American Anthropological Association, "all races possess the ability needed to participate fully in the democratic way of life and in modern technological civilization."[33]

With the development of systematic methods of investigation and a scientific orientation toward social life itself, the ideas that certain groups are born to lead and others to follow, that xenophobia is rooted in the genes, have been found to be theoretically and empirically untenable. However, this conclusion does not mean that research on the relationship between racial background and behavior has ceased. On the contrary, it has taken new forms—often variations on old themes that seek by use of such culturally biased instruments as intelligence tests, to demonstrate persisting differences between Blacks and Whites.

Intelligence testing began in the 1890s and was used extensively in the early decades of this century. The most famous measures were the Stanford-Binet scales and the Yerkes Alpha and Beta tests used to assess American soldiers in World War I. Other psychologists, including Carl C. Brigham, who already assumed Blacks to be inferior in intelligence took data from Army tests claiming that native-born White Americans "proved" more intelligent than new immigrants. Brigham was one of several behavioral scientists whose contentions about the deleterious effects of allowing newcomers to enter the United States lent considerable academic legitimacy to the restrictive immigration legislation of the 1920s discussed in Chapter Two.

While later research clearly contradicted Brigham's claim regarding the differential scores of "natives" and immigrants (and their children), the black-white dichotomy still remained evident. Perhaps the best examples of such reasoning were to be found in the work of Audrey Sheuey, a Columbia University-trained psychologist and author of *The Testing of Negro Intelligence*,[34] and in the debates over the work of Harvard University psychologist Arthur Jensen.[35]

Sheuey, after an extensive review of the literature in which I.Q. test scores of White and Black subjects were compared, concluded that the data clearly belie the claim that there are no native differences. The biggest problem was the leap she made between the consistency of the findings that Blacks scored proportionately lower and the argument that this was attributable to innate intellectual inferiority.

In perhaps the most pointed gibe at Sheuey's work (and the work of others who made similar claims) Adrian Dove, a social worker from the Watts section of Los Angeles, clearly illustrated that the vast majority of White people would flunk his Black-oriented "Dove Counterbalance Intelligence Test," while most Blacks, Dove claimed, would do quite well. The test consisted of 30 multiple-choice questions, including the following:

Which word is out of place here? (a) splib, (b) blood, (c) gray, (d) spook, (e) black.

A "handkerchief head" is a(n) (a) cool cat, (b) porter, (c) "Uncle Tom," (d) hoddi, (e) preacher.

Cheap "chit'lin's" . . . will taste rubbery unless they are cooked long enough. How soon can you quit cooking them to eat and enjoy them? (a) 15 minutes, (b) 2 hours, (c) 24 hours, (d) 1 week (on a low flame), (e) 1 hour.

Hattie Mae Johnson is on the county. She has four children and her husband is now in jail for nonsupport, as he was unemployed and was not able to give her any money. Her welfare check is now $286 per month. Last night she went out with the biggest player in town. If she got pregnant, then 9 months from now, how much more will her welfare check be? (a) $80, (b) $2 less, (c) $35, (d) $150, (e) $100.

"Hully Gully" came from (a) "East Oakland," (b) Fillmore, (c) Watts, (d) Harlem, (e) Motor City.[36]

Not all critics of the Sheuey argument used humor to counter it. Systematic research indicated the persisting cultural biases of the traditional tests.[37] Sometime after the debates over Sheuey's book had simmered down, psychologist Arthur Jensen gained widespread attention for an article, "How Much Can We Boost I.Q. and Scholastic Achievement?" published in the *Harvard Educational Review* in the Winter of 1969 in which, on the basis of his research, he stated that it is "a not unreasonable hypothesis that genetic factors are strongly implicated in averaged Negro-White intelligence difference." This hypothesis was based on findings that alleged to show that (1) compensatory education programs designed to improve intellectual performance of those euphemistically called "culturally disadvantaged" failed to raise I.Q. scores; (2) children with low I.Q.'s tend to be handicapped genetically as well as culturally (or environmentally); (3) the genetic proclivity for certain types of performances is an important factor not merely in determining potential differences in intelligence ratings from the same group but also differences between groups; and (4) one should recognize and compensate for the fact that rote learning seems easier for some than abstract learning.[38] Aware that he might raise, once again, the specter of "scientific racism," Jensen nevertheless felt that a number of important questions about the relationship between nature and nurture needed consideration especially by people who were concerned with the attainment of improved education for all children.

Reactions, especially to the shakiness of some of Jensen's assertions, as expected, were harsh—in some cases quite extreme. "Jensenism" became a word that was linked to "imperialism" and "fascism" and "genocide" by militant critics. Even those who attended the annual business meetings of the American Anthropological Association found themselves asked to vote on the censure of the *Harvard Educational Review* for publishing Jensen—and they proceeded to do so without protest. (The protest came later, and it was not only from reactionary quarters.)[39]

As Christopher Jencks, an authority on educational research, noted in a lengthy review of Jensen and his critics:

Were there a dispassionate observer, who could look at these arguments without political or personal bias, I think he would conclude that neither Jensen nor his critics have offered a persuasive explanation of IQ differences between blacks and whites. He would probably also conclude that neither geneticists nor social scientists know enough about the determinants of IQ scores to design a study which would fully resolve our present confusion. Nonetheless, Jensen's decision to re-open this ancient controversy without first gathering more evidence strikes me as a serious political blunder.[40]

An even more thorough assessment of Jensen's work was made by political scientist Philip Green, who, in three lengthy articles published in *Dissent*, challenged what he called "the fallacy of heritability."[41] In a few pointed paragraphs, Green suggested *two* ways of defining heritability. First he offered the "standard" definition:

> The heritability of a trait refers to the extent to which variations in measurement from the average value of the trait may be traceable to genetic variation in the measured population.[42]

Noting that the key word is "population," Green pointed out that this has generally meant "specific breeding and rearing populations"—at least according to most geneticists—but he suggests,

> . . . the heritability of a trait can equally be conceived of as nothing more than a function of the extent to which salient features of the *environments* the observed population lives in are themselves alike or unlike.[43]

In his three essays, Green proceeded to elaborate on this contention that, after a review of the literature he found "not a single aspect of the history of inherited deficiency is ascribable to genetics: it is all a product of social conditions and thus potentially susceptible to social amelioration."[44]

However valid Jencks' and Green's conclusions may be, the topic has been reopened and the debates have forced us to examine a number of important assumptions, not the least being those related to the persistent blurring of the study of race per se (and of race differences) and the study of prejudice and discrimination and their effects. The significance of the distinction becomes clearly apparent when one moves away from the emotionally charged realm of "intelligence" and "performance" to that of health and illness.

It has long been asserted by some that racial purity is a virtue and that, by sticking to one's own race, many problems can be avoided. Perhaps, as some Blacks now argue (and as many Whites have long contended) there is a psychological truth embedded in the assumption but not necessarily a physiological one. Recent medical research has shown several important negative results of endogamy (marriage to a member of one's own group, especially an ethnic or racial one) in the so-called race-based diseases, such as sickle-cell anemia, thalassemia, and Tay-Sachs disease, which are prevalent among Blacks, Mediterranean peoples, and Ashkenazic Jews, respectively.

The suggestion here is that, as the famous geneticist Theodore Dobzhansky has noted, "Faced with a revival of 'scientific' racism, one is tempted to treat the matter with the silent scorn it so richly deserves ... [Yet] it may perhaps be useful to add a warning against exaggerations which some writers bent on combatting racism are unwittingly making."[45] In one sense, making official statements such as the unanimous declaration of the American Anthropological Association cited above, denies to the discreditors the notion that those categorized as members of a given racial group (such as the far from "pure" American Blacks), are innately inferior, but in another sense it begs several questions that remain scientifically legitimate.[46] The study of race and the ideology of racism must be dealt with as separate phenomena.

Social Structure and Individual Personality

Concern about racism is clearly at the center of most current discussions of prejudice in American society. But various students of the subject tend to concentrate their attention on one or another aspect of the overall problem. Some focus on the social system and its various parts (organizations, classes, and institutions), its rules or norms, and its purported values. Society itself is often the principal unit of analysis. Others eschew so grand a scope of study, preferring to concentrate on individual behavior and personality. George A. Kourvetaris has called these polar approaches "macroscopic" and "microscopic."[47] As George Simpson and J. Milton Yinger and Gordon Allport have indicated, there are "levels" in between. In their well-known text, *Racial and Cultural Minorities*, Simpson and Yinger begin where we left off above:

To say simply that there is an "instinct" or natural tendency toward prejudice, or that there is an inevitable "dislike of the unlike," or that so-called prejudice against minority groups is a natural reaction to their factual inferiority—explanations that abound in the literature—is to fail to bring the study of prejudice into the framework of contemporary theory of human behavior.[48]

They suggest posing a set of questions:

Do groups differ in the direction and amount of prejudice that they exhibit? If so, why?
Is there change, through time and space in the groups, and kinds of groups toward which prejudice is directed?
What is the process by which an individual acquires prejudice?
What forces, in the lives of individuals and of groups, operate to sustain, and to reduce prejudice?[49]

Simpson and Yinger then attempt to answer the questions they pose by looking from the micro- (or the individual) level, focusing on personal needs, to the macro-level, examining the structure of society—power arrangements and economic, political, religious and other structural variables. In between they look at culture and cultural values and norms and the way in which these are transmitted.[50] This latter category is concerned with socialization, a most significant factor in the writing of the late Gordon W. Allport, author of *The Nature of Prejudice*.[51]

Allport, too, described levels in discussing his diagram reproduced in Table 5 at the bottom of this page.[52]

The approaches mentioned by Allport include examining the rationalized self-interests of upper classes in various societies; studying traditions that lead to conflict; upward mobility, and the challenge of certain elements in society; looking at population density and various types of contact, all of which occur when social change is intensive as in the case of rapid urbanization. But, said Allport, in addition to these approaches, comprehensive analysis must consider social climates, the settings of social interaction where rules are interpreted and acted upon. Moreover, Allport recognized the importance of the characteristics placed upon groups who are often the very objects of discrimination itself. (For example, in medieval Europe, Jews, denied the right to own land or to work in any occupations other than those involving high risk such as petty

Table 5 Theoretical and Methodological Approaches to the Study of the Causes of Prejudice.

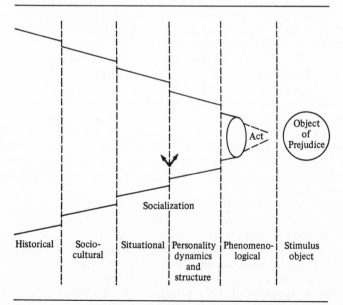

Source: G. W. Allport. "Prejudice: A Problem in Psychological and Social Causation," *Journal of Social Issues*, Supplement Series, No. 4, 1950.

finance, became money-lenders and tax-collectors, thereby fulfilling the prophecy that Jews are money brokers.) In the last instance we almost come full circle for, according to Allport, the minority-group member is the stimulus object, the object of prejudice, and the target of discrimination. (Here is the classic case of scapegoating to rationalize the self-interest mentioned above.)[53]

In the sections to follow, we look at some of these ares of concern with special attention to economic and class factors, culture and personality, and the socialization process itself.

Economic Interpretations

Followers of Marx and a good many other social scientists view prejudice as primarily the result of the strained relationship between the exploited and the exploiter. Carey McWilliams, for example, argued that anti-Semitism has traditionally been "a mask for privilege" and is based on the efforts of those in economically advantageous positions to exclude rising groups.[54] Oliver Cox and others have hypothesized that the whole system of race relations and segregated patterns, especially in the United States, is directly related to the maintenance of a cheap labor supply.[55] In not very different terms many contemporary analysts of American racial patterns argue that they are a form of domestic colonialism based on a continuing policy of exploitation of poor people, especially those who belong to such "Third World groups," as Blacks, Puerto Ricans, Mexican-Americans, Asian-Americans, and Native Americans.[56]

The *colonial model*, at least when applied to the situation of Third World Americans, according to William J. Wilson, involves four fundamental components: (1) The racial-group's entry into the dominant society is forced and involuntary. (2) The members of the dominant group administer the affairs of the suppressed or colonized group. (3) The culture and social organization of the suppressed group are destroyed. (4) Racism exists, that is, "a principle of social domination by which a group seen as inferior or different in terms of alleged biological characteristics is exploited, controlled and oppressed socially and psychically by a superordinate group."[57]

While all social scientists do not agree that economic interests play the most important role in bringing about and maintaining prejudice and discrimination, many have found that the intergroup conflict continues in large part because of the gains—both material and psychological—that are realized by assuming an attitude of superiority and enforcing social distance between one's own group and others. Early studies of "social distance" suggested that the principal basis for differential ranking of ethnic groups is the desire to maintain or enhance one's social position by associating with groups considered to be of high status and by disassociating from those low in the prestige hierarchy.[58] More recent investigations have found anti-Semitism and anti-Black sentiments to be most common among people dissatisfied with their own economic position or among those whose status has declined.[59]

Psychological Interpretations

In 1945 Bruno Bettelheim and Morris Janowitz documented the relationship between downward mobility and increased antipathy toward Jews and Blacks.[60] In *Social Change and Prejudice*, a volume published years after the initial study, they summarized the findings of various national-sample surveys conducted to reexamine the relationship.[61]

In their original investigation Bettelheim and Janowitz suggested that from among the 150 young veterans they interviewed in Chicago, those enjoying moderate upward mobility were more tolerant than those who had experienced no change in status, those who were rising very rapidly, or, especially, those experiencing downward mobility. In explaining these differences the authors said that "one can argue that, given American values which legitimate social mobility . . . the moderately upwardly mobile person is likely to have relatively effective personal controls." This theme of effective controls was crucial to the revised theoretical orientation of the investigators. In their more recent work they place heavy stress on new developments in ego psychology in which the person is viewed as part of, not apart from, his wider social milieu. In these terms prejudice is no longer seen as a reflection of an inherently weak ego straining against unacceptable inner strivings (as many psychologists have long contended); rather the emphasis is on the protective shield prejudice affords to those whose identity is threatened, as in the case of those experiencing sudden changes of status.

In societies such as our own, where prejudice is a "normal" rather than an "abnormal" fact of social life, Bettelheim and Janowitz assert that it must be understood in functional terms. In popular parlance, prejudice helps to pump up the egos of those who feel deprived or threatened; it reduces anxiety about one's own status; it adds in the assertion of superiority. "Unless other means of ego support are found for the person seeking identity and fearing its loss, prejudice can be expected to exist in one form or other."

The notion that prejudice may prove advantageous to certain individuals is something that bigoted demagogues and militant minority leaders have long known. This idea also has long been explored by social scientists. Thus in the 1930s in his classic study of race relations, *Caste and Class in a Southern Town*, John Dollard examined the functions of prejudice. Dollard was particularly impressed with the level of "social inertia," the reluctance to change traditional patterns mainly because of the gains accruing to those middle-class Whites who maintained the institutions of segregation.[62] Among the advantages he saw were those in the spheres of economics, sexual activities, and ego gratification linked to what Dollard called "prestige."

The psychological advantages of prejudice can be demonstrated more clearly in Freudian than in Marxian terms. Some writers have explained prejudice as a means of deflecting aggressions created by personal frustrations.[63] The thesis develops as follows: One goes through life seeking gratification for felt needs and, while many such needs have their origin in the organic structure of the individual, there are others which are culturally determined. These are learned early in life and are channeled and directed toward certain goals. When goal-directed behavior is blocked, hostile impulses are frequently created in the individual who, unable to determine the real source of his frustration but in an attempt to overcome it, manifests "free-floating aggression."[64] Such undirected aggression finds a "legitimate" point on which to focus which becomes a substitute for the actual frustrating agent. Usually the target is weak and unable to strike back. This process is well known: The boss berates his employee, who takes it out on his wife, who in turn berates the children. And so it goes.

Free-floating aggression is often directed toward a minority group or outgroup whose status in society puts it in a vulnerable position. One observer has made the point in graphic—though extreme—terms:

The rich take to opium and hashish. Those who cannot afford them become anti-Semites. Anti-Semitism is the morphine of the small people. . . . Since they cannot attain the ecstasy of love they seek the ecstasy of hate. The Jew is just convenient. . . . If there were no Jews the anti-Semites would have to invent them.[65]

When aggression is displaced in this manner the target is a scapegoat. In sociological parlance, scapegoating is the expression used to describe the psychological mechanism of displacing aggression. It refers to placing one's own "iniquities" or "sins" upon others. The scapegoat is therefore a whipping boy for the frustration-invoked hostility of the individuals or groups who use it. And, as Albert Camus has suggested, anyone and anything can become a scapegoat:

We are all exceptional cases. We all want to appeal against something. Each of us insists at all costs that he is innocent even if he has to accuse the whole human race and heaven itself.[66]

The reader who examines these economic and psychological explanations of the basis of prejudice may ask what predisposes certain individuals to attempt to exploit others or to seek scapegoats upon whom they can transfer their own inadequacies. One attempt to answer this question was made by a group of behavioral scientists who hypothesized "that the political, economic, and social convictions of an individual often form a broad and coherent pattern as if bound together by a 'mentality' or 'spirit' and that this pattern is an expression of deep-lying trends in his personality."[67] This statement is taken from the well-known study of *The Authoritarian Personality*, which, more than twenty years ago, presented a new approach to the investigation of prejudice. The major concern of this large-scale research, conducted in the United States during and after World War II, was to understand the "potentially fascistic individual, one whose structure is such as to render him or her particularly susceptible to anti-democratic propaganda."[68]

Both quantitative and qualitative research techniques were employed in this investigation. Questionnaires administered to groups of college students (and later to noncollege groups) provided background information about the respondents. Stereotype-laden questions were used as bases for the development of scales of anti-Semitism, ethnocentrism, politicoeconomic conservatism, and fascism. Two types of interviews were administered to the extreme scorers on these scales: one, nondirective, aimed at getting at basic ideology; the other, clinical-genetic, designed to elicit case history material.

Analysis of data thus obtained suggested that antipathy toward minorities and ethnocentric thinking—called "social discrimination" by the authors—are generalized ideological systems pertaining to groups and group relations. Highly prejudiced individuals were found to possess the following personality characteristics: glorification of power; the tendency to view people as good or bad, and things as black or white; deep concern with status and toughness; repression of sexual feelings; conception of the world as a jungle; cynicism about human nature; the proclivity to blame others rather than themselves for misdeeds and trouble. Outgroup hostility was especially prominent among the defense mechanisms of the "authoritarians." Concerning these extreme scorers, the authors wrote:

... The basically hierarchical, authoritarian, exploitative parent-child relationship is apt to carry over into a power-oriented, exploitively dependent attitude toward one's sex partner and one's God and may well culminate in a political philosophy and social outlook which has no room for anything but a desperate clinging to what appears to be strong and disdainful rejection of whatever is relegated to the bottom.[69]

This study, in other words, concluded that many, perhaps most, highly prejudiced persons are mentally disturbed.[70] This conclusion no doubt holds for many individuals of "rigid personality," including at least some of the leaders of extremist hate movements and, perhaps, quite a few of their followers.[71] But these all-weather bigots are hardly representative of the vast number of Americans who manifest racial and ethnic prejudice and discriminate against minority groups. In fact, follow-up studies of hypotheses presented in *The Authoritarian Personality*, using similar or identical research instruments (especially the "F scale"), report that prejudice and discrimination characterize the attitudes and behavior of many "normal" people.[72] Moreover, careful testing of the hypotheses of this pioneering work suggests that bigotry is by no means confined to politically conservative or reactionary individuals, and that authoritarian personalities are to be found among both the right and the left segments of the nation's citizenry.[73] Given the fact that these patterns are widespread, adequate sociological explanation of prejudice and discrimination cannot be confined to psychological deviation alone. Prejudice and discrimination constitute a major social problem precisely because most of their practitioners *conform to established beliefs and values.*

Socialization and Social Conformity

Rather than conceiving of group prejudice as an inborn tendency or a characteristic rent in one's basic personality, most sociologists today view it as a social habit. This thesis derives from the general proposition that cultural traits are learned. In the process of learning the ways of their groups—the process of socialization——individuals acquire both self-perceptions and images of others. If the teaching is effective, the individual internalizes (in substantial measure, but never fully) the sentiments and customs of his social milieu—including the "appropriate" prejudices. As sociologists MacIver and Page have written:

The individual is not born with prejudices any more than he is born with sociological understanding. The way he thinks as a member of a group, especially about other groups, is at bottom the result of social indoctrination, in both its direct and its indirect forms, indoctrination that inculcates beliefs and attitudes, which easily take firm hold in his life through the process of habituation.[74]

An old southerner put it this way:

I grew up just 19 miles from Appomattox. The teaching I received both in school and from my parents was hard-core South, with no chance of insight into the thinking and ways of other peoples. I was taught to look down upon Negroes, tolerate Jews (because we had to do business with them) and ignore Catholics.

We celebrated Jefferson Davis's birthday, but ignored Lincoln's; the name Robert E. Lee was spoken with reverence and Appomattox was a shrine. The Golden Rule only applied to others who were either Methodist or Baptist, white and without a foreign-sounding name. . . .[75]

The internalization of social prejudices does not require direct contact between the learner and the members of groups held in low esteem. If the agents of socialization—parents or peers or community leaders—are themselves prejudiced people, they are apt to be effective teachers of group antipathies whether the objects of their attitudes are immediate neighbors or distant outgroups.

The lessons learned in this "natural" process of acculturation constitute a serious problem for those educators and other persons who attempt to make more realizable the values of the American ethos. They are competing with the home, playground, and, sometimes, the mass media, which for many people represent the normal and desirable way of life, a way of life that all too often is inconsistent with and disruptive of ideals of freedom, social equality, and unhampered opportunity. This situation is aggravated by the fact that group antipathy has been found to exist not only among upper-status individuals but, more significantly perhaps, among members of the rank and file. Both feel that they have material or psychological stakes in institutionalized patterns of prejudice—and act accordingly.

Culture and Institutionalized Racism

Many contemporary writers and most militant minority-group leaders consider institutionalized racism to be the principal source of prejudice against non-White peoples (or those treated as a "racial" group like Jews in Nazi Germany). Their explanations find expression in many forms— from academic rhetoric to the argot of the street—but the theme remains more or less the same. The core argument is that a faulty belief in their own superiority is deeply ingrained in the minds of White people and in their social mores. They have internalized the same views as those promulgated by the early anthropologists and perpetuated by those who, for several centuries, claimed to be lifting and carrying "the White man's burden." The late Whitney M. Young put it succinctly when he wrote that "racism . . . is the assumption of superiority and the arrogance that goes with it."[76]

As noted earlier, many southerners found scientific racism a justification for the exploitation of Africans during the first half of the nineteenth century, a time when the institution of slavery was being severely challenged. Increasing evidence suggests that others shared their views but, instead of putting down the Blacks, they put them out, out of their minds. Joel Kovel, for example, in his psychohistory White Racism contends that in this country racism is still manifest in efforts to control (or what he calls the pattern of "dominative racism") or to avoid ("aversive racism").

He explains that:

In general, the dominative type has been marked by heat and the aversive type by coldness. The former is clearly associated with the American South, where, of course, domination of blacks became the cornerstone of society; and the latter with the North, where blacks have so consistently come and found themselves out of place. The dominative racist, when threatened by the black, resorts to direct violence; the aversive racist, in the same situation, turns away and walls himself off.[77]

To pursue the point one step further, it is interesting to note that, like Alexis de Tocqueville long before him, Kovel asserts that aversive racists have been more intense in their reaction than their dominative countrymen. De Tocqueville had suggested: "The prejudice of race appears to be stronger in the states that have abolished slavery than in those where it still exists; and nowhere is it so intolerant as in those states where servitude has never been known . . . "[78] In recent years, the degree of compliance with school desegregation orders reflects, at least in some measure, levels of prejudice; and, in keeping with the observations of de Tocqueville and Kovel, southern districts, in many of which attitudes appear to be changing rapidly, are desegregating more rapidly than many communities in the North.

In the North, people who long overlooked what was happening in their midst, while condemning Southerners for their racial prejudice, are revealing that they are by no means immune to racism themselves.

Institutionalized racism thus pertains to discriminatory practices reflected in customs and laws concerning what is expected, what is required, what is forbidden—and with whom. As shall be noted in the next chapter, various segments of society have systematically denied equal opportunity to certain specific groups in such a way that many are involved, including the reluctant discriminators previously mentioned.

Conclusion

Prejudice, as we have seen, has been attributed to basic economic interests, to authoritarian personality structure, to reactions to frustration, to social conformity, to poor education. There are, of course, other interpretations; for example: the emphasis upon the symbolic significance of the presence of a particular minority in a certain area;[79] the idea that contact with certain minorities under certain circumstances increases rather than decreases prejudice;[80] and what Allport has called "earned reputation"—the notion that individuals react to ethnic traits that are in fact menacing and threatening and therefore evoke realistic hostility.[81]

Each of these interpretations possesses more than a kernel of truth, and each may help to explain prejudice of a particular sort. Group prejudice is not a unidimensional phenomenon. Although we have not exhausted the various explanations for its occurrence, one thing appears certain: Prejudice is learned, not inherited.

NOTES

1. Rudyard Kipling, "We and They," in *Debits and Credits* (London: Macmillan, 1926), pp. 327–328. By permission of Mrs. George Bambridge, the Macmillan Co. of London & Basingstoke, the Macmillan Co. of Canada, and Doubleday & Co., Inc.
2. *Idem.*
3. William Graham Sumner, *Folkways* (Boston: Ginn, 1906), p. 13.
4. Robert Louis Stevenson, "Foreign Children," In *The Works of Robert Louis Stevenson* (New York: Walter Black, Inc., 1926) (originally published in 1883).
5. Margaret Mead, *And Keep Your Powder Dry* (New York: William Morris 1965), p. 11.
6. For further discussion of this phenomenon, see W. Lloyd Warner and Leo Srole, *The Social Systems of American Ethnic Groups* (New Haven: Yale University Press, 1945), pp. 283–296.
7. See, for example, these early discussions and studies of "social distance": Robert E. Park, "The Concept of Social Distance," *Journal of Applied Sociology*, 8 (1924), 339–344; and E. S. Bogardus, *Immigration and Race Attitudes* (Boston: D. C. Heath, 1928); and his articles "Measuring Social Distance," *Journal of Applied Sociology*, 9 (1925), 299–308; "A Social Distance Scale," *Sociology and Social Research*, 19 (1933), 265–271; and, "Stereotypes vs. Sociotypes," *Sociology and Social Research* 34 (1950). See also E. L. Hartley: *Problems in Prejudice* (New York: Kings Crown Press, 1946); and James W. Vander Zanden, *American Minority Relations*. 3rd ed. (New York: The Ronald Press, 1972), p. 101.
8. Hartley, *ibid.* See also R. Zeligs and G. Hendrickson, "Racial Attitudes of 200 Sixth-Grade Children," *Sociology and Social Research* (September–October 1933), pp. 26–36.
9. Sigmund Freud, *Group Psychology and the Analysis of the Ego* (New York: Boni and Liverright, 1950), p. 55.
10. Catton and Hong have found that "after social dominance has been taken into account, the appearance of ethnocentrism in minorities is a further factor in the development of majority hostility." William R. Catton, Jr., and Sung Chick Hong, "The Relation of Apparent Minority Ethnocentrism to Majority Antipathy," *American Sociological Review*, 27 (April 1962), 190.
11. Joseph G. Gittler, "Man and His Prejudices," *The Scientific Monthly*, 69 (July 1949), 43–47. See also Herbert Blumer, "Race Prejudice as a Sense of Group Position," *Pacific Sociological Review*, 1 (Spring 1958), 3–7.
12. Daniel Wilner *et al.*, "Residential Proximity and Intergroup Relations in Public Housing Projects," *Journal of Social Issues*, 8 (No. 1, 1952), 45. For several discussions of the definition of prejudice, see Gordon W. Allport, *The Nature of Prejudice* (Cambridge: Addison-Wesley, 1954), pp. 3–16; Brewton Berry, *Race and Ethnic Relations* (Boston: Houghton Mifflin, 1958), pp. 363–371; John Harding *et al.*, "Prejudice and Ethnic Relations," in Gardner Lindzey

(ed.), *Handbook of Social Psychology*, Vol. II (Cambridge: Addison-Wesley, 1954), pp. 1021–1061; George Simpson and J. Milton Yinger, *Racial and Cultural Minorities*, rev. ed. (New York: Harper & Row, 1958), pp. 14–19; and Robin M. Williams, Jr., *The Reduction of Intergroup Tensions* (New York: The Social Science Research Council, Bulletin No. 57, 1947), pp. 36–43.

13. See Bernard M. Kramer, "Dimensions of Prejudice," *Journal of Psychology*, 27 (April 1949), 389–451.

14. Arnold M. Rose, "Anti-Semitism's Root in City Hatred," *Commentary*, 6 (October 1949), p. 374.

15. This is essentially the same definition used by Robin M. Williams, Jr., *op. cit.*, p. 39.

16. As reported in *Time* (September 29, 1958), p. 58. Italics supplied.

17. As reported in *The New York Times* (October 21, 1966), p. 28.

18. John P. Dean and Alex Rosen, *A Manual of Intergroup Relations* (University of Chicago Press, 1955), p. 58.

19. Robert K. Merton, "Discrimination and the American Creed," In R. M. MacIver (ed.), *Discrimination and National Welfare* (New York: Harper & Row, 1949), pp. 99–126. The passages to follow are largely summary statements of Merton's thesis. Only direct quotations will be noted.

20. *Ibid.*, p. 105.

21. See, for example, Robert O. Blood, "Discrimination Without Prejudice," *Social Problems*, 3 (October 1955), 114–117.

22. Merton, *op. cit.*, p. 108.

23. *Ibid.*, p. 109.

24. See Allport, *op. cit.*, p. 68.

25. See, for example, E. Terry Prothro and John A. Jenson, "Interrelations of Religious and Ethnic Attitudes in Selected Southern Relations," *The Journal of Social Psychology*, 32 (August 1950), 45–49.

26. See, for example, Herbert J. Gans, "Negro-Jewish Conflict in New York," *Midstream* (March 1969).

27. See, for example, Gerhard W. Ditz, "Outgroup and Ingroup Prejudice Among Members of Minority Groups," *Alpha Kappa Deltan* (Spring 1959), 26–31; and Catton and Hong, *op. cit.*, pp. 178–191.

28. Harry Golden, *You're Entitle'* (Cleveland: World Publishing Company, 1962), p. 259.

29. For a more detailed discussion of various explanations of the causes of prejudice, see Allport, *op, cit.*, pp. 206–216; Arnold M. Rose, "The Causes of Prejudice," in Francis E. Merrill (ed.), *Social Problems* (New York: Knopf, 1950), pp. 402–424; Arnold M. Rose, "The Roots of Prejudice," in *The Race Question in Modern Science* (a UNESCO publication) (New York: Whiteside, Inc., and William Morrow and Company, 1956), pp. 215–243; and Robin M. Williams, Jr., *op. cit.*, pp. 36–77.

30. See especially Peter I. Rose, *The Subject Is Race* (New York: Oxford University Press, 1968). Also see Oscar Handlin, "The Linnean Web," in *Race and Nationality in American Life* (Garden City, N.Y.: Doubleday, 1957), pp. 57–73; and Cyril Bibby, *Race, Prejudice and Education* (New York: Praeger, 1960), pp. 40–62.

31. E. B. Reuter and C. W. Hart, *Introduction to Sociology* (New York: McGraw-Hill, 1963), p. 263.

32. Robert E. Park and Ernest W. Burgess, *Introduction to the Science of Sociology* (University of Chicago Press, 1924), p. 578. Italics supplied. Park later modified his position. For example, in "The Nature of Race Relations," in Edgar T. Thompson (ed.), *Race Relations and the Race Problem* (Durham, N.C.: Duke University Press, 1939), pp. 3–45, he wrote: "Race consciousness, therefore, is to be regarded as a phenomenon, *like* class or caste consciousness that enforces social distances." Italics supplied.

33. This is the closing sentence of a resolution passed by the Fellows of the American Anthropological Association, November 17, 1961. A similar resolution was adopted at the annual meeting of the Society for the Study of Social Problems in 1961.

34. Audrey Sheuey, *The Testing of Negro Intelligence* (Lynchburg, Va.: Randolph-Macon Women's College, 1958).

35. Arthur R. Jensen, "How Much Can We Boost I.Q. and Scholastic Achievement?" *Harvard Educational Review*, 39 (Winter 1969), 1–123. See also *Educability and Group Differences* (New York: Harper & Row, 1973).

36. As reported in *The New Republic* (December 16, 1967), p. 7. N.B. The answer is (c) in each case. The full text of the "test" appeared in *The Denver Post* (July 8, 1968), p. 6.

37. See, for example, Melvin M. Tumin (ed.), *Race and Intelligence*, (New York: Anti-Defamation League, 1963).

38. Jensen, *op. cit.* See also Christopher Jencks, "Intelligence and Race," *The New Republic* (September 13, 1969), pp. 25–29.

39. The sharpest barb came from anthropologist Jerry Hyman, who facetiously suggested that the Association had not gone far enough. He suggested "That it is incumbent on all members dedicated to Truth to seek out and destroy any remaining copies of publications that include the views of Herrnsteins, Shockley and Jensen so that our libraries and institutions of learning not be used to disseminate such unscientific and potentially damaging material. That special attention be paid to the destruction of *The Atlantic Monthly, Harvard Educational Review* and *New York Times* in that their complicity in this deception has been more energetic and more constant than other publications. That the method of destruction shall be left to the conscience of the individual fellow or voting member but that fire is a particular symbolic and therefore appropriate mechanism." (Quoted from *Newsletter of the American Anthropological Association*, 13 [February 1972], 2–3.)

40. Jencks, *op. cit.*, p. 29. See also H. J. Eysink, *The I.Q. Argument* (New York: Library Press, 1972).

41. Philip Green, "Race and I.Q.: Fallacy of Heritability," *Dissent* (Spring 1976); "The Pseudo Science of Arthur Jensen," *Dissent* (Summer 1976); and, "I.Q. and the Future of Equality," *Dissent* (Fall 1976).

42. Philip Green, "Race and I.Q.," *op. cit.*, p. 183.

43. *Ibid.*, p. 184.

44. *Ibid.*, p. 192. For another useful summary of the controversy see Berry and Tischler, *op. cit.*, Chap. 4, pp. 63–86.

45. Theodore Dobzhansky, "Comment," *Current Anthropology*, 2 (October 1961), 31.

46. Rose, *The Subject Is Race, op. cit.*, p. 41.

47. George A. Kourvetaris, "Prejudice and Discrimination in American Social

Structure," in P. Allan Dionisopoulos (ed.), *Racism in America* (DeKalb, Ill.: Northern Illinois University Press, 1971), pp. 32–41.

48. George Eaton Simpson and J. Milton Yinger, *Racial and Cultural Minorities*, 4th ed. (New York: Harper & Row, 1972), p. 63.

49. Idem.

50. Simpson and Yinger, *op. cit.*, pp. 63–102 and 139–164.

51. Allport, *op. cit.*

52. Gordon W. Allport, "Prejudice: A Problem in Psychological and Social Causation," *Journal of Social Issues*, Supplement Series, No. 4, 1950.

53. Allport, *The Nature of Prejudice*, pp. 201–212.

54. Carey McWilliams, *A Mask for Privilege: Anti-Semitism in America* (Boston: Little, Brown, 1948).

55. Oliver C. Cox, *Caste, Class and Race: A Study in Social Dynamics* (Garden City, N.Y.: Doubleday, 1948).

56. See, for example, Jack Forbes *et al.*, *The Third World Within* (Belmont, Calif.: Wadsworth, 1972); and Joan W. Moore, "Colonialism: The Case of the Mexican-Americans," *Social Problems*, 17 (Spring 1970), 463–472.

57. William J. Wilson, "Race Relations Models and Explanations of Ghetto Behavior," in Peter I. Rose (ed.), *Nation of Nations* (New York: Random House, 1972), p. 262. The definition of "racism" is from Robert Blauner, "Internal Colonialism and Ghetto Revolt," *Social Problems*, 16 (Spring 1969), 396.

58. See, for example, studies by E. S. Bogardus, including: "Social Distance and Its Origins," *Journal of Applied Sociology*, 9 (1925), 216–226; "Analyzing Changes in Public Opinion," *Journal of Applied Sociology*, 9 (1925), 372–381; "Social Distance: A Measuring Stick," *Survey*, 56 (May 1926), 169–170; and "Race Friendliness and Social Distance," *Journal of Applied Sociology*, 11 (1927), 272–287.

59. See, for example, A. A. Campbell, "Factors Associated with Attitudes Toward Jews," in T. M. Newcomb and E. L. Hartley (eds.), *Readings in Social Psychology* (New York: Holt, Rinehart and Winston, 1947), pp. 518–527.

60. Bruno Bettelheim and Morris Janowitz, *The Dynamics of Prejudice* (New York: Harper & Row, 1950).

61. Bruno Bettelheim and Morris Janowitz, *Social Change and Prejudice* (New York: Free Press, 1965).

62. John Dollard, *Caste and Class in a Southern Town* (New Haven: Yale University Press, 1937), esp. Chaps. 6 to 8.

63. See John Dollard *et al.*, *Frustration and Aggression* (New Haven: Yale University Press, 1939). "When Marxists have described the dynamic human interrelationships involved in the class struggle . . . they have introduced unwittingly a psychological system involving the assumption that aggression is a response to frustration." *Ibid.*, p. 23.

64. See, for example, Clyde M. Kluckhohn, "Group Tensions: Analysis of a Case History," in L. Bryson, L. Finkelstein, and R. M. MacIver (eds,), *Approaches to National Unity* (New York: Harper & Row, 1945), p. 224.

65. Quoted by Allport, *op. cit.*, p. 343.

66. Albert Camus, *The Fall* (Justin O'Brien, tr.) (New York: Vintage Brooks, 1963), p. 81.

67. T. W. Adorno *et al.*, *The Authoritarian Personality* (New York: Harper & Row, 1950), p. 1.

68. *Ibid.*
69. *Ibid.*, p. 971.
70. See Bettelheim and Janowitz, *op. cit.*; and Selma Hirsch, *The Fears Men Live By* (New York: Harper & Row, 1955).
71. See, for example, Leo Lowenthal and Norbert Guterman, *Prophets of Deceit* (New York: Harper & Row, 1949).
72. See, for example, Richard Christie, "Authoritarianism Reexamined," in Richard Christie and Marie Jahoda (eds.), *Studies in Scope and Method of "The Authoritarian Personality"* (New York: Free Press, 1954), pp. 123–196. See also Muzafer and Carolyn Sherif, *Groups in Harmony and Tension* (New York: Harper & Row, 1953).
73. See Edward A. Shils, "Authoritarianism: 'Right' and 'Left,'" in Christie and Jahoda, *op. cit.*, pp. 24–49. See also Stanley Rothman and Robert Lichter, *Radical Christians, Radical Jews* (New York: Oxford University Press, 1981).
74. Robert M. MacIver and Charles H. Page, *Society: An Introductory Analysis* (New York: Holt, Rinehart & Winston, 1949), p. 407.
75. Letter to the Editor of *The New York Times* (May 16, 1963). The letter was signed by Tom Wilcher.
76. See Whitney M. Young, Jr., *Beyond Racism: Building on Open Society* (New York: McGraw-Hill, 1969).
77. Joel Kovel, *White Racism: A Psychohistory* (New York: Pantheon, 1970), pp. 31–32.
78. Alexis de Tocqueville, *Democracy in America* (New York: Vintage Books, 1945), Vol. I, p. 373.
79. See, for example, Lewis Browne, *How Odd of Jews* (New York: Macmillan, 1943); and Arnold M. Rose, "Anti-Semitism's Roots in City Hatred," *op. cit.*
80. See Allport, *op. cit.*, Chap. 16.
81. *Ibid.*, p. 217.

5

DISCRIMINATION

Patterns of Discrimination

Eenie, meenie, miney, moe.
Catch a nigger by the toe.

Not a tiger, a "nigger." Until very recently, the bit of doggerel chanted by children throughout the English-speaking Western world contained an explicit racial epithet. It may have been an "unintended indiscretion" but it was clearly an insult.

Insults are but one of a range of actions we call discriminatory. In this chapter we will examine various expressions of behavior that fall under the rubric of *discrimination*, the singling out of people for separate and unequal treatment.[1] The treatment itself is often institutionalized as in the denial of the franchise, separate and unequal education, selective hiring practices, restrictive neighborhoods, and exclusive social clubs. It may be *de jure*, supported by law, or *de facto*, supported in practice or by custom. Moreover, those who maintain the practices of discrimination may not do so out of deep-seated hatred but through a reluctance to change what, to them, are economically, psychologically, and socially acceptable or necessary arrangements. Thus it is not surprising to find that many Americans are fair-weather liberals who more often do what is "expected" than what is "right," who often engage in behavior which, to the objective outside observer, would appear to be downright contradictory.

Not so long ago many middle- and upper-class Whites in the South regularly employed Black servants whose jobs involved intimate contact with the family, such as cooks, maids, even wet-nurses for the children. Yet these very same people were reluctant to allow Blacks to drink from the same water fountain, swim in the same pool, or go to school with their youngsters. Northern Whites, more self-righteous perhaps but equally inconsistent, were less concerned with "pollution" yet kept Blacks from their neighborhoods, clubs, and churches. The height of northern hypocrisy was most clearly manifest each Sunday morning when loyal parishioners faithfully proclaimed the "Brotherhood of Man"—in segregated churches.

These inconsistent behavior patterns demonstrate the segmental quality of discrimination and the fact that large numbers of people subscribe to those forms of behavior that are acceptable according to the social and cultural definitions of the situations in which they find themselves. Relatively few are willing to cut the cake of custom, especially when they feel (or are made to feel) that their vested interests are threatened. In this way the fair-weather liberal often ends up being a reluctant discriminator.

In addition to an understanding of its institutional settings, it is important to recognize the varying degrees of discrimination and the specific ways in which individuals are denied their civil and social rights. *Defamation, avoidance, threat, coercion, segregation, colonization, relocation,* and *annihilation* describe points along the continuum of discriminatory practices. Of these practices, the present chapter deals with three distinctive modes, which we call *derogation, denial,* and various forms of *aggression.*[2] This listing is not exhaustive, for the varieties of discrimination, as the continuum above suggests, are numerous. Yet these three patterns—ranging from name-calling to genocide—should serve to indicate both the varying degrees of intensity and the social forms discrimination may take.

Derogation

Ethnophaulism is a technical word for a derogatory term used by the members of one ethnic group to describe the members of another. Ethnophaulisms are at the core of the language of prejudice and, when openly expressed, become a form of discrimination known as *antilocution,* a fancy word for name-calling. The old saying that "sticks and stones may break my bones but names will never hurt me" is misleading, for articulated antagonisms may serve to reinforce the images we hold of others and may have serious psychic consequences for those on the receiving end. The repeated reference to the adult Black male as "boy" or the married Black woman as "miss," to cite examples graphically portrayed by Richard Wright, is like a stain that leaves an indelible imprint on the recipient's personality.[3]

Unintentional references to color, verbal slips, and testimonials are frequently construed by minority-group members as derogatory. Included here are such old-fashioned expressions as "Free, White, and Twenty-one," "He treated me white," and "Your face may be black, but your heart is as white as mine." Color-laden phrases are closely related to those expressions that slip out, often with no intent to harm or disparage. Examples are numerous: "nigger toes" (referring to Brazil nuts); "jew him down" (to bargain sharply); "He's scotch all right" (referring to the stereotype of tight-fistedness); "I've been gypped" (a reference to Gypsies). Sometimes, in an attempt to indicate friendliness, the White person may say to the Black, "You're as good as I am"; or a Gentile, speaking to a Jew: "You Jews are a fine race. . . . " Such testimonials are often received by the listeners as patronizing gestures; so are the statements that begin, "Don't get me wrong, why, some of my best friends are . . . "[4]

Humor is found in all societies, and ethnic humor is particularly prevalent in ours. Americans are all familiar with ethnic jokes and frequently tell them with abandon—forgetting or failing to consider what they mean to those joked about. In an article pointedly titled "The Sting of Polish Jokes," philosopher and writer Michael Novak discussed the matter in some detail. One of his main points was that "Not all humor is humorous." As he explained:

Ethnic humor is one of the great resources of this nation. There are forms of laughing at oneself and at others, usually based on the daily absurdities of mutual noncomprehension or double meaning. These are truly amusing, probably the most amusing jokes in the American repertoire. In this humor, all ethnic groups are equal; the barbs are shared by everybody at the same time.

But there is a second genus of ethnic joke. It does not gain its force from that double understanding of the same word or doubly misapprehended event that characterizes multi-cultural perception. It is based on demeaning the character of one ethnic group, in line with a stereotype, and its function is to make the majority feel superior to the minority. Told in the presence of the minority, these jokes further require those who are their butt to acquiesce in their own humiliation, to laugh obediently, to accept their ascribed inferiority. (Nudging elbow: "No offense, friend. Only a joke.") The tactic is structurally the same as those techniques that force inmates to embrace their own degradation. Rage is not permitted. One must stand there helplessly and acquiesce.

Southern and Eastern Europeans in the United States are subject to the last respectable bigotry.[5]

The last phrase, coined by Michael Lerner,[6] refers to the fact that many liberal people who supposedly "know better" than to tell jokes about Blacks and other non-White minorities seem to have no compunction about telling them about Southern and Eastern Europeans.

Members of minority groups often affect accents and tell jokes and stories among themselves seemingly at their own expense. Among Jews it is not uncommon to hear stories that describe the conflict between the desire for acceptance and the ties to the Jewish community.[7] Blacks frequently joke about their low status, the difficulty of advancement, the special significance of "soul," and the White man's image of their lives.[8] Some stories are tinged with the bitterness of self-abasement; others stress the virtues of marginality. Such intragroup humor has subtle social and psychological functions, including the reinforcement of group identity. The fact remains, however, that to laugh at yourself is very different from listening to an outsider tell stories about you or the members of your group.

Over the past forty years, in an attempt to deal more forthrightly with ethnic pluralism, a number of television networks introduced comedy programs with "intergroup" themes. In addition to "The Life of Riley," "The Goldbergs," and "Bridget Loves Bernie" and an increasing number of sitcoms starring Blacks (such as "Julia," "Sanford and Son," "The Jeffersons," and "Good Times,"[9]), there was "All in the Family." This controversial show, based on an English program called "Til Death Do Us Part," pulled few punches. It (purposely) dealt directly with contemporary issues—the role of women, sexual deviance, and, especially, ethnic interaction.

Like "The Cosby Show" in the late 1980s, in the 1970s "All in the Family" was one of America's most popular t.v. programs. Millions of people put aside other things to watch Archie Bunker, the bumbling bigot who didn't trust anybody regardless of race, creed, or color; his wife Edith, the "dingbat"; daughter Gloria, the child/woman caught between parental love, "wifely" responsibility, and cravings for independence; son-in-law, Mike, the "liberal meathead" and Polish-American sociology graduate student; his friends; and his enemies. The program was filled with epithets used in direct reference to minorities—"spic," "greaser," "jigaboo," "hebe," "a-rab," and the like.

Because it was assumed that those so labeled would see such expressions as an extreme form of derogation, many critics argued that "All in the Family" served to legitimize the use of such terms. Moreover, and more important, some argued that Archie Bunker made bigotry somehow respectable.[10] Others disagreed. Those who supported the program contended that it is healthy to make fun of such serious matters; it releases tensions and, perhaps, even creates a climate of understanding.

The few studies that were conducted for the Columbia Broadcasting System (CBS), the network that produced the show, indicated that most of those maligned by Archie Bunker appeared to *like* the program. One reason may be that the minority individuals portrayed usually came out on top (and even Archie seemed to learn something each time). Some of those who identified themselves with Archie Bunker said that he reminded them of what they used to be like.

Other studies of "All in the Family" came to the conclusion that a process of selective perception seems to take place when one is exposed to certain derogatory material or interracial satire. Thus, "nonprejudiced viewers and minority-group members may perceive and enjoy [the program] as satire, whereas prejudiced viewers may perceive and enjoy the show of "telling it like it is." The researchers, Neil Vidman and Milton Rokeach, explained that "by making Archie a 'lovable bigot' the program encourages bigots to excuse and rationalize their own prejudices."[11] Vidman and Rokeach come close to the position taken by Michael Novak and discussed above.

Erdman Palmore, on the basis of a careful study of ethnophaulisms, concludes that:

All racial and ethnic groups use ethnophaulisms. The greater the number of ethnophaulisms used against a group, the greater the prejudice. When the outgroup is a different race, most ethnophaulisms express and support the stereotypes of highly visible physical differences. When the out-group is the same general racial type, most ethnophaulisms express and support stereotypes of highly visible cultural differences. The derivations of most ethnophaulisms express some negative stereotypes.[12]

Since ethnophaulisms appear to be essential to the support and spread of ethnocentrism, they provide one indication of the relationship between ideas and action. As noted in Chapter Four, the conative dimension of prejudice is that aspect of the attitude construct concerned with predispositions for behavior. There is little question that referring to people in particular derogatory ways or portraying them in terms of negative stereotypes or caricatures heightens one's sense of animus and, if supported by appropriate norms allows—even encourages—the acting out of one's predispositions. Today such expressions are often labeled "fighting words," so incendiary that they are said to exceed the constitutional protection of free speech.

Palmore notes that ethnophaulisms are used by some members of all groups at one time or another. Thus not only do some Whites have favorite expressions for Blacks but some Blacks have their own terms for Whites— "whitey," "Mr. Charlie," "the Man,"—and some with seemingly obscure origins such as "Honky." "Honky" was originally "Hunky," used to describe Hungarians (Bohemians were "Bohunks"). By the 1960s the term came to refer to all Whites, regardless of national origin. Another ethnophaulism used by some Blacks is "Ofay," pig Latin for "foe."

The use of derogatory language, of defamation, of carefully chosen ethnophaulisms, is often of a piece, particularly in the hands of racist demagogues. Throughout history name-calling, trumped-up charges, distortions of social roles, and guilt by association have been used by those wishing to find scapegoats and to teach others to use them.

The Roman historian Tacitus explained this practice as well as anyone. Describing the burning of Rome, an act that most historians (and many Romans) attributed to Nero himself, Tacitus wrote:

Heaven could not stifle scandal or dispel the belief that the fire had taken place by order. Therefore, to scotch the rumour, Nero substituted as culprits, and punished with the upmost refinements of cruelty, a class of men, loathed for their vices, whom the crowd styled Christians.[13]

It should be noted, however, that Tacitus himself was ambivalent about the Christians, if not about their alleged deed. Thus he further wrote:

Christus, the founder of the name, had undergone the death penalty in the reign of Tiberius, by sentence of the procurator Pontius Pilatus, and *the pernicious superstition* was checked for a moment, only to break out once more, not merely in Judaea, the home of the disease, but in the capital itself, where all things horrible or shameful in the world collect and find vogue. First, then, the confessed members of the sect were arrested: next, on their disclosures, vast numbers were convicted, not so much on the count of arson as for hatred of the human race.[14]

The practice of using demagoguery is very old. Many examples are to be found during the Crusades, the Middle Ages, the periods of colonization, and throughout the nineteenth century. In various times and places different groups have been the targets for defamation and other forms of discrimination. Jews, however, hold the dubious distinction of having been the most persistently vilified throughout the centuries—from ancient times to the present day. It was in Germany during the 1930s that anti-Semitic propaganda was refined to an "art" under the direction of Joseph Goebbels and through the pen of Julius Streicher. This kind of "art" (and the characterization of Jews as parasites, money-grubbers, imperialists) did not disappear with the end of the Nazi regime. In the Soviet Union, similar caricatures were presented with one notable difference. Some of the Soviet propaganda portrayed Jews as *Nazis*, a curious juxtaposition but one that clearly served the needs of the demagogues who presented it.

Our own country has not been immune to anti-Semitic writing or speech. In the early days of World War II several social scientists conducted a study of anti-Semitic demagoguery in the United States. In the volume *Prophets of Deceit* they described the mind and ideology of the hate-monger. The book provides many examples of the sort of message being delivered by such anti-Semites as Gerald L. K. Smith and Father Coughlin. Here are samples:

When will the plain, ordinary, sincere, sheeplike peoples of America awaken to the fact that their common affairs are being arranged and run for them by aliens, Communists, crackpots, refugees, renegades, Socialists, termites, and traitors? These alien enemies of America. . . .

•••

Hitler and Hitlerism are the creatures of Jewry and Judaism. The merciless programs of abuse which certain Jews and their satellites work upon people who are not in full agreement with them create terrible reactions.

•••

We are going to take this government out of the hands of these city-slickers and give it back to the people that still believe that 2 and 2 is 4, that God is in his heaven and the Bible is the Word . . . [15]

Despite denials by his brother, President Jimmy Carter, the late Billy Carter seemed to echo some of these sentiments when he claimed that

Jews had too much power and influence in America, especially in what he termed "the Jewish media."[16] Others in prominent positions have made similar public utterances in recent years signaling a resurgence of anti-Semitic populism.

In 1969 Seymour Martin Lipset and Earl Raab published a political history of right-wing activities. In *The Politics of Unreason* they describe in detail the activities and mentalities of such nativistic movements as the Anti-Masonic League, the American Protective Association of the 1890s, the Ku Klux Klan in its various incarnations, the Coughlinites of the 1930s, the McCarthyites of the 1950s, and the followers of George Wallace and other reactionary leaders in the 1960s.[17]

Summing up their views of those who listened to the demagogues and joined the movements, Lipset and Raab suggest that:

> The adherents of extremist movements have typically felt deprived—either they have never gained their due share or they are losing their portion of power and status. We might call these two groups the "never-hads" and the "once-hads." These deprived groups are not necessarily extremist, but *extremism usually draws its strength from them.*[18]

When the demagogue speaks, somebody listens.

While in the past the "once-hads," especially, felt outraged by the thought of newcomers and outsiders getting what they believed to be legitimately theirs, in recent years the "never-hads" seem to be particularly incensed by what they see as people demanding privileges that, they claim, they never had. Much anti-Black sentiment, especially by "White ethnics," is couched in these terms. But many southern Whites and middle Americans also are attracted by the appeals of those who blame the Blacks not only for their alleged personal failings but for wreaking changes throughout society. Some hark back to the turbulent days of the Klan when "nigger-baiting" words were spoken from a stump or written in *The Fiery Cross.* Others have a more contemporary view, linking Black demands with communist conspiracies. One of the favorite charges of the radical right in the late 1950s and early 1960s was that Daisy Bates, the president of the NAACP in Little Rock, Arkansas, who helped to bring about school integration there, and others like her, were fronting for "commies."[19]

Used by demagogues, ethnophaulisms serve well as vehicles for venting the wrath of the bigot, for stirring up latent prejudices, for fomenting hate, and for calling people to take action against their "foes." Name-calling is a widely used and highly effective form of discrimination.

Denial

Discrimination, of course, consists of more than ethnic labels, humorous anecdotes, embittered oratory, and defamation. Words are inflammatory and, as the Nazi propagandist Joseph Goebbels diabolically demonstrated, they can have far-reaching effects. As noted previously, the saying about "sticks and stones" denies the fact that name-calling does hurt. Still, there are more direct means used to break one's bones (and one's spirit). Most discriminatory behavior involves establishing and maintaining some measure of physical and social distance from minorities, either by avoiding contact as much as possible or by "keeping them in their place." *Avoidance* and *segregation* are two effective techniques of institutionalized discrimination. And, in many ways, they are related.

Discrimination often involves the practice of eschewing face-to-face relations with members of this or that minority group. Fundamental lessons in avoidance are learned early in life when children are taught by their parents or playmates, sometimes intentionally, often inadvertently, about groups with whom they should—or should not—associate. In adulthood these lessons manifest themselves in a variety of devices used to prevent or minimize contact with group members socially defined as being of low repute, unpleasant, or even untouchable. The diversity of avoidance taboos is well known.

One method of avoidance is the economic boycott. In the not so distant past, stores, restaurants, and conveyances known to be owned, operated or frequented by certain minority-group members on an equal basis with those in the dominant group were boycotted as a protest against their integrated policies. Fear of this kind of protest led quite a few department store owners (many of whom were themselves fair-weather liberals) to refrain from desegregating certain facilities such as lunch counters. In turn they often became the targets of civil rights groups seeking a redress of grievances. Two techniques were used in challenge: one was the sit-in, which forced proprietors to bring in police and, ultimately, to seek adjudication in the courts; the other was a counterboycott to discourage members of the minority from using other facilities in the targeted stores. Further examples of boycotting as a weapon *against* discrimination are discussed in Chapter Six.

Discriminatory boycotts have also been used in public places such as playgrounds, parks, and beaches abandoned by those who used them in protest against new integrated policies. Frequently leading to a self-fulfilling situation, a common pattern is for certain groups to withdraw from participation or utilization of such facilities as others move in. Ultimately what is most feared takes place. The minority takes over and the initial boycotters say, "We told you so!"

In some cases such boycotting is seen as a worthwhile inconvenience ("You can always go farther up the coast to another beach") or a necessary evil ("Nobody in his right mind would go *there*!"). But the beginning of an end of segregated schools created a setting for a somewhat more permanent pattern. In the urban centers of the North and in many parts of the South, white parents responded to the threat of integrated schooling by sending their children to private schools or by establishing such schools where they had not existed previously—sometimes with the tacit support of local and state authorities. The implementation of busing to achieve greater racial balance intensified the use of the boycott. In city after city newspapers noted the *Washington Post's* headline of December 20, 1972: "8000 Boycott Prince George's Classrooms" (in protest against court-ordered desegregation).[20] That was only the beginning. The pattern continued in many areas throughout the decade. One of the most serious examples occurred in Boston, Massachusetts, where many working-class Whites felt their sanctuaries were being invaded by court-ordered integration of the schools. Angry mobs and organized groups of local residents tried to disrupt the process and end busing. That failing, many simply refused to go to school, or to send their children.

The most widespread method of avoidance is that of movement away from neighborhoods into which minority-group members are entering. Thus, for many decades, the ecological history of large American cities has been marked by the "invasion" of residential areas by ethnic and racial minorities, by resistance of earlier inhabitants, by attempts to frighten or cajole people to sell out in response to the perceived threat, and by the eventual abandonment of the block or neighborhood and the succession of the newcomers.[21] In recent decades, once all-White areas in northern and west coast cities have turned into "Black" neighborhoods. Not infrequently the exodus of Whites is prompted by the panic of those residents who will not accept Black neighbors under any circumstances. (A similar pattern exists when the incoming group is Puerto Rican or Mexican-American or Native American or even a particular type of "Whites" like mountain people or "hillbillies.") While the process of changing neighborhoods is far from uniform and the time sequence is highly variable—depending upon such factors as the size of the incoming group, the nature of residential mobility already under way, and the extent of prejudice—many move simply because of the perceived threat of "invasion."[22]

A theme runs through all the methods employed for maintaining distances by avoidance. It involves *action or movement on the part of the dominant group rather than the minority*. To do something about "them" means, in these cases, doing something to one's self, one's family, or one's group.

Although related, segregation differs from avoidance. In segregation, instead of doing something to one's self or group, action is directed *against* others. A variety of devices is used to set up and maintain barriers between one's own group and those considered unworthy of normal social interaction. Segregation involves restrictive and exclusionary policies established to keep minorities out of private clubs, certain vocations, schools and colleges, churches, and neighborhoods, and, in many instances, to place and hold them in particular areas such as reservations, barrios, and ghettos.

Segregation has sometimes evolved on a voluntary basis as did the famous ghetto of Cologne, Germany, where the Jews of the thirteenth century sought and obtained permission to set up their own community within the city walls.[23] Most segregation, however, is not voluntary, as suggested by the term itself and by its definition as a "form of isolation which places limits or restrictions upon contact, communication, and social relations."[24] With several notable exceptions—for example, the communities of Hasidic Jews, the Amish, and the Mennonites—most of the segregation practiced in the United States is of an involuntary nature. The castelike restrictions that apply to Black Americans are the most obvious examples.

Involuntary segregation usually involves both spatial and social barriers. Social distance is most easily maintained through physical distance. Native Americans, in the past, have been forcibly restricted to reservations, as many Blacks and "colored peoples" in South Africa are being restricted today. Jews have been barred from purchasing homes in certain urban and suburban neighborhoods. Mexican-Americans have had to live in certain parts of several cities in the southwestern cities. Blacks have been denied easy escape from ghettos, large and small. Clearly, this physical separation serves to limit the interaction with members of other groups. Residential segregation accounts for many other patterns of separation—even when these are unenforceable by law, as in the case of education where school districts tend to follow neighborhood patterns.

Among the various devices used to maintain discriminatory housing patterns are restrictive covenants, neighborhood pressures, and "gentlemen's agreements." In some parts of the country one can still find deeds to property with provisions such as the following:

. . . and, furthermore, no lot shall be sold or leased to, or occupied by, any person excepting of the Caucasian race.

• • •

Provided further, that the grantee shall not sell to Negroes or permit use or occupation by them, except as domestic servants.

• • •

. . . shall not permit occupation by Negroes, Hindus, Syrians, Greeks, or any corporation controlled by same.[25]

Perhaps the most infamous of neighborhood restrictive policies was the "point system" maintained as recently as a quarter of a century ago for admittance to residence in exclusive Grosse Pointe, Michigan. There, all prospective residents had to be screened and evaluated on the basis of race, religion, education, occupation, accent, "swarthiness," and similar invidious criteria, and were allotted points for each "favorable" attribute. Only high scores were allowed to purchase property. The Grosse Pointe pattern is an extreme example of an established, though declining practice in many communities in the United States.[26]

Housing is not the only area where restrictive regulations, formal and informal, official and sub rosa, prevent outsiders from entering the circle of the dominant group. City clubs and country clubs, sororities and fraternities, lodges and service organizations, have required applicants or initiates to be "members of the Christian faith," or to "believe in Jesus Christ," or to be "White Caucasian." Not long ago there were Greek-letter college fraternities that went so far as to exclude Greeks.[27]

Admission to some private schools and colleges has also been limited by quota systems under which only certain percentages of the members of specified groups are considered eligible—irrespective of academic abilities. Since the 1940s, anti-discrimination legislation has prohibited colleges and universities in some states (and those receiving federal support) from requesting photographs, indications of religious preference or affiliation, or information about national origin from applicants. Still, such restrictions have been circumvented through the implementation of "area quotas." By accepting only a certain percentage of city-dwellers or easterners, for example, schools are able to limit the number of Jewish students. (In the past, Blacks and other non-Whites have been discriminated against in a variety of ways. Under new directives from the Department of Health and Human Services—brought about by forceful civil rights agitation—institutions of higher learning are being required to establish "plans of affirmative action," involving the setting of minima that, as we shall see in Chapter Seven, some call nothing other than "reverse discrimination.")

In spite of the increasing salience of performance standards in occupational life, some business corporations (especially, smaller, family-controlled firms), professional organizations, and many labor unions disqualify members of minority groups from employment or membership, severely hampering their opportunities to pursue occupations for which they are trained. The timeworn practice of hiring minorities last and firing them first still holds in many industries.

The following statements from an annual official government document, "The Social and Economic Status of the Black Population in the United States," reveal the legacy of discrimination and the effects of segregation in this country:

In the 1960s significant advances were made by the black population in many fields—notably, income, health, education, employment, and voter participation. The current statistics indicate continued progress in some areas of life, while other areas remained unchanged. Overall, however, in 1972, blacks still lag behind whites in most social and economic areas, although the differentials have narrowed over the years.[28]

That pattern, Whites behind Blacks in almost every sphere—education, voting, political participation as well as employment and income—persisted well into the next decade.[29] Indeed, despite gains on some fronts, such as greater access to higher education through the initiation of more far reaching recruitment schemes to make campuses "more diverse," much of this triggered by the requirements of affirmative-action rules, the overall picture, especially in the crucial areas of employment and income, offered little evidence of significant breakthroughs.

The generally sluggish economy and inflationary pressures in the mid- and late 1970s had a dampening effect on the chances of the able bodied poor in all cohorts, White, Black, Hispanic, or Asian. As for the working class, that is those already steadily employed, Whites in the aggregate made some slight gains, Blacks hardly any. In 1977, for example, about 30 percent of Black families in the United States had incomes of $15,000 or over, compared to some 57 percent of White families. Moreover, the median income of Black males in the labor force at that time was $6,290, compared to $10,600 for White males. (The figures for the median income Black and White women in 1977 were $3,460 and $4,000, respectively.) Most dramatic of all was the statistical corroboration of the widely held assumption that, "while most of the poor in the United States are White, a much larger percentage of the Black population is poor!"

Many conservative citizens believed that things could be dramatically changed if the "tired old policies of the 1930s" were finally replaced with new, innovative economic strategies. The opportunity to effect such changes came to pass with the election of Ronald Reagan whose new administration sought "to get the country moving again" convinced that the trickle-down effects of supply-side economics would help all Americans realize the dream of a better life. Yet, even the economic boom of the 1980s which did occur had little direct impact on the hard-core sufferers, many of whom were members of minorities. Much of the blame for the failure to reach them has been placed directly at the feet of the government.

In a hard-hitting statement, John Jacob, president of the Urban League in 1986, put it this way:

What columnist David Broder called the "fatal blend of ignorance and arrogance" [regarding such foreign policy blunders as "Irangate"] also describes the administration's civil rights policies. It tried to win tax exemptions for segregated schools, fought extension of civil rights laws, undermined affirmative action, destroyed the U.S. Civil Rights Commission, stacked the judiciary with right-wingers, and refused to budge from its support for South Africa's apartheid government—all the while implementing a public relations policy designed to convince Americans that we are now a color-blind, racially neutral society.

At the same time, it ignored mounting black poverty. In place of substantive domestic policy, it substituted demonstrably false statements designed to convince the public that unemployment was no longer a problem, that the poor don't want to work, and that social programs simply compound social problems instead of helping to resolve them.[30]

Jacob's remarks were offered in a preface to a lengthy report on the state of Black America in 1986. Based on data gathered from a wide variety of sources, the document underscores a widening gap in the society. For example, it points to labor department statistics showing that at the height of the economic "recovery" nearly four million parttime workers wanted to work full time, and almost 1.2 million discouraged workers gave up search for jobs. It points to a U.S. Census Bureau report that, in 1985, over 33 million people were poor in this country—a rise of four million since 1980. At the same time, more than one of every five American children were classified as poor; for Blacks, the ratio was one in two.

There was a growing employment gap, a growing income gap, and a growing wealth gap. Again, according to the Census Bureau, the typical White family in the mid-1980s had a net worth twelve times as great as the net worth of the typical Black family. And almost one third of all Black families had no assets at all.

While Jacob does indicate that the gaps between rich and poor cut across racial lines, a point forcefully argued by the sociologist William Julius Wilson in his thoughtful volume, *The Declining Significance of Race*,[31] neither Jacob nor Wilson denies the persistence of discrimination—both blatant and subtle—that continue to hobble non-Whites in their effort to find a securer place in the wider society.

Many social scientists contend that while discrimination is no longer a sufficient explanation for all the problems of ghetto living—street crime, delinquency, drug abuse, unwanted pregnancies, child abuse, and "welfare dependency"—so often discussed in the press, it is surely necessary to take into account the effects of patterns of institutionalized racism so deeply woven into the fabric of this society.

Despite a number of positive changes in the behavior and attitudes of increasing numbers of those in the dominant sector who have come to accept the reality of America as a multiracial, multiethnic society, the categorical disparities manifest in one area of life after another are related to long-institutionalized patterns of discrimination which still make it more difficult for Blacks (and, in many instances, other non-Whites) to run an equal race. They have known it for years; so, as numerous studies have shown, have policy makers. This last point was made abundantly clear over twenty years ago when, in the wake of the urban riots that erupted in city after city during the summers of 1966 and 1967, a Presidential Commission was invited to investigate their causes. Asked to find out why these outbreaks had taken place and what could be done to prevent them in the future, a group of leading citizens headed by then Governor Otto Kerner of Illinois carried out an extensive study of 24 disorders in 23 different American cities. A year later the report was published. In one version, Tom Wicker, columnist for *The New York Times*, wrote a special introduction in which he focused on the central issue that constantly confronted the commissioners and the investigative staff. "In the end," wrote Wicker, "not without dispute and travail and misgiving, in the clash and spark of human conflict and human pride, against the pressures of time and ignorance, they produced not so much a report on the riots as a report on *America—one nation divided.*[32]

Wicker based his conclusion on his assessment of the report, which included the following summary statements about the explosive mixture that contributed to the potential for upheaval:

> *Pervasive discrimination and segregation* in employment, education and housing, which have resulted in the continuing exclusion of great numbers of Negroes from the benefits of economic progress.
>
> • • •
>
> *Black in-migration and white exodus,* which have produced massive and growing concentrations of impoverished Negroes in our major cities, creating a growing crisis of deteriorating facilities and services and unmet human meets.
>
> • • •
>
> *The Black ghettos* where segregation and poverty converge on the young to destroy opportunity and enforce failure. Crime, drug addiction, dependency on welfare, and bitterness and resentment against society in general and white society in particular are the result.[33]

Pathology for many non-Whites is doubtlessly still related to the patterns of life they are forced to adopt. Upheaval may be construed as a desperate cry for help; it may also be viewed as one of the few healthy alternatives to despair in a sick society. Whichever view one takes (and there is considerable controversy over this fundamental question), there is little question that the barriers erected to keep non-Whites in their place have done more than isolate large numbers of people.

> Segregation and poverty have created in the racial ghetto a destructive environment totally unknown to most white Americans.
>
> What white Americans have never fully understood—but what the Negro can never forget—is that white society is deeply implicated in the ghetto. White institutions created it, white institutions maintain it, and white society condones it.[34]

Practices of segregation, such as those reported by the Kerner Commission, are easier to observe than the more subtle patterns of social separation. Yet these are of equal, if not more, sociological significance. In many communities, where direct physical contact between Whites and non-Whites is far more frequent than in the riot cities, and where spatial separation is not nearly as pronounced, local customs serve to insulate the groups from one another. Pre-World War II studies of "Negro-White" relations in the United States provide numerous examples of southern "etiquette" which enhanced the separation of the races. Some of the practices described by Gunnar Myrdal four decades ago are still to be found:

> In *content* the serious conversation should be about those business interests which are shared (as when a white employer instructs his Negro employee or when there is a matter to be discussed concerning the welfare of the Negro community) or it should be polite but formal inquiry into personal affairs. There can generally be no serious discussion.
>
> •••
>
> The conversation is even more regimented in *form* than in content. The Negro is expected to address the white person by the title of "Mr." or "Miss." . . . From his side, the white man addresses the Negro by his first name, no matter if they hardly know each other or by the epithets "boy," "uncle," "elder," "aunty," or the like.[35]

Here we see a direct linkage between derogation and denial. The main function of racial etiquette is to remind Blacks, in their day-to-day contacts with Whites, of their place in the social hierarchy, which persistently demeans them and weakens their willingness to resist. Such institutionalized intimidation, with respect to its psychological consequences, is one of the cruelest forms of discrimination.

Aggression

Intimidation is sometimes subtle. Most of the time it is blatant. ("Just try stepping out of line!") Violence or the threat of violence has long been used to keep racial and ethnic minorities mindful of their subordinate status. Tied to both derogation and denial, there are many forms of aggressive action in which individuals or groups participate, ranging from the jeering at and threatening of little children to gang fights or organized terror and mob rule. The lexicon of racial conflict is filled with words related to violent aggression: "lynch," "pogrom," "genocide," and hundreds of others—and examples of their use are not hard to find.

> A Puerto Rican is savagely beaten for trespassing on "white turf" . . .
> A synagogue is symbolically smeared with swastikas and the slogan "Hate Jews."
> A black man is lynched for having stepped out of line.
> Thousands of Indians are exterminated to make the country safe—and profitable—for white men.
> Millions are murdered by the Third Reich in the name of racial purity.

"Violence," Gordon Allport once wrote, "is always an outgrowth of milder states of mind. Although most barking does not lead to biting, yet there is never a bite without previous barking."[36] Led by the demagogue, the ardent segregationist, and the fanatic patriot, solid and respectable citizens have done unspeakable violence to their enemies.

Even in our society of "law and order" the social conditions for mob violence still exist, as does the violence itself. Not long ago many southern Blacks lived in terror of the lynch mob. Their anxiety was well justified for, according to the records of the NAACP, there were 5,112 lynchings between 1882 and 1939 (3,657 of the victims were Black).[37] In the past, lynchings occurred mainly in those areas where the practice of segregation was maintained by the harshest forms of intimidation. Some social scientists have interpreted lynching as a means of venting frustrations against a convenient scapegoat. For example, it has been argued that the falling price of cotton portended an upsurge in the number of lynchings in the South. Whether one can make a causal reference from the correlation, the wide use of lynching indicates a tacit acceptance of such activity as a legitimate way to maintain the castelike social system. The facts—that lynchings were often not prevented even when known of by the authorities and that when culprits were known and apprehended they were seldom punished to a degree commensurate with the crime—give ample evidence to support the contention that such behavior was condoned by those in official positions of authority.[38]

While the number of lynchings remained relatively negligible from the end of World War II to the late-1970s, in those same years vigilantes sometimes took the law into their own hands, meting out "cracker barrel justice." The desire to fight against changes in the status quo saw a rebirth of mob aggressiveness in the South. In the 1950s, Black parents attempting to send their children to schools desegregated by court decision in Clinton, Little Rock, New Orleans, and more than a score of other southern cities were met with angry crowds of White demonstrators who burned crosses, threatened them, and severely beat them. All too frequently the local authorities failed to provide adequate protection for the Black citizens. In some cities, once law and order were established or reestablished—sometimes with the aid of federal troops—segregation was maintained by Whites who withdrew their children from public schools.[39]

Sit-in demonstrators who sought equal service in restaurants, kneel-in demonstrators desiring to attend integrated church services, wade-in demonstrators wishing to swim in areas restricted to Whites, read-in demonstrators wanting to take books from segregated libraries, and freedom riders challenging the policy of segregated interstate transportation and separate terminal facilities met with similar outbursts of aggression and violence. In the spring of 1961, for example, a busload of freedom riders was greeted by an angry mob in Anniston, Alabama, who threw rocks, smashed windows, and eventually burned the bus. Another group that had gone to Birmingham was attacked by White men armed with clubs, and several riders were brutally beaten.

In the early fall of 1962 an especially ugly incident in the long fight for desegregation occurred at Oxford, Mississippi, when, aided by several hundred U.S. marshals and 24,000 soldiers, James Meredith was forcibly admitted to the university under a court order restraining the school from denying his admission. His presence on the campus triggered a series of riots that took several hours to quell. By the time order was restored by the imposition of virtual martial law, two adults had been killed and over one hundred people injured.

Only two weeks earlier, four Black churches in rural Georgia were burned to the ground. All but one were being used for registering new voters. On September 17, 1962, the Student Nonviolent Coordinating Committee sent the following telegram to President Kennedy:

> Another church burned this morning. Four churches burned in the past month, reminiscent of Nazi burning of synagogues. Imperative you investigate and apprehend arsonists. Halt the outrageous terror of peaceful American citizens. The national shame must be ended.[40]

The President's own violent death a little over one year later indicated that terror remained rampant in our society. And we were to see more and more senseless killing—much of it related to racial tensions—in the years to come.

The annals of civil rights martyrdom are filled with names of young Black and White civil rights workers gunned down by those who could not tolerate the changes in the status quo that they represented: among them Herbert Lee, Medgar Evers, Mickey Schwerner, Andrew Goodman, James Chancy, and the Nobel prize-winner Reverend Martin Luther King, Jr., the "apostle of nonviolence." In addition to the sensational killing of these men (and many others), hundreds of other acts of violence continued to be perpetrated in big cities and rural towns. Crops were burned, workers were fired, women and children were threatened. Even policemen, sworn to uphold the law, sometimes ran amuck, venting their wrath on unarmed protesters and innocent bystanders. The whole world reeled at the image of young Blacks being attacked by police dogs in Birmingham and elsewhere in the South.

A headline in the December 12, 1972, issue of The New York Times stating "City Unit Sees Violence Pattern by Whites Against Minorities," was a stark reminder that vigilantism persisted in a period many have viewed as a time of interracial progress. The article described a study conducted by the City Commission of Human Rights that revealed eleven cases in which homes owned by Blacks or Puerto Ricans in New York City had been set afire or vandalized and instances of arson in churches and attacks on school buses. Blaming white gangs, the Commission wrote:

> We can no longer maintain the myth that violence and pathology of Southern racism is totally absent in the North. These occurrences, while unconnected, none-

theless suggest an ominous trend that could mean that continued integration in the North will be resisted as forcefully and violently as in the South.[41]

The commentary proved prophetic. In the years that followed America witnessed further evidence of the persistence of violent resistance along with other forms of reaction against moves toward desegregation. The major arena of confrontation was the northern school district and the basic issue was busing, the movement of Black and White children to schools that were sometimes far from home in order to achieve "racial balance."

A debate has continued over the effects of such policies on attitudes and behavior relating to race relations and their effectiveness on the educational process itself. Sociologist James Coleman, an early advocate of desegregation and author of one of the most widely quoted reports on the problems of separate schooling, argued along with others that forced busing was counter-productive, especially since it accelerated "White flight," the movement from city to suburb.[42] Others said the evidence, including evidence from a later study conducted by Coleman himself, belied such claims, that, in fact, Whites were leaving the cities whether busing was being imposed or not. And some continued to suggest that, while desegregation would not be accomplished by school integration alone, it still was essential to get people to know one another even if it meant requiring them to leave the neighborhood to do so.

While the debate over techniques of breaking down what the English call "the color bar" continued in many quarters, there were those who seemed to be little interested in weighing the issues. "Righteous racists," as some called them, sought to maintain closed communities, White bastions, often White Christian bastions. They opposed "race mixing" in any form. Some such protesters joined the ranks of a revitalized Ku Klux Klan. Others found their ideological home in other right-wing groups.

In the late 1970s both the KKK and the neo-Nazis gained some strength and considerable publicity. Perhaps the most widely discussed case was the proposed pro-Nazi march scheduled to be held in Skokie, Illinois, a suburb of Chicago with many Jewish residents, including a number of concentration camp survivors. The Nazis sought and, through the intercession of the American Civil Liberties Union (ACLU), obtained a permit to demonstrate, speak their piece freely—blatant anti-Semitism and attacks on others they, like those whose banner they carried, deemed inferior and parasitic. The question of whether they should have been given a permit or not evoked a debate of its own and much soul-searching on the part of many civil libertarians. While the American Civil Liberties Union defended the right to march, a number of ardent supporters of free speech (including several prominent former members of the ACLU) reminded their fellow liberals that, in the words of Chief Justice Holmes, the First Amendment does not give one the right to shout "Fire" in a crowded theater. And, they argued, calls for the expulsion, even the annihilation, of Jews were surely more than expressing opinions.[43]

While the Skokie March was finally called off, it represented a clear case of how our first concern with antilocution is (or may be) linked to the last, genocide, the planned elimination of an entire people.

Lynchings, cross burnings, calls to arms, rallies to whip up attacks on racial, religious and ethnic minorities in this country are painful reminders of the crimes against humanity perpetrated in Nazi Germany. Genocide was the national policy of a sovereign state less than half a century ago. Over nine million Jews lived in Europe before World War II. Nazi leaders were determined to eradicate this group and nearly succeeded.

Forced to wear identifying yellow stars with the word JEW (Jude in German, Jood in Dutch, Juif in French, and so forth), driven from homes and families, passed through transit camps, herded into concentration camps, used as forced labor, experimented upon, violated in countless ways, and ultimately shot down or liquidated in gas chambers, the Jews of Europe suffered the most repressive of all fates that can befall a group, a "Final Solution," the slaughter of an entire people. Death camp survivor Primo Levi, an Italian Jew, describes his recollection of the steps taken to break the spirit of the healthier camp inmates, those who it turned out, were to be used for forced labor and then executed, joining the others who had been killed earlier.

A dozen SS men stood around, legs akimbo, with an indifferent air. At a certain moment they moved among us, and in a subdued tone of voice, with faces of stone, began to interrogate us rapidly, one by one, in bad Italian. They did not interrogate everybody, only a few: "How old? Healthy or ill?" And on the basis of the reply they pointed in two different directions. . . .

In less than two minutes all the fit men had been collected together in a group. What happened to the others, to the women, to the children, to the old men, we could establish neither then nor later: the night swallowed them up, purely and simply. Today, however, we know that in that rapid and summary choice each one of us had been judged capable or not of working usefully for the Reich; we know that of our convoy no more than ninety-six men and twenty-nine women entered the respective camps of Monowitz-Buna and Birkenau, and that of all the others, more than five hundred in number, not one was living two days later.[44]

The initiation rite continued. Heads were shaved, the people were thrown in boiling showers, then immediately forced to run, naked and barefoot, in the icy snow. Finally they were given uniforms to put on.

There is nowhere to look in a mirror, but our appearance stands in front of us, reflected in a hundred livid faces, in a hundred miserable and sordid puppets. . . .

Then for the first time we became aware that our language lacks words to express this offense, the demolition of a man. In a moment, with almost prophetic intuition, the reality was revealed to us; we had reached the bottom. It is not possible to sink lower than this; no human condition is more miserable than this nor could it conceivably be so. Nothing belongs to us anymore; they have taken away our clothes, our shoes, even our hair; if we speak, they will not listen to us, and if they listen they will not understand. They will even take away our name. . . . [45]

And they did take away their names. In many camps, including Auschwitz, where Levi was finally taken, inmates were tattooed on the forearm with prison numbers, their only form of identification. They carried their numbers to the grave.

The word "genocide" itself emerged during the war trials at Nuremberg, where it was defined as "a denial of the right of existence of entire human groups in the same way as homicide is the denial of the right to live for individual human beings." Although the term is newly coined, the practice itself is very old. It was known in biblical times when Menahem smote Tiphsah,[46] it was practiced by the British when they destroyed the Tasmanians in the "triumph of 'civilization' over 'savagery' ";[47] a version was used in early America when settlers offered bounty for the scalps and sometimes the heads of Indians[48] and when Lord Jeffrey Amherst distributed smallpox-laden blankets to the indigenous peoples.

As we have seen, in recent times violence has raged in our society—much of it based on racial hatred—and although the word is frequently used by militant critics, there is no evidence that genocidal policies have been advocated or carried out by agencies of the United States government *within the borders of the society.* The prolonged situation in Indochina was quite another matter and many contend that what was done there by the United States and, later, in Kampuchea by fellow Cambodians and Vietnamese occupiers fall clearly under the definition set forth at Nuremberg.

Conclusion

These cases of discrimination have been cited not to indicate how inconsiderate and brutal people can be (though such might be purpose enough), but rather to describe briefly the varying degrees of discrimination—*derogation, denial,* and *aggression.* Each, except *mass murder,* is a contemporary example of discrimination in the United States and an expression of both unwitting and willful behavior to which too many Americans, including fair-weather liberals, subscribe.

We have examined some formal and informal policies of those with majority status and some ways in which they seek to maintain it. Little attention has been paid to the reactions of those discriminated against. The following chapter examines the impact of discriminatory treatment and some sociological implications of minority status.

1. Robin M. Williams, Jr., *The Reduction of Intergroup Tensions* (New York: Social Science Research Council, 1947), p. 39.
2. See, for example, Gordon W. Allport, *The Nature of Prejudice* (Cambridge: Addison-Wesley, 1954), esp. pp. 14–15 and 49–51; and Ernest Works, "Types of Discrimination," *Phylon* (Fall, 1969), 223–233.
3. Richard Wright, *Black Boy* (New York: Harper & Row, 1945), esp. pp. 128–129 and 163–170.
4. A good summary of the language of prejudice is to be found in John P. Dean and Alex Rosen, *A Manual of Intergroup Relations* (University of Chicago Press, 1955), Chap. 2. This chapter was written in collaboration with Robert B. Johnson and the ideas expressed are largely based on Johnson's unpublished Ph.D. dissertation, "The Nature of the Minority Community" (Ithaca, N.Y.: Cornell University, 1954).
5. Michael Novak, "The Sting of Polish Jokes," *Newsweek* (April 12, 1976), p. 13.
6. Michael Lerner, "Respectable Bigotry," *The American Scholar*, 38 (Autumn 1969).
7. Bernard Rosenberg and Gilbert Shapiro, "Marginality and Jewish Humor," *Midstream*, 4 (Spring 1958), 70–80.
8. See, for example, Russell Middleton and John Morland, "Humor in Negro and White Subcultures: A Study of Jokes Among University Students," *American Sociological Review*, 24 (February 1959), 61–69. See also John H. Burma, "Humor as a Technique in Race Conflict," *American Sociological Review*, 11 (December 1946), 710–715; Milton L. Barron, "A Content Analysis of Intergroup Humor," *American Sociological Review*, 15 (February 1950), 88–94.
9. For an excellent analysis of such shows, see Henry Louis Gates, Jr., "T.V.'s Black World Turns But Stays Unreal," *The New York Times* (November 12, 1989) Section II, pp. 1, 40.
10. Laura Hobson, *The New York Times* (September 12, 1971), Section II, p. 1 and continuation. See also Robert Alter, "Defaming the Jews," *Commentary*, 45 (January 1973), 77–83.
11. Neil Vidman and Milton Rokeach, "Archie Bunker's Bigotry: A Study of Selective Perception and Exposure," *Journal of Communication*, 24 (Winter 1974).
12. Erdman Palmore, "Ethnophaulisms and Ethnocentrism," *American Journal of Sociology*, 67 (January 1962), 442–445. See also William B. Helmreich, *The Things They Say Behind Your Back*, (New Brunswick, N.J.: Transaction Books, 1984).
13. Clifford H. Moore [tr.], *The Annals of Tacitus* (Cambridge: Harvard University Press, 1937), Vol. IV, Book XV, p. 285.
14. *Ibid.*, pp. 285–287. Italics supplied.
15. These phrases are part of a composite speech made up of actual statements by American demagogues; they serve as introduction to the study by Leo Lowenthal and Norbert Guterman, *Prophets of Deceit* (New York: Harper & Row, 1949), pp. 1–2. Current examples of inflammatory writings are *Common Sense, America's Newspaper Against Communism*, published in Union, N.J.,

and *The American Nationalist,* published in Inglewood, Calif. The support given to such publications is analyzed in an article by Hans H. Toch, Steven E. Deutsch, and Donald M. Wilkins, "The Wrath of the Bigot: An Analysis of Protest Mail," *Journalism Quarterly,* 37 (Spring 1960), 173–185, 266.

16. Martin Tolchin, "President Won't Condemn Brother's Remarks on Jews," *New York Times* (February 28, 1979), p. A16.
17. See Seymour Martin Lipset and Earl Raab, *The Politics of Unreason* (New York: Harper & Row, 1969).
18. Seymour Martin Lipset, "Prejudice and Politics in America," in Charles Y. Glock and Ellen Siegelman (eds.), *Prejudice U.S.A.* (New York: Praeger, 1969), p. 18. Italics supplied.
19. See, for example, *Common Sense* (September 15, 1958), p. 1.
20. *Washington Post* (December 20, 1972), p. C1.
21. See, for example, Charles Abrams, *Forbidden Neighbors* (New York: Harper & Row, 1955); and Oscar Handlin, *The Newcomers: Negroes and Puerto Ricans in a Changing Metropolis* (Cambridge: Harvard University Press, 1959).
22. Two summaries of the problems of "race and housing" are Morton Grodzins, *The Metropolitan Area as a Racial Problem* (Pittsburgh: University of Pittsburgh Press, 1958); and Eunice Crier and George Crier, *The Impact of Race on Neighborhoods in the Metropolitan Setting* (Washington, D.C.: Washington Center for Metropolitan Studies, 1961).
23. See, for example, Louis Wirth, *The Ghetto* (Chicago: University of Chicago Press, 1956), pp. 18–19.
24. Brewton Berry, *Race and Ethnic Relations,* 2nd ed. (Boston: Houghton Mifflin, 1958), p. 273.
25. Allport lists these and other examples of restrictive covenants, *op. cit.,* p. 53.
26. See Benjamin R. Epstein and Arnold Forster, *Some of My Best Friends . . . (New York: Farrar, Straus & Cudahy, 1962),* esp. pp. 106–139.
27. This practice has lessened in recent years, largely as a result of college administration action. See Epstein and Forster, *ibid.,* pp. 165–167. See also Alfred McClung Lee, *Fraternities Without Brotherhood* (Boston: Beacon, 1955); and, "A Study of Religious Discrimination by Social Clubs," *Rights,* 4 (January 1962), 83–96.
28. *The Social and Economic Status of the Black Population in the United States,* Current Population Reports, Series P-23, No. 42 (Washington, D.C.: Department of Commerce, 1971), p. 1.
29. *The Social and Economic Status of the Black Population in the United States: An Historical Overview 1790–1978,* Current Population Reports, Series P-23, No. 80 (Washington, D.C.: Department of Commerce, 1979), pp. 168–169.
30. John E. Jacob, *The State of Black America* (New York: National Urban League, Inc., 1987), pp. 7–14.
31. William J. Wilson, *The Declining Significance of Race* (Chicago: University of Chicago Press, 1978).
32. Tom Wicker, "Introduction," *Report of the National Advisory Commission on Civil Disorders* (New York: Bantam Books, 1968), p. xi.
33. *Report of the National Advisory Commission on Civil Disorders* (New York: Bantam Books, 1968), p. 10.
34. *Ibid.,* p. 2.

35. Gunnar Myrdal, *An American Dilemma* (New York: Harper & Row, 1944), pp. 610–612. See also John Howard Griffin, *Black Like Me* (Boston: Houghton Mifflin, 1961).
36. Allport, *op. cit.*, p. 57.
37. As reported in George E. Simpson and J. Milton Yinger, *Racial and Cultural Minorities*, rev. ed. (New York: Harper & Row, 1958), p. 515.
38. See Allport, *op. cit.*, pp. 61–62.
39. For descriptions of several instances of school desegregation crises, see the following *Field Reports on Desegregation in the South*, written by social scientists and published in New York by the Anti-Defamation League of B'nai B'rith: A report on Beaumont, Texas, "College Desegregation Without Popular Consent," by Warren Breed; a report on Sturgis, Kentucky, "A Tentative Description and Analysis of the School Desegregation Crisis," by Roscoe Griffin; on Mansfield, Texas, "A Report on the Crisis Situation Resulting from Efforts to Desegregate the School System," by John Howard Griffin and Theodore Freedman; and, on Clinton, Tennessee, "A Tentative Description and Analysis of the School Desegre-Crisis," by Anna Holden, Bonita Valien, and Preston Valien.
40. Reprinted in *The New York Times* (September 18, 1962), p. 27.
41. *The New York Times* (December 12, 1972), pp. 1, 54.
42. See, for example, James Coleman, "Liberty and Equality in School Desegregation," *Social Policy*, 6 (January 1976), 9–13.
43. See, for example, David Goldberg and others, "Thoughts about Skokie," *Dissent* (Spring 1979), pp. 226–230.
44. Primo Levi, *Survival in Auschwitz*, trans. by Stuart Woolf (New York: Orion Press, 1959), pp. 21–22.
45. *Idem.*
46. II Kings 15:16.
47. G. P. Murdock, *Our Primitive Contemporaries* (New York: Macmillan, 1934), p. 18.
48. See Berry, *op. cit.*, pp. 187–194. See also Alain Locke and Bernhard Stern, *When Peoples Meet* (New York: Progressive Education Association, 1942), pp. 165–170.

6

IN THE MINORITY

The View from Outside

Henry James, the American novelist, spent 20 years of his life, from 1883 to 1904, away from his native land. Between his departure and return the country had undergone profound changes, most noticeably in the quality of urban life. When he left, it was English (or Anglo-American) in style and in sound. When he returned to New York the modest city had been transformed into a bustling metropolis, and homogeneity no longer marked the character of the social structure.

The old streets of the city had become warrens of poor immigrants, Little Italies and Little Jerusalems—polyglot enclaves even more strange than the shanty towns of the Irish who had come during James' youth, already signaling the beginning of the end of Protestant preeminence and Anglo conformity.

James was especially moved by the Jews he observed on the Lower East Side of New York City. His firsthand account of impressions gleaned from a visit to "that outpost of Jerusalem" was vivid as well as pointed. He likened the Jews to squirrels and monkeys. He was awed and repulsed by the crowded conditions in which they lived, enchanted and dismayed by their exotic ways and lively manners. He drank deeply of the summer-city scene and then departed, as if from a voyage to the moon. (One is tempted to say as if from "abroad" but, more surely than not, he would have found London or Edinburgh or Paris less foreign than the Lower East Side of his own New York.)

If Henry James were to come back to life and visit Rutgers Street today, he might have a haunting sense of déjà vu. To be sure, the "squirrels" and "monkeys" he would now observe scampering up and down the fire escapes of the tenements would be even darker than the "swarthy Orientals" he saw eighty years ago. The argot of the street would be marked by a Spanish accent or a soft-southern English and jive talk rather than the babble of Yiddish. And the kitchen odors would be of paella and plantain or chit'lin's and collard greens rather than the soups and pickled herrings of the "Israelites." Still, it would strike him that, once again, his fair New York was "swarming" (a favorite word) with alien elements.

Pushing this fantasy a bit further, James, if he listened carefully, might hear some outlandish proposals: demands for group rights and recognition, schemes for resisting the untenable choice of either completely conforming to the ways of the dominant society (his society) or continuing to be excluded. He might hear rumblings about slumlords who overcharge, politicians who take bribes, teachers who make fun of those who have difficulty with the language. He might even hear of plots to organize against the bosses, plans for greater community control within the ghetto, notions of developing local political organizations or bloc power.

There are many parallels to what was going on in James' New York at the turn of the century and in the New York of recent years as described in Tom Wolfe's best selling novel *Bonfire of the Vanities*.[1] There are differences, too. To understand these, one must carefully examine the nature of minority status as it affected (and continues to affect) the various groups of white immigrants, who, for whatever reason, chose to come to these shores from Europe; and as it affected other non-White peoples like the Native Americans, Black Americans, Asians, and many Latin Americans.

Minority Status

For most Europeans migration to America was followed by successive stages of contact, competition, and some form of accommodation with the Old Settler population. For some (such as the Protestants from northern Europe and Scandinavia) accommodation led to gradual assimilation into the dominant society, leaving but a vestige of ethnic difference. For others (including many Africans, Latin-Americans, Asians, and Jews) the process stopped short of full assimilation. In spite of the fact that there has been increasing intermarriage in recent years, especially between members of various Catholic ethnic groups and between Protestants and Catholics, clearly identifiable ethnic communities continue to exist. The most prominent of these are those sociologists call *minority communities*. As noted, such communities have several distinguishing characteristics, not least the fact that members are both differentiated from others and discriminated against in some fashion.

Minority status is sometimes "given," often it is inherited. It may stem simply from the ascription of a differentiating label to a category of individuals who share certain social and physical traits deemed inferior to those of the dominant group—for example, persons with dark skin, atheists, women, or, in some circles, "intellectuals." Statistical aggregates such as these are not social groups in the sociological sense of the term. They do, however, possess the potentialities for becoming groups or collectivities, especially when they are categorically singled out for differential treatment.

Minority status is often ascribed to those social groups who have a history of patterned interaction, shared or similar beliefs and values, a sense of ingroup solidarity, and who are *also* relegated to subordinate positions in the prestige hierarchy.[2] The two words *subordinate positions* are central, for all sociological minorities—no matter how tightly knit—share the fact that they have only limited control over their destinies.

In 1945, sociologist Louis Wirth spelled out the concept of minority group in some detail and, implicitly, noted its relation to the concept of power. Stressing both its internal characteristics and the relation of the subordinate group to the wider society, Wirth wrote:

... A minority must be distinguishable from the dominant group by physical or cultural marks. In the absence of such identifying characteristics it blends into the rest of the population in the course of time.

• • •

Minorities objectively occupy a disadvantageous position in the society. As contrasted with the dominant group they are debarred from certain opportunities— economic, social and political.

• • •

The members of minority groups are held in lower esteem and may even be the objects of contempt, hatred, ridicule and violence.

• • •

They are generally socially isolated and frequently spatially separated.

• • •

They suffer from more than the ordinary amount of social and economic insecurity.[3]

Because of these attributes, Wirth felt that "minorities tend to develop a set of attitudes, forms of behavior, and other subjective characteristics which tend further to set them apart.[4]

In an earlier chapter it was noted that while Wirth was greatly concerned about the deleterious effect of the inferior status position of particular ethnic groups, he and others, such as E. K. Francis, stressed the fact that most ethnic groups, including many "minorities," frequently shared a positive sense of unity or "we-feeling," an ideology (however vague and unreflective it may be), and an interdependence of fate (whether based upon religious or political or cultural or racial characteristics). Moreover, ethnic-group ties are maintained as long as individuals feel bound to the community, "a community dependent as much upon the idea of communality as on actual proximity; a community one can 'feel' if not 'touch.' "[5]

One of the arguments that persist among students of racial and ethnic relations concerns the extent to which minority status is injurious to the individuals who occupy such a position and the benefits, if any, of prescribed separateness. This debate is most clearly joined in discussions of *marginality*, the concept that refers to those who appear to be on the edges of the dominant society.

Marginality

More than a few sociologists have suggested that those whose group identity is determined in part by external pressure, who are categorically excluded from opportunities for equal status, who are barred from assimilation and thus must live on the periphery of the dominant society, are "marginal men . . . whom fate has condemned to live in two societies and in two not merely different from antagonistic cultures."[6]

Perhaps the clearest articulation of this viewpoint was offered by the sociologist W. E. B. Du Bois in 1897 when he spoke of his people, Black Americans, in the following way:

After the Egyptian and Indian, the Greek and Roman, the Teuton and Mongolian, the Negro is a sort of seventh son, born with a veil, and gifted with second sight in this American world—a world which yields him not true self-consciousness, but also lets him see himself through the revelation of the other world. It is a peculiar sensation, this double-consciousness, this sense of always looking at one's self through the eyes of others, of measuring one's soul by the tape of a world that looks on in amused contempt and pity. . . .[7]

Max Weber, Werner Sombart, Georg Simmel, and Thorstein Veblen all described the ambiguous role of the "stranger." Usually referring to European Jews, their prototypes also seemed both to enjoy and to suffer from the double-consciousness Du Bois used to describe the paradoxical situation of Blacks in the United States. Simmel, for example, wrote of the "stranger" in the following manner: "His position in the group is determined, essentially by the fact that he has not belonged to it from the beginning, that he imparts qualities into it which do not and cannot stem from the group itself."[8]

Robert E. Park gave a new label to this phenomenon. He called it, *marginality*. Park suggested that members of many racial and ethnic groups suffer from the ambivalence of values created by their longing for the old and their desire to participate in the new. Park and Everett Stonequist, author of *The Marginal Man*, described such persons as "cultural hybrids."[9] One of the results of their marginality, Park and Stonequist suggested, was personal maladjustment; another was the tendency to engage in deviant behavior.

Critics of the Park-Stonequist thesis have argued that belonging to a minority group in and of itself does not necessarily predispose one to inner strain, personal disorientation, psychic difficulties, or various types of deviance such as crime.[10] Moreover, problems in one era do not necessarily mean groups or their members are destined to repeat them time and again. As many historians have pointed out, the well-known term "Paddy Wagon" (for police vans) originated because of the large number of once-marginal Irish immigrants who got in trouble with the police in the late nineteenth century. Today it is often said that "Paddy drives the wagon" and others ride in the back. This does not mean that minority status is irrelevant; rather it is often relative and many sociologists think the main problem is related to status consistency and inconsistency. Personal stability depends, in large measure, on the sense of security the individual members feel within the community as well as within the society.[11] Who one thinks he or she is and where he or she belongs are crucial matters; so, too, is the support system provided for the person growing up in a minority setting.

Recently, for example, economist Thomas Sowell has suggested that the differential mobility of various ethnic groups is often unrelated to the amount of discrimination they suffered. On the basis of his analysis of available statistical data, Sowell asserted that

Groups may be subject to very similar treatment by society at large and yet differ enormously in their economic achievements and social problems. Japanese-Americans and Mexican-Americans, for example, came to the United States in large numbers at about the same time (the early 1900's), settled in the same region (the Southwest), and faced discrimination in schools and on the job. Yet today Japanese-Americans' incomes are almost double the incomes of Mexican-Americans, and their crime rates and broken homes are only a fraction of the figures for Mexican-Americans. As for how they were treated by "society," the Japanese suffered more—being legally denied citizenship and land ownership for many years, and being interned with great loss of property during World War II. They were also much easier targets for racism. . . . [12]

Similar findings are reported in comparing other groups who, at one time or other found themselves on the margins of society. For some minority status has proved functional, or, at the least, a rallying point around which to mobilize.

Minority status repeatedly has been found to intensify already existing group identity or to create it where it has not existed prior to discrimination. Forced to live in particular areas and to associate with one another, members of minority groups frequently come to view themselves as a community, to feel a keen sense of responsibility for their fellow members, and to build institutions that contribute to the protection of individuals and to further the sense of fellow-feeling.[13] Such a development suggests that the concept of *marginal man* is too narrow; it may even be inappropriate for vast numbers of minority-group members.

Thus, in one of the many attempts to reformulate the marginal man notion, Milton M. Goldberg, relying in large measure on the work of the anthropologist Alexander Goldenweiser and his idea of "marginal cultural areas," suggested that:

> If (1) the so-called "marginal" individual is conditioned to his existence on the borders of two cultures from birth, if (2) he shares the existence and conditioning process with a large number of individuals in his primary groups, if (3) his years of early growth, maturation, and even adulthood find him participating in institutional activities manned largely by other "marginal" individuals like himself, and finally, if (4) his marginal position results in no major blockages or frustrations of his learned expectations and desires, then he is not a true "marginal" individual in the defined sense, but is a participant member of a *marginal* culture, every bit as real and complete to him as is the nonmarginal culture to the nonmarginal man.[14]

Contrary to the views of Park and Stonequist, Goldberg (and those sharing his conception) does not see most minority-group members as maladjusted products of cultural ambivalence, but as adjusted participants in a *marginal culture*, itself a product of accommodation to differential treatment. This interpretation is consistent with our own conviction that members of American minority communities manifest certain common characteristics normal to groups with similar marginal experiences, including certain traits that outsiders sometimes define as pathological.

While minority communities may differ from one another in racial and ethnic composition, their levels of socioeconomic status, patterns of social mobility, and local customs—those retained and those newly created—they tend to possess a transmitted remembrance of how the community developed. Everyone, of course, is "ethnocentric" to some degree. Moreover, spokespersons for almost every group engage in "the creative distortion of history" to emphasize their group's historical legacy and to underscore its unique contributions.[15] Thus references are frequently made to the first members of the group to arrive and the conditions under which they came, how they were received and how they fared, the discrimination they encountered and how they coped with it, the grounds on which the community was established in this country, and the deeds of important leaders.

Many minorities have their own territorial bases, sometimes marked by physical boundaries ("the other side of the tracks," "down by the riverside," "in the hollow"), sometimes by psychological or social walls that set them apart from the larger community. In his novel *A Walker in the City*, Alfred Kazin explains:

> We were the end of the line. We were the children of the immigrants who had camped at the city's back door, New York's rawest, remotest, cheapest ghetto, enclosed on one side by the Carnarsie flats and on the other by the hallowed middle-class districts that showed the way to New York. "New York" was what we put last on our address, but first in thinking of the others around us. *They* were

New York, the Gentiles . . .; we were Brownsville—*Brunzvil*, as the old folks said. . . .[16]

Today Brownsville is predominantly Black and those who now write of their estrangement often describe Kazin's people, the Jews, as the *they* who represent the Establishment![17]

When separated from the dominant society, minorities frequently maintain their own traditional and social institutions. Some of these run counter to the ways of the larger community and are viewed as deviant, mysterious, dangerous or simply un-American. One thinks of the ways various people "use" time (for example, the *mañana* spirit of many Spanish-surnamed Americans), worship (the practices of Orthodox Jews, Pentecostalists, Zen Buddhists), and relax (perhaps through various sorts of gambling and gaming activities), to say nothing of the myriad differences in ways of perceiving themselves, each other, and the society in which they live.

The last point was most poignantly expressed through the research of the late Oscar Lewis. Here is a short excerpt from his famous essay in which his Puerto Rican respondents compare life in New York with that on the home island. The passage begins with Lewis asking, "Have you ever been in New York, Hector?"

"Yes, yes, I've been to New York."
"And what did you think of life there?"
"New York! I want no part of it! Man, do you know what it's like? You get up in a rush, have breakfast in a rush, get to work in a rush, go home in a rush, even shit in a rush. That's life in New York! Not for me! Never again! Not unless I was crazy.
"Look, I'll explain. The ways things are in New York, you'll get nothing there. But nothing! It's different in Puerto Rico. Here, if you're hungry, you come to me and say, 'Man, I'm broke, I've had nothing to eat.' And I'd say, '*Ay, Bendito!* Poor thing!' And I'd give you some food. No matter what, you wouldn't have to go to bed hungry. Here in Puerto Rico you can make out. But in New York, if you don't have a nickel, or twenty cents, you're worthless, and that's for sure. You don't count. You get swallowed by a horse."[18]

But even such harshness of urban life is coped with by hundreds of thousands of Puerto Ricans and others who feel the centripetal attraction of places like New York. While often disillusioned by what they find, many stay and attempt to survive. They do so in part by modifying old ways or by instituting new ones, engaging in a process that has been called "ethnogenesis."[19]

The street culture of Spanish Harlem, the tight-knit social organization of Chinatowns in San Francisco and Seattle, New York and Boston, the ubiquity of storefront churches in poor, Black areas, the twang of western music in Chicago neighborhood bars, the array of ethnic newspapers found on the stands of every large city, all indicate that many Americans carry on by retaining or reviving that which they once knew. Others, as noted, develop new patterns and organizations such as juvenile gangs (like the "Mexican Marauders"), athletic clubs (the "Jewish Marvels"), ethnically based patriotic organizations ("Polish-American Veterans"), religious bodies ("African Methodist Episcopal Church"), social agencies (the "Catholic Youth Organization"), schools (such as those offering Chinese, Hebrew, and Greek), and many kinds of businesses—some set up specifically to serve the minority community or, at the least, to benefit from desires for particular foods and special services.

Many members of minority groups make their living and spend much of their money within the ethnic community itself. Some, including those who have become quite successful, find themselves in what Norbert Wiley calls an "ethnic mobility trap."[20] Having chosen to make his or her way within the confines of the ethnic enclave, the individual may become locked in with a skill or a specialty that is difficult to transfer to the wider world. Norbert Wiley begins his discussion of this phenomenon by reminding the readers of William Foote Whyte's famous study, *Street Corner Society*, a detailed description and analysis of a working-class Italian area in the north side of Boston. There, Whyte noted, two avenues of socialization led to two sorts of "opportunity ceilings." If one was a "corner boy" one could aspire to work in local (ethnic) politics or to a high position in the rackets; if one was a "college boy" he was groomed for professional and managerial positions. Many, frustrated by the seeming remoteness of middle-class jobs, opted for following the line of least resistance. Some of them even became big men in the local community, but they were nothing on the outside.[21]

Many members of minority groups fall somewhere between the "corner boys" and the "college boys." While some spend their lives inside the enclave and some break away completely, a common pattern is to make one's living away from the neighborhood. It is in the workaday world that one tends to have the greatest amount of interaction with members of other groups and with representatives of the wider society. When night falls, as the saying goes, "The WASPs return to their nests—and the others return to their own." Ethnic nests vary, of course, from old law tenements to high rise apartments to ranch homes in what some sociologists call "gilded ghettos."[22]

On-the-job participation is frequently quite formal and segmentalized, with each person playing his appropriate role. The minority-group member is often seen as an "ambassador of his people" by those with whom he has contact.[23] Because exposure is frequently limited to outstanding figures (such as athletes, entertainers, professionals), to workers or to servants, and rarely involves intimate or informal exchanges, individuals in the dominant group tend to have distorted images of minority peoples and of their personal existence. Their views are frequently a combination of hunches (based on limited observation) and prejudices (which they have learned through contact with other prejudiced people).

The pattern is frequently asymmetrical, however, for minorities are continually exposed to the values and norms of the dominant group through public schooling, mass media, employment, advertising, and just living. They inevitably learn the ways of the dominant group even though they may not accept them all.

Although it is not unusual to hear blanket indictments of the entire Establishment, members of minority groups learn fairly early in life that the dominant group itself is highly differentiated in various ways. They are surprised when they find that so many of those beyond the confines of their communities are unaware that they, too, have their own hierarchies, interest groups, leaders and followers, successful members and ne'er-do-wells, poets and preachers, artisans and laborers, professionals and provocateurs.

Like most communities in complex societies, minority enclaves consist of differentiated clusters of subgroupings, varying in socioeconomic status, occupational interest, and political proclivity.[24] Certain ethnic groups, to be sure, put more stress on one activity than on another and certain occupations hold greater prestige than others. One thinks of the role of the priesthood in a French-Canadian village, of law and politics in an Irish community, teaching and the professions for Jews, or of business and science for the parents of Chinatown's children. While not every French-Canadian child aspires to be a priest nor every Irish-American wishes to be a "pol," there is no question that many members of their communities get a certain amount of satisfaction from seeing one of their own people become successful, especially in those areas toward which they feel particularly partial for sentimental, ideological, or practical reasons.

Even where there are relatively parallel systems of social stratification, there is no assurance that persons considered to be upper class by members of their own group would be accorded the same status by outsiders; nor does it mean that the respected members of a given minority would be held in the same esteem by those in the dominant group. Consider a well-known historical example: As the Irish and Italians moved into the political arena in cities dominated by Yankee interests many Brahmins moved aside. In time the latter began to define politics as dirty business more suited to the "saloon culture" of the newcomers than to their drawing rooms and clubs. Today, many an American is highly suspect of those who decide to pursue a career in local politics.[25] This discrepancy between the views of the members of dominant and minority groups serves to intensify the most pervasive attribute of any minority community: group identification. Group identification is revealed in intragroup attitudes and actions; it is reflected in expressions of intergroup behavior and minority reaction to treatment by others.

Pride

Pride in one's ethnic or racial identity may be illustrated in the fellow feeling that predisposes many young Blacks to identify with brothers and sisters they have never met. When introduced they may go through an elaborate handshake, signifying to one another that they are together. Members of other groups perform similar rituals to indicate their sense of identification and their group-based pride.

In the author's study of small-town Jews and their Christian neighbors, each Jewish participant was asked what first came to mind when he or she read the following newspaper headline: MISCHA GOLDBERG LAUDED FOR CONCERT PERFORMANCE. The most frequent response emphasized pride in seeing a fellow Jew receive recognition. Many echoed the sentiment expressed by one of them who said, "I'm glad when it's one of ours who does well, it makes me feel good." When the same individuals were then asked their reactions to a second headline—MAX COHEN INDICTED FOR FRAUD—the characteristic responses were vexation, embarassment, and anger. "It's bad for us when a Jew gets in trouble."[26]

Not surprisingly many Jews, whatever their political proclivities, take special pride in the prominence of Sol Linowitz, Henry Kissinger, and Morris Abrams and, whatever their taste in entertainment, identify with the celebrity of Paul Newman, Ed Asner, Beverly Sills, and Itzak Perlman. They also share a sense of collective embarrassment over the notoriety of the likes of David Berkowitz, the convicted murderer, or Ivan Boesky, the discredited "inside-trader."

In similar fashion many Mexican-Americans are pleased when the champion of the farm laborer is named Cesar Chavez and the leading golfers are Lee Trevino and Nancy Lopez but upset when the accused in a celebrated mass murder case is named Corona. Italian-Americans often display special feelings of identity with Frank Sinatra, Joe DiMaggio, John Sirica, and Associate Justice Anthony Scalia; Irish-Americans with Phil Donahue, Daniel Patrick Moynihan and many a Kennedy.

Two factors are operating in these cases: a sense of interdependence of fate with others with whom one is identified; and a vicarious connection with those in the limelight. Minority-group members often see themselves as part of a whole community, of those they know intimately and those they know only by sight or sign or name. The group identity is expressed in innumerable ways. Perhaps it is best expressed through the immediate response to the question many ask themselves about a stranger being met for the first time: "Is he a 'brother'?" "Is he a *landsmann*?" "Is he a *compadre*?" "Is he a *paisano*?" Social intercourse is apt to be shaped by this definitive beginning.

Self-Hatred

It has been hypothesized that "the greater the pressure of prejudice and discrimination, the greater is likely to be the feeling of interdependence of fate within the minority community."[27] While this relationship has been found to apply to many members of minority groups, it does not necessarily hold for all. Some individuals, objects of severe discrimination, may internalize the negative stereotypes held of them by others and, as a result, display little ingroup solidarity. In fact, rather than drawing into the ranks of the minority, they may seek to withdraw from it.

Those with a positive sense of group identity may feel self-conscious at the thought of "one of theirs" getting into trouble since it puts the whole minority in a bad light. Those who possess a low degree of morale stemming from minority status are sometimes so anxious about their subordinate position that they attempt to disavow membership. To such persons the minority community is not a source of pride but of self-hatred. In order to combat their inability to adjust to minority status they may change their names, deny their racial or ethnic origins, alter their physiognomy (which in the case of Jews, was once facetiously called "cutting off your nose to spite your race"), refuse to associate with group members, attempt to pass as a member of the majority group. If they still find themselves rejected, they are caught between two social worlds—one that they reject, the other that rejects them—suffering the plight of the original marginal man as described by Du Bois and Park and Stonequist.

Reactions to Discrimination

What sorts of individual and collective action can minority-group members take to deal with or alter their social position in a society such as our own? Or, putting the point in the words of Langston Hughes, "What happens when a dream is deferred?" Hughes' poetic answer is offered first; mine, which follows, is largely an elaboration on his metaphors.

What happens to a dream deferred?

Does it dry up
like a raisin in the sun?
Or fester like a sore—
And then run?
Does it stink like rotten meat?
Or crust and sugar over—
like a syrupy sweet?

Maybe it just sags
like a heavy load.

Or does it explode?[28]

Many attempts have been made by sociologists to describe the responses of minority-group members to their social situation. While, to be sure, various minorities suffer greater or lesser discrimination, nonetheless, within most minorities in the United States there are those who "want in" and are willing to do anything to obtain entry, there are those who simply want to be left alone, there are those who want what they feel they are rightly entitled to. Thus, as George Simpson and Milton Yinger suggest, most discussions of minority responses consider at least the following models: those who favor "acceptance," those who seek "accommodation," and those who are "aggressive,"[29] (They may be aggressively for reform to get themselves in; they may be aggressively for radicalization to get themselves out or to form something entirely new.)

My position is slightly different. While taking into consideration these three models it is suggested here that reactions to minority status are most fully understood when *two* questions are posed. Answers to the questions reveal at least four types of reaction that, as shall be shown, may be further broken down and, in some ways, represent points on a spectrum through which some individuals may pass at various stages of their lives. The questions are these: (1) Does the minority-group member accept or reject the image of subordinate status imposed on him or her by the majority? (2) Is he or she willing to play a humble role as expected by those in positions of power?

Table 6 presents the four possible types of reaction suggested here: submission, withdrawal, separation, integration. (The first two incorporate what Simpson and Yinger call "acceptance"—at least on one axis; the latter two only partially parallel the categories of "accommodation" and "aggression" for, as noted below, *both* may involve the process of detente and militant action to achieve certain defined goals.)

Before examining these types it should be reiterated that all of these reaction patterns are possible, and a given individual may manifest two or more of them at different times or in different circumstances. Since it is the largest single minority group in the United States at present, illustrations of these types will be drawn from the experiences of Black Americans.

Table 6 Four Types of Reaction to Discrimination by Members of Minority Groups.

	Dominant Image of Minority Member's "Inferior Status"	
Segregated Role:	Accepted	Rejected
Accepted	1. *Submission*	3. *Separation*
Rejected	2. *Withdrawal*	4. *Integration*

Submission

The Black leader Malcolm X once said that "the worst crime the white man has committed is to teach us to hate ourselves." There is little question that one of the first things many Black Americans learn is their "place" and the roles they are expected to play in the white man's world. They learn "to be Negro" (or, in currently popular terms "to be black"). In 1929 A. L. Holsey wrote,

> At fifteen I was fully conscious of the racial difference, and while I was sullen and resentful in my soul, I was beaten and knew it. I knew then that I could never aspire to be President of the United States, nor governor of my state, nor mayor of my city; I knew that I could only sit in the peanut gallery at our theater and could only ride on the back seat of the electric car and in the Jim Crow car on the train. I had bumped into the color line and knew that so far as white people were concerned, I was just another nigger.[30]

Recognizing one's fate as "just another nigger" among Whites has led some Blacks to accept their inferior status and to play the segregated roles socially assigned to them. American folklore is filled with stories of "Uncle Toms," the defeated persons who knew the score and could play the tune as well. They bow and scrape, crack jokes, and play dumb to please the white folks. Uncle Toms exist in real life too.

Some minority people feel that the best way to live is to accept second-class status and do the bidding of those in the dominant positions. One such individual is described by Richard Wright in his famous autobiography *Black Boy*. Wright tells of a Black elevator operator with whom he worked in a Memphis hotel. One day Shorty needed lunch money and told Wright to watch him get it from the first White man who came along. When such a person eventually got into the elevator, Shorty said to him:

"I'm hungry, Mister White Man. I need a quarter for lunch."

The white man ignored him. Shorty, his hands on the controls of the elevator . . .

"I ain't gonna move this damned old elevator till I get a quarter, Mister White Man."

"The hell with you, Shorty," the white man said, ignoring him and chewing on his black cigar.

"I'm hungry, Mister White Man. I'm dying for a quarter," Shorty sang, drooling, drawling, humming his words.

"If you don't take me to my floor, you will die," the white man said, smiling a little for the first time.

"But this black sonofabitch sure needs a quarter," Shorty sang, grimacing, clowning, ignoring the white man's threat.

"Come on, you black bastard, I got to work," the white man said, intrigued by the element of sadism involved, enjoying it.

"It'll cost you twenty-five cents, Mister White Man, just a quarter, just two bits," Shorty moaned.

There was silence. Shorty threw the lever and the elevator went up and stopped about five feet shy of the floor upon which the white man worked.

"Can't go no more, Mister White Man, unless I get my quarter," he said in a tone that sounded like crying.

"What would you do for a quarter?" the white man asked, still gazing off.

"I'll do anything for a quarter," Shorty sang.

"What, for example?" the white man asked.

Shorty giggled, swung around, bent over, and poked out his broad, fleshy ass.

"You can kick me for a quarter," he said, looking impishly at the white man out of the corner of his eyes.

The white man laughed softly, jingled some coins in his pocket, took out one and thumped it to the floor. Shorty stooped to pick it up and the white man bared his teeth and swung his foot into Shorty's rump with all the strength of his body. Shorty let out a howling laugh that echoed up and down the elevator shaft.

"Now, open this door, you goddam black sonofabitch," the white man said, smiling with tight lips.

"Yeess, siiiir," Shorty sang, but first he picked up the quarter and put it into his mouth. "This monkey's got the peanuts," he chortled.

He opened the door and the white man stepped out and looked back at Shorty as he went toward his office.

"You're all right, Shorty, you sonofabitch," he said.

"I know it!" Shorty screamed, and then let his voice trail off in a gale of wild laughter.[31]

There are, of course, two possible interpretations of Shorty's acceptance of his role as buffoon. On the one hand, he was manipulating the white man—he got what he wanted; on the other, his behavior served to demonstrate the depth of his submissiveness, for he played his role according to his image of the white man's expectations.

For many minority-group members, acceptance of subordinate status is the only way to eke out a living. The "red cap" with a master's degree and the Puerto Rican waiter with a high school diploma are well-known examples.

In many cases, submission to the inferior status imposed by others is a rational acceptance, a seeming necessity for survival. Berry, for example, states that "it is not uncommon for one to conform externally while rejecting the system mentally and emotionally."[32] Yet, there are significant exceptions to this generalization.

Contemporary sociology and cultural anthropology have shown that people can learn to adjust to, and even accept extremely diverse circumstances that seem strange, painful, or evil to those who have received different training. Standards of value by which the desirability of a given status is judged, as well as the status itself, are a product of the society. A whole group may accept what to others seems to be an inferior role. . . . [33]

For some individuals, acceptance of such inferior roles is simply conformity to the traditions of the community in which they happen to be raised. While Whites may learn that they are superior to Blacks as part of a more general socialization experience, some Blacks similarly may accept the standards of racial inequality. Thus, acceptance of inferior status may be seen as a conditioned reaction in a prejudiced society. Today many of their militant children and grandchildren disparagingly refer to such people as "Nee-groes," in contrast to Blacks or African-Americans.

Withdrawal

One reaction to discrimination is submission to inferior status; another is the denial of identity. In this case the individual accepts the majority image of his group[34] and—because of self-hatred or expediency—withdraws from the group. In rejecting the segregated role that they are supposed to play, some light-skinned "Negroes," Jews who wish to be taken for Gentiles, Puerto Ricans who claim they are Spanish, and others attempt to pass into the dominant group. Not infrequently they hold ambivalent attitudes toward themselves and others, and their conflicting allegiances are apt to induce anxiety, which is further provoked by the constant threat of exposure. Thus a fictional character asks himself:

—But what if a lot of people know it already? Or can detect the Negro in me? I hear lots of Southerners claim they can do that. That man goggling at me down the car—can he see I'm part Negro? Has everybody always guessed it?[35]

In 1945, St. Clair Drake and Horace Cayton estimated that each year at least 25,000 persons permanently leave the Negro population to become assimilated into white society.[36] While one suspects that number would not be as high today, still there are innumerable individuals who pass on a part-time or segmental basis, for example, working as Whites by day and returning home to the Black community. In this way they avoid the strain of breaking contact completely and turning away from lifelong friends and neighbors.

"Passing," a course open to those who possess no identifying racial or ethnic characteristics or those who can mask them, is the only method of assimilation available to persons who wish to enter an environment that would reject them out of hand if their true identity were to be revealed. In some areas of society, racial identity is relatively unimportant, and individuals can withdraw from the minority community while still being associated with it by others. Black athletes who attend big universities or join the armed forces, Black artists who become expatriates or entertainers, others who engage in such illicit activities as gambling and prostitution, frequently find acceptance in the White world because of the special skills or characteristics that they bring to the situation. Many such individuals, while not denying their minority identity, prefer not to be "professional race men"; they wish to be accepted in spite of—rather than because of—their racial or ethnic background. In most instances assimilation for such exceptional members of minority groups is only partial, for when they step out of their specialized roles they are considered by many Americans as "just another nigger."

Separation

The reaction patterns of both submission and withdrawal used by certain minority-group members presume acceptance of the inferior image held of them by the majority. Yet, accepting their plight as members of a group considered by the majority to be of lower status does not necessarily mean total capitulation to the stigma of second-class citizenship. In recent years, a large percentage of minority-group members have rejected the idea that they are inferior and have attempted either to avoid contact with the enemy camp or to integrate and take their place alongside those in the dominant group. Here we consider the former response pattern.

For many years some Blacks who attained a moderate amount of security and rose to relatively high status within their own segregated community seemed resentful of those who submitted to the indignities imposed upon them. Long ago, Hortense Powdermaker reported:

> Those at the top deplore the others' submission to white assumptions of superiority and their recalcitrance to white standards of behavior. They decry the loose morality and the ignorance by which, they feel, the lower class of Negro lends credence to unfair notions about the race.[37]

Although these attitudes are still prevalent in certain circles, a qualification is in order: In rejecting white assumptions of superiority, many Blacks accept pervasive white middle-class cultural standards and frequently establish parallel social institutions that mimic the presumed manners and mores of Whites, sometimes to the extent of becoming distorted parodies. Such efforts—often exaggerated accounts of the achievements of individuals—have been described as flights of fantasy. The late E. Franklin Frazier, speaking of middle-class urban Negroes, claimed that "their escape into a world of make-believe with its sham 'society' leaves them with a feeling of emptiness and futility which causes them to constantly seek an escape in new delusions."[38]

The extent to which old "Negro" newspapers and magazines (some of which still exist) were imitative of White society was evidenced by the advertisements and articles that appeared in them. *Ebony, Jet, Tan,* and others used to be filled with pages for ads for skin whiteners and hair straighteners. Furthermore, stories of fancy cotillions and exclusive clubs, of expensive homes and problems with the help, were reported. The preeminence of White standards, even among those who by subscribing to such journals supported their own institutions, was manifest.

Discussing the general problem, Maurice Davie once wrote: "Avoidance is thus a protective device, a way of adjusting to . . . [segregation] with the least pain and uneasiness. It may be carried to the point of almost complete voluntary segregation."[39]

What might be considered a conventional response to separate treatment, namely, the development of institutions paralleling those of the dominant society, is not uncommon, especially by middle-class members of minorities (the White *nouveaux riches* are little different from the Black bourgeoisie). But it is surely not the only reaction pattern of people who reject others' views of their alleged inferiority but see little point in trying to enter their social world.

Some, most often those too poor to emulate middle-class Whites or too disgusted to want to, have taken what seem to many to be more drastic measures. They not only seek to maintain separation and a sense of communal integrity, they also foster the rejection of "White" standards. This type of response is frequently an active and sometimes aggressive method of furthering the goals of the group as a group, strengthening its position, and justifying its separate existence. To combat discrimination, exponents of this reaction pattern sometimes adopt a chauvinistic doctrine of their own superiority. Rather than paralleling dominant institutions and values they challenge them—often acting out certain stereotypes in the process. Jeremy Larner has addressed himself to this last point when he notes the tendency of certain Black nationalists and their spokesmen to engage in a self-indulgent (and, to him, self-deluding) game of mirroring, particularly in playing on three common White themes: "the noble savage" (with its emphasis on creativity, spontaneity, and willingness to fight); "the hipster" (a black Negro to replace Norman Mailer's famous "white Negro," portrayed as a sort of nihilistic superman who is the cock of the walk); and "the Black proletarian" (who is part of the vanguard of the revolution to come).[40] Another key concept marking separation is "soul." In the late 1960s the Swedish anthropologist Ulf Hannerz made a careful study of a Black neighborhood in Washington, D.C. His observations offer one interesting view. He concluded that "soul as solidarity is a reaction to the threat of a split in the community" among those whose lives are circumscribed by the values and norms of mainstream (or wider American) society and those values more specific to ghetto living. Thus Hannerz argues that:

In order to make [the] solidarity encompass even the least privileged, it must be symbolized by those most undiluted forms of black proletarian experience which everybody can claim as his heritage, and to give it a positive valence weakness must be turned into strength. Thus poverty, oppression, and troubled relationships are interpreted as the foundation of an endurance which can only be appreciated by those who have passed the same way.[41]

Others contend that "soul" is simply a label broadly applied to the shared perspective of all Blacks, the basis of their "cultural" character.

As shall be shown in the next chapter, at various stages Blacks have opted for revitalization through separation, through the exaltation of all that is Black and the denigration of all that is White, and, frequently, through making capital of what outsiders (and some high-status insiders) consider to be lower-class cultural traits specific to the Black ghetto.

Thus under the general heading of avoidance one must consider the paths of both parallel participation and of ethnic chauvinism.

Integration

Protest is not always manifest in attempts to pull away, to go it alone. As James Baldwin indicated, however, the appeal for such action is very great.

> The brutality with which Negroes are treated in this country simply cannot be overstated, however unwilling white men may be to hear it. In the beginning . . . a Negro just cannot believe that white people are treating him as they do; he does not know what he has done to merit it. And when he realizes that the treatment accorded him has nothing to do with anything he has done, that the attempt of white people to destroy him—for that is what it is—is utterly gratuitous, it is not hard for him to think of white people as devils.[42]

Despite such sentiments, and they are still widespread, not all Blacks have attempted to solve the problem of inequality by joining the cause of Black Nationalism and rejecting the possibility of eventual integration. In fact, a very large percentage of African-Americans, even today, seek equality without any strings. They do not want to be separate and equal or separate and superior. They want what is constitutionally guaranteed and are willing to fight to get it.

Here, again, such integrationists may try one of two routes. The first is essentially integration-at-a-distance, the kind that most other minorities (namely so-called white ethnics) enjoy; the second is full integration or, better stated, amalgamation.

Most of those we call ethnics in this society do live in two distinct, though not necessarily antagonistic, worlds (as pointed out above). One world is that of their kith, kin, and community; the other is the broader society in which they study and work and sometimes play. The former comes closer to possessing what sociologists call a *gemeinschaftlich* character, a sense of total involvement, of real belonging or "weness"; the latter is more *gesellschaftlich*, that is, marked by secondary relationships, impersonal ties, partial involvement and remoteness. Thus a surprising number of ethnics (White and non-White) keep to their own neighborhoods and enjoy their own activities even when the formal barriers are removed. What they want, at least what many want, is the *right* to do as they please. Once they have that free choice they often opt for life with their own people.

Now there are some members of minority groups who wish to live in a truly color-blind, ethnically neutral society, a society where no one is judged, considered, or even recognized on the basis of skin color or any other potentially invidious criterion. They differ from those in the "withdrawal" category in Table 6, for they desire not to leave their own group but to abolish the idea of group difference itself. In terms introduced in Chapter Three, they are the true advocates of amalgamation—the legatees of Crèvecoeur and Zangwill—and wish their children to be the best that the crucible can pour out.

In both instances militance may mark the road to emancipation. For whether people want the right to decide whether or not to integrate at a distance or to foster fusion, they must often work to convince others that it is their choice to make, not that of others. Since both of these responses are well within the value framework of the American ideal, many of the activities of the civil rights movement were and are oriented toward these goals and many of the important pieces of legislation—including the Civil Rights Acts of 1964, 1967, and 1968—were testimony to the efficacy of integrationist pressure for many Americans.

Mixed Responses

There are times when those in the minority find that they cannot really go it alone (seeking separation or co-existence), nor can they abide the slowness of change as advocated by those whose perseverance is ever tempered by the call for patience and good-will, as in the civil rights movement. Feeling stifled by recalcitrant institutions and reluctant officials, hampered by powerful opponents and anxious neighbors, some leaders have pressed their followers to push beyond the tolerance limits and have advocated radical tactics designed to force society to give in to their demands, to play not only on sympathy but also on fear of disruption, to appeal not merely to charity and righteousness but to countervailing power marshaled by those considered powerless. America has long been witness to such movements: the struggle for women's rights, the labor movement, and the Black Power Revolution. It is the last-named that concerns us here.

In the preceding section we looked at four typical ways minority peoples, including Blacks, have reacted to their treatment. We noted variations within each type, (1) such as unconscious as well as intentional (or calculated) submission; (2) partial or complete withdrawal; (3) avoidance, that is, mimicking the majority but avoiding contact, or opting for nationalism and putting emphasis on real, imagined, or created differences; (4) partial integration (or what was earlier called structural pluralism) or full integration (or amalgamation). Discounting those in the first two general categories because they accept dominant-group definitions of their group's inferiority, it may be said that the third and fourth responses and their variations are permissible, even expected, within our normative structure. Like them or not, most Americans would acknowledge that people have the right to remain separate as long as they do not make trouble; to seek to integrate as long as they accept the values of others—and it does not cost too much. The trouble appears to begin when the limits are broached. Integrating a park is one thing; a neighborhood is quite another. Of course, as noted in Chapter One, these limits—and the norms that define them—vary from region to region and from community to community. Still, in general, one can say that when Blacks (or Chicanos or Puerto Ricans or Native Americans) become nationalistic at least some Americans approve (they may even find it quaint or amusing) so long as they do it in their own area, on their own turf. Likewise, when integrationists press to have the country honor its own ideals, to force the door open through the slow, tedious, and expensive process of litigations, well and good. Liberals applaud; conservatives complain—but generally they go along once a decision is made.

In other words, both "ethnocentric blackwardness" and "soul-less militancy" are tolerable from the majority viewpoint, even if not warmly welcomed. (Numerous public opinion polls bear testimony to this response.) But when chauvinism is joined with direct action (even nonviolent direct action), when pride and protest are linked together, the critical balance is upset and new responses are devised.

The latter situation was invoked by the Black Power movement in the mid-1960s, for reasons discussed in Chapter Seven. In the present context, however, it is instructive to consider what Table 6 (on page 144) would look like if one thinks in terms of *radical responses* to minority status. Table 7 represents this view.

Of course, "Black Power" and similar derivative movements are not historical accidents. They grew out of the mounting realization that unidi-

Table 7   Black Power in Relation to Two Typical Reaction Patterns.

	Separation
a. "Parallel participation"	
b. "Ethnocentric blackwardness"	------------------------------➝
	BLACK POWER
	Integration
a. "Soul-less militancy"	
b. "Color-blind fusion"	-------------------------------➞

mensional programs—whether chauvinistic or reformistic—are usually inadequate to meet the basic challenge, the challenge posed by those who have
the power to control the lives of others. And the lack of power, as noted at
the beginning of this chapter, is a fundamental attribute of minority status.

NOTES

1. See Tom Wolfe, *Bonfire of the Vanities* (New York: Farrar, Strauss and Giroux,
   1987).
2. For a more thorough discussion of groups and statistical aggregates, see Ely
   Chinoy, *Society*, rev. ed. (New York: Random House, 1967), pp. 40–43.
3. Louis Wirth, "The Problem of Minority Groups," in Ralph Linton (ed.), *The
   Science of Man in the World Crisis* (New York: Columbia University Press,
   1945), p. 348.
4. *Ibid.*
5. Peter I. Rose, *The Subject Is Race* (New York: Oxford University Press, 1968),
   p. 71.
6. Robert E. Park, "Human Migration and the Marginal Man," *American Journal
   of Sociology*, 33 (May 1928), 891: see also Everett V. Stonequist, *The Marginal
   Man* (New York: Scribner, 1937), p. 217.
7. From W. E. B. Du Bois, *The Souls of Black Folk* (1903), reprinted in *Three
   Negro Classics* (New York: Avon, 1965), p. 215.
8. Kurt H. Wolff (tr. and ed.), *The Sociology of Georg Simmel* (Glencoe, Ill.: Free
   Press, 1950), pp. 402–408.
9. See Robert E. Park, *Race and Culture* (New York: Free Press, 1951), p. 354.
10. For example, Golovensky's study of the Jewish community contradicts many
    of Park's contentions. See David I. Golovensky, "The Marginal Man Concept:
    An Analysis and Critique," *Social Forces*, 30 (October 1951 to May 1952),
    333–339.
11. George E. Simpson and J. Milton Yinger, *Racial and Cultural Minorities: An
    Analysis of Prejudice and Discrimination*, 4th ed. (New York: Harper & Row,
    1972), p. 186.
12. Thomas Sowell, "Myths About Minorities," *Commentary*, (August 1979), 34–
    35.
13. See Kurt Lewin, *Resolving Social Conflict* (New York: Harper & Row, 1941),
    esp. pp. 145–216; and a recent critique of Lewin's thesis, Jack Rothman, "Mi-
    nority Group Status, Mental Health and Intergroup Relations: An Appraisal
    of Kurt Lewin's Thesis," *The Journal of Intergroup Relations*, 3 (Autumn 1962),
    299–310.
14. Milton M. Goldberg, "A Qualification of the Marginal Man Theory," *American
    Sociological Review*, 6 (February 1941), 52–58.
15. See Chapter Seven of this text.
16. Alfred Kazin, *A Walker in the City* (New York: Grove Press, 1951), p. 12.
17. See, for example, Candice van Ellison, "Introduction," in Allon Schoener (ed.),
    Harlem on My Mind (New York: Random House, 1968). The author's remarks
    were adapted from Nathan Glazer and Daniel Patrick Moynihan's *Beyond the
    Melting Pot* (Cambridge: M.I.T. Press, 1963).

18. Oscar Lewis, "In New York You Get Swallowed by a Horse," *Commentary* (November 1964), p. 69.
19. See, for example, L. Singer, "Ethnogenesis and Negro Americans Today," *Social Research*, 29 (Winter 1962), 419–432.
20. Norbert F. Wiley, "The Ethnic Mobility Trap and Stratification Theory," *Social Problems*, 2 (Fall 1967), 147–159.
21. *Ibid.*; see also William Foote Whyte, *Street Corner Society* (University of Chicago Press, 1943).
22. See Judith R. Kramer and Seymour Leventman, *Children of the Gilded Ghetto* (New Haven: Yale University Press, 1961). See also Part I, "Jews, Gentiles and the American Dream," in Peter I. Rose (ed.), *The Ghetto and Beyond* (New York: Random House, 1969), pp. 21–97, *passim*.
23. See, for example, Peter I. Rose, *Strangers in Their Midst: Small-Town Jews and Their Neighbors* (Merrick, N.Y.: Richwood Publishing Company, 1979), especially pp. 76–79. Most of the small-town Jews interviewed by the author were keenly aware of the role they were forced to play as "ambassadors to the goyim."
24. Edward A. Suchman, John P. Dean, and Robin M. Williams, Jr., *Desegregation: Some Propositions and Research Suggestions* (New York: The Anti-Defamation League of B'nai B'rith, 1958), p. 67.
25. See, for example, E. Digby Baltzell, *The Protestant Establishment* (New York: Random House, 1964), pp. 329–334.
26. See also, Peter I. Rose, "Small-Town Jews and Their Neighbors in the United States," *Jewish Journal of Sociology* 3 (December 1962), 1–17.
27. Suchman *et al.*, *op. cit.*, p. 198. See also Arnold M. Rose, *The Negro's Morale* (Minneapolis: University of Minnesota Press, 1949), pp. 85–95.
28. Langston Hughes, *Selected Poems* (New York: Alfred A. Knopf, 1951).
29. Simpson and Yinger, *op. cit.*, pp. 205–233.
30. A. L. Holsey, "Learning How to Be Black," *The American Mercury*, 16 (April 1929), 421–425.
31. Richard Wright, *Black Boy* (New York: Harper & Row, 1945), pp. 198–200.
32. Brewton Berry, *Race and Ethnic Relations*, 3rd ed. (Boston: Houghton Mifflin, 1965), p. 483.
33. Simpson and Yinger, *op. cit.*, p. 251.
34. "Individuals may belong to membership-groups which are different from their reference-groups, and thereby manifest positive prejudice toward a social category other than that to which they apparently belong." Robin M. Williams, Jr., "Racial and Cultural Relations," in J. B. Gittler (ed.), *Review of Sociology* (New York: Wiley, 1957), p. 428.
35. Sinclair Lewis, *Kingsblood Royal* (New York: Random House, 1947), p. 69.
36. St. Clair Drake and Horace Cayton, *Black Metropolis* (New York: Harcourt, Brace, 1945), p. 160.
37. Hortense Powdermaker, *After Freedom* (New York: Viking, 1939), p. 357.
38. E. Franklin Frazier, *Black Bourgeoisie* (New York: Free Press, 1957), p. 213.
39. Davie, *op. cit.*, p. 440.

40. Jeremy Larner, "To Speak of Black Violence," *Dissent* (Winter 1973), pp. 76–78.
41. Ulf Hannerz, *Soulside: Inquiries into Ghetto Culture and Community* (New York: Columbia University Press, 1970), p. 157; also pp. 144–158.
42. James Baldwin, *The Fire Next Time* (New York: Dial Press, 1963), pp. 82–83.

7

BLACK CONSCIOUSNESS

Red, White, Blue—and Black

History is often written in terms of the images people, or peoples, wish to project. American history, for example, was long recounted as if the English, Scottish, Irish, Welsh Protestants—and a few Dutchmen—were the only ones to have had an impact on the growth and development of the country. Early textbooks and classroom lectures dealt almost exclusively with the "Anglo-American Tradition" or "Our Christian Heritage." Throughout most of the eighteenth and nineteenth centuries, newcomers from northwestern Europe were encouraged to forget about the customs of Germany or Scandinavia and to adapt themselves to eminently superior *American* lifeways. Other immigrants were often considered beyond the pale of social acceptance. In story and song Irish Catholics, Italians, Poles and Russian Jews—and, those who came from China or Japan—were referred to as "unassimilable aliens." Many politicians expressed serious doubts about whether such immigrants would ever have the makings of "real Americans." Several noted social scientists endorsed the Dillingham Commission reports that supported the restrictive immigration legislation of the 1920s.

In time, historians and social scientists adopted a different viewpoint. Pluralism became in vogue and school children and college students were then told that "our differences make us strong," or that "America is a multiplicity in a unity," or, as John Dewey once put it, in the United States "the hyphen connects instead of separates." It even became fashionable to teach about the Judeo-Christian heritage and to consider Catholics as Christians, too! Indeed, as if to bear public witness to such a revisionist view, the single Protestant preacher who had always intoned opening prayers at official gatherings was supplanted by a ubiquitous triumvirate: minister, priest, and rabbi, representatives of "Our three great religions." (In time some sociologists gave expression to this new conception as a symbolic recognition of the "triple melting pot" phenomenon.)[1]

In the early 1960s yet another figure stepped onto the dais—and another culture was "added" to the heritage. It is said that behavior rises to meet expectations and the behavior of historians and social scientists seems to be no exception. By mid decade bookstores were flooded with hundreds of volumes on "the Negro problem." The problem wasn't new. It was as old as America. But, worried about the future, once again the past was to be reexamined and, to some extent, rewritten.

The textbooks that were prepared for the 1970s began to indicate that there was much more to Black history than the slave blocks; the old plantations; Emancipation and "the grateful darkies;" the Freedmen's Bureau; the Hayes-Tilden Compromise; *Plessy v. Ferguson;* Booker T. Washington; race riots during the two world wars; Marian Anderson, the opera singer; Jackie Robinson, the baseball player; Ralph Bunche, United Nations official; Thurgood Marshall, former counsel to the NAACP and now Associate Justice of the Supreme Court; and the Court's "Brown Decision" of 1954. Rather, they dwelt on the role played by Black Americans who, "under the most adverse conditions, fought and died to gain their own freedom" and who (paradoxically it seemed to some reviewers) "were enlisted in every major battle to save this Republic."

The new texts continued to tell a story of life in the ante-bellum South. But the readers were to learn that things were not so tranquil beneath the mimosa trees, that not all Negroes sought to emulate the ways of their masters, and that none enjoyed decent relations with them ("no matter what the romantics say"). They also learned that Black people did not really move "North to freedom," but exchanged one kind of hell for another.

As more and more of these new histories appeared, a far different picture of Black Americans emerged. And it was not limited to the celebration of the martyrdom of Crispus Attucks or to the achievements of George Washington Carver. The new books included discussions of Black soldiers who fought in the Union Army; they told of Black politicians in the turbulent days of Reconstruction; they praised the Black cowboys who helped to open the West, the Black troopers who rode with Teddy Roosevelt, the Black workers who toiled along the railbeds and in the factories and on the farms. Some went further, too, extolling the virtues of blackness and the solidarity of soul and exposing the pallid character of White culture in contrast to Black.

The reconsideration of American history and the assignment of Blacks to an honored place along with other minorities were largely the consequences of the civil rights movement and the campaign to eliminate segregation. The demand for an entirely new view of the African-American, however, was an offshoot of a larger struggle.

Feeling that many of the hard-won victories of the 1950s and 1960s had not made that much difference, angry Black spokespersons began challenging a number of basic assumptions of the reform-minded, civil-rights advocates. First, they argued, liberal White leaders (whatever their personal goals) could rarely offer much more than palliatives that, often as not, were viewed as programs to keep their cities from erupting rather than being expressly designed for helping poor Blacks. Second, they claimed that traditional Black leaders rarely were much better: they were either out of touch with the people for whom they claimed to speak (as many felt about the late Dr. King) or were too willing to play the Establishment game (as was often said of Roy Wilkins, then head of the National Association for the Advancement of Colored People). Arguing that their people had been deluded by Whites who had taken up the "burden" and by Negroes who were trying to lighten it, the new militants wanted to turn them "blackward," wanted them to have an identity that was truly their own. They began their campaign by excoriating white liberals, Uncle Toms, and, especially, "Honkie society." They carried it forward with appeals to Black Nationalism and by making (and, in some cases, making up) history itself.

Of course, since no group has a monopoly on ethnocentrism, it should not be surprising to find that many of the new views of Black history were similar to most paeans to a cloudy past: compilations of vague memories that had become legends, of vague legends that became memories, of isolated incidents swelled to monumental significance, and a good deal of hard evidence of what actually happened and, for various reasons, had been overlooked or purposely ignored. The history of African-Americans, like that of people from Europe, is—and must inevitably be—a potpourri of fancy and fact. What makes it different is that the new versions began to serve two functions: helping to strengthen communal ties among Blacks and, simultaneously, teaching other Americans that those who came from Africa also had a noble past and are a proud people.

To tell it like it really was, of course, is a difficult and frustrating task. It is difficult because there is so little information that is untainted by the biases and romanticism of those who capture the oral tradition or the written record; it is frustrating because even the sketchy story that does emerge is so terribly ambiguous—ambiguous not with respect to the well-known patterns of oppression, but with respect to the effects of these patterns upon the oppressed. But one thing is fairly clear: much of the old African heritage was replaced by a new orientation. Western ways and Southern values were imposed and absorbed and hundreds of thousands of Black Africans became "Negroes."

The great Black sociologist W. E. B. Du Bois once suggested that "there is nothing so indigenous, so made in America, as me." And yet, too few Black Americans have been able to enjoy the freedoms that most other Americans take for granted. Few have ever gotten away from the stigma attached to the color of their skins. As Du Bois and others repeatedly pointed out, every Black American child has always asked, "Who am I?" "What am I?"

Self, Segregation, and Soul

In the early 1960s, James Baldwin wrote an essay entitled "Nobody Knows My Name."[2] In a sense, it dealt with only half of the problem. White people did not know what to call him and he did not know either. Baldwin's people—variously called African, Colored, Negro, and Black—had little to look forward to and even less to look back upon, or so it seemed.

Still, saying they had little is not to say they had nothing. There is such a thing as African-American culture, shared in some measure by every Black person in this country. Like all cultures it is made up of many things—memories and moods and myths. What makes it different is that the memories and moods and even the myths remembered are unique: slavery and its aftermath; spiritual uplift and over-Jordan imagery;[3] and continued subjugation by those who repeatedly tried to prove that white was always right.

Against and, in some ways, in response to these factors there was considerable social integration and cultural resilience, marked by richness and romance. The Black world had (and has) its cuisine ("soul food"), its oldtime religion, its rules and conduct, its lingo, its literature, its sound. Some who now study the Black experience in America contend that it left Blacks with different conceptions of time and space and property—and life.

Resistance was another matter. Being frozen into the rigidity of a caste-like system and unable to become full partners in the society from which so much of their own customs, beliefs, and values were derived, black people lacked the organizational apparatus characteristic of many other minority groups in America—the very groups with which they had long been compared and, perhaps more significantly, with which they had often compared themselves. For years they talked about organizing and fighting their tormentors, but faced with both entrenched institutions and powerful men, they usually had no recourse but to adapt themselves to the system that kept them in servitude. Even acts of defiance often involved playing roles that reflected the stereotypes—feigning illness, acting the fool, slowing down on the job. Except in the isolated cases of such revolts as Gabriel's Insurrection and Nat Turner's Rebellion, frontal attacks were rarely attempted.

Segregation kept many Blacks humble and sometimes their own leaders aided and abetted "The Man." Both Black preachers and White segregationists spoke of their children, both tended their flocks. (Of course, not all White men and not all leaders of Blacks acted in such a manner. But these were the most significant role models available for the vast majority of Black people, especially in the Old South.)

In the 1960s a parallel began to be drawn between the plight of some Blacks in this country and that of mental patients. By that time few well-educated white people would argue that all Blacks were innately inferior;

they knew better—or knew better than to express such sentiments. Yet, the new conventional wisdom sounded strikingly like that of the old planters and ministers of God. Acting as if "only we know what's good for them," many social workers and school teachers have held to this view to the present day. Disadvantaged Black people were viewed and treated as "culturally deprived" victims or patients in need of care and succor. And many Blacks, in turn, like the inmates of most mental institutions, continued to internalize the roles ascribed to them and acted accordingly. Considering the situation, some psychiatrists suggested that what was needed was what they labeled *reality therapy*, the technique used to shock patients into the realization that the world *is* cruel and if they are going to make it, they are going to have to do more than play out the sick role which "enlightened doctrine" had ascribed to them and which, quite understandably, many accepted.

Slaves were not and their descendants are not simple "Sambos," but many did learn to act out the stereotypes others held of them and many, even in putting the White man down by seeming to play along, came to believe that they were in fact inferior. It was in this context that, as noted previously, the late Malcolm X wrote that self-hatred was the worst of all the legacies of racist policies.[4]

Knowing this, perhaps one can understand the bitterness of those who argued that there had really been no progress for Blacks, only expanded "welfare colonialism." And one should be able to understand why young Black radicals began to choke on that noblest of all words in the lexicon of human relationists: brotherhood. Brotherhood, to too many, came to mean: "When you become like me, then we'll be as one." They had a point. Time and again Blacks found that there was one more river to cross; white people would offer the boats if the Black rowers did not rock them too hard.

This situation presented a terribly difficult choice for a potential leader: tell your people to remain supplicants in the hope that someday the white people would overcome their prejudices, lower the barriers, and welcome you into their big *white* house; or become a firebrand in the hope that you might force the White community's capitulation. And once having made the decision, where were you left? Dead on the inside or dead all over.

To solve the dilemma of supplication versus rebellion, most efforts to redress the grievances of the past were channeled into campaigns for integration (not quite supplication and not quite rebellion). Most Black people, it seems, wished to give the impression (and many believed) that, someday, somehow, color would really be overlooked. And, as noted in Chapter Three, those held in contempt today by the angriest Black spokespersons—the White liberals[5]—helped to perpetuate this assumption without, for the most part, realizing what they were doing and without having very much personal contact with those they claimed to accept as equals.

The foregoing observations refer to "most" Blacks, and "many" Blacks, but not to all. There were many who had "made it"; some by the same techniques used by members of other minority groups, including the exploitation of those whose identity they shared; some by becoming athletes and jazz musicians and soul singers performing for both their own people and a wider audience; some—undoubtedly the largest group—by sheer determination to overcome the barriers of segregation, working their way up by entering government service as postmen and clerks, secretaries and soldiers, and, of course, as teachers. Together, these members of what had come to be called the "Black bourgeoisie," the "Colored entertainers," and the "Negro respectables" represented to many white people (especially middle-class Whites) living evidence that Black people could succeed if they tried hard enough and were willing to thicken their skins against whatever abuses the system and its agents meted out.

It is true that many such people have taken pride in their progress and, for all their difficulties, seemed quite stable, even happy in American society. They also belied the claims of others that Blacks were characteristically lazy or ignorant or overly aggressive.[6] Many seemed to be the essence of middle-class respectability: friendly, hard-working, religious, and community-minded.

Many of the children of successful Blacks, however, who entered college in the mid-1960s began to think differently. They, and not merely the poor residents of Watts or Harlem, knew what nationalist spokesman Ron Karenga meant when he cried; "There are only three kinds of people in this country: white people, black people, and Negroes. Negroes? They are black people that act like white people."[7]

The message was not lost. Black college students, particularly of northern schools and the larger southern ones, knew that part of Karenga's rhetoric was addressed to them and their parents. ("Which side are you on?") Those who had suffered least from the stigma of color began to feel the strain the most. Many reacted by forming Afro-American organizations on the campus or by going "home" to Harlem or Hattiesburg (often places they had never been) to work and teach and organize. Some, to resolve their race/class schizophrenia, joined ranks of the most militant members of the Black community. Stressing both poverty and race, the disorganized "Black lumpen" became their cause. With the poor, they argued, one could put to use some of the direct and fringe benefits of a college education. And for them one could try to offer a new and different view of the Americans who came from Africa.

The Past, the Present, and the Future

The young Black militants were "a new breed of cat." They saw themselves as the vanguard of a movement to erase once and forever the stigma imposed by white slave masters and perpetuated by segregationists over the last hundred years. They wanted everyone—parents and peers, White liberals and conservatives—to know that times had changed and that *they were Black men, not Black boys.* Often using the future as a guide to the past, they called for a new view of the Black experience, "one in which the real truth about Black people would finally be known."

In response to mounting pressure, colleges and universities (and some public schools) introduced African-American programs and curricular innovations geared to the special needs of Black students. From among the welter of proposals and pronouncements requesting or as often, demanding such programs, one message came across loud and clear: "We will be *Negroes* no more." This mood, its strategy and its rhetorical style, signaled the end of an old era and the beginning of a new phase in Black-White relations in the United States.

The new ideology was the culmination of years of struggle and crisis during which Black people were trying to come to grips with their unique problems and their constantly thwarted desires to become full-fledged Americans. Among the various techniques of protest, two types of action were most prevalent from the time of Emancipation to its centennial. One centered on Black people themselves and was concerned with "uplift"— the learning of useful skills, the instilling of pride in self and neighbor and emphasizing such puritan virtues as thrift and practicality. The other focused on integration and the gaining of civil rights. In the first instance, the underlying notion was that Black people would show Whites that they were responsible, upright, and talented citizens and that, in time, they would be ready to take their place beside anyone. In the latter the argument was that the problem was not the Blacks' but the Whites' and they should be made to change.

Uplift

The first sustained challenge to Jim Crow laws and the entire system of segregation was to come from highly-educated and remarkably well-integrated northern Blacks. Men like Monroe Trotter and W. E. B. Du Bois challenged what they saw as the tendency of southern Blacks and their leaders to acquiesce and accept their second-class status.

A prime target was Booker T. Washington, who, before the turn of the present century, had sought to come to terms with the problem of Black alienation. Washington, himself born a slave, saw the hope of his people— at least in a southland of deeply rooted segregation—in the development of pride and self-esteem, in the puritan virtues of thrift and practicality, and in the learning of skills of the honest tradesman. His famous speech delivered at the Atlanta Exposition in 1895 has been branded as a classic in accommodationist thinking.[8] The implication was clear: Black people were not ready to take their place beside Whites.

What Washington and others saw, however, was not simply the "Uncle Tomism" his critics (such as Trotter and Du Bois) claimed. Rather, it was, to some at least, a sort of live-and-let-live pluralism. As Washington himself put it: "In all things that are purely social we can be as separate as the fingers, yet as one in hand in all things essential to mutual progress."[9] He also said, in the same speech, that "the wisest among my race understand that agitation of questions of social equality is the extremist folly, and the progress in the enjoyment of all the privileges that will come to us must be the result of severe and constant struggle rather than of artificial forcing."[10]

It was Washington's unwillingness to advocate agitation that won for him contempt in the minds of several generations of radical leaders. Yet, he did begin to come to terms with two of the most serious problems plaguing Black Americans, acceptance of self and the question of racial solidarity, especially in the economic arena.

At Tuskegee Institute, which he established, Washington sought and in many ways succeeded in implementing his plan. For a time he became the idol of millions of Blacks and to this day he remains the symbol for many Whites (especially older school teachers) of the "responsible and reasonable Negro." Today, few of his Black cousins share these sentiments, although, as we shall see, a growing number have reverted to the argument of self-help and, in some instances, even to the very values Washington promulgated.

Washington's famous theme of accommodation turned toward one of separation for some lower-class Blacks, especially those in the urban centers. They joined the ranks of Marcus Garvey's "Back-to-Africa" movement in the 1920s, followed Daddy Grace and other charismatic evangelists in the 1930s, and joined the Black Muslims and other separatist sects more recently. All were, in their own way, considerably militant—and in their militancy very different from those who first followed Washington. Yet each group, including the Muslims, was—and is—an uplift organization: giving a sense of identity to downtrodden followers, a measure of importance, lessons in proper decorum and, above all, a purpose for living. Not long ago it was argued, "Washington's separatist ideology functioned both as a mechanism of accommodation to American racism and as a device for overcoming it."[11] Yet, until very recently, the latter point was not at all apparent or, at least, acknowledged by Washington's critics who saw accommodation and separatism as blind alleys that merely gave support to segregationist sentiment.

The Burden of Responsibility

Washington's most vocal early critic was W. E. B. Du Bois, Harvard graduate, professor of sociology at Atlanta University, and cofounder of the then radical Niagara Movement, an all-Black organization set up explicitly to oppose Washington and his program. Taking an entirely different tack, the radicals argued that the burden of redressing grievances was not the Blacks' but the Whites' and that *they* should be made to change. (It should be pointed out that on certain issues Du Bois and Washington did agree. Both believed firmly in the idea of racial solidarity. Indeed, Du Bois the integrationist went considerably further than Washington in proposing a Pan-African movement to unite Black people everywhere.)

Washington and his followers were able to stop the Niagara Movement of 1905 from getting started, but they were unable to do the same with its successor, the National Association for the Advancement of Colored People (NAACP), founded in 1909, "with the announced goal of fighting for the Black man's constitutional rights and the undeclared aim of curbing Booker T. Washington's power."[12] The NAACP, like the Urban League (founded in 1910), was an organization of Black and White progressives who sought to fight the battle for justice and civil rights through education, politics, and, especially, litigation. Closely associated with the organization was its Legal Defense and Education Fund, which, supported by the general membership, brought numerous suits against various parties accused of violating the Constitution through adherence to state and local statutes upholding segregation.

The lawyers were skilled and persistent and, in time, one barrier after another was to fall as the Supreme Court ruled in favor of the complainants. The culmination of the legal movement came in 1954 when in a unanimous decision the high court overturned the old *Plessy* ruling and proclaimed that separate could never be equal. Many Black and many White integrationists believed that the critical point had been passed and that rapid compliance with the court's mandate for "desegregation with all deliberate speed" would toll the death knell of segregation in the United States. They were wrong.

Alternatives

As far back as the 1920s a number of Black intellectuals had begun to question the advisability of following the slow and deliberate course of taking cases up through the courts while, as they saw it, black people were suffering without relief. Some, even then, questioned any piecemeal approach of attacking one institution—for example, the educational system—instead of trying to alter the entire social order. Such people as A. Philip Randolph and other socialists branded leaders like Du Bois as "a handkerchief head," that is, a hat-in-hand Negro. In *The Messenger*, which Randolph edited, the NAACP was attacked as a bourgeois organization and an alternative, a workingman's movement, was advocated. With capitalism defined as the enemy of all poor people, Randolph sought to rally Blacks and Whites. He did not succeed. As August Meier and Elliott Rudwick point out, Randolph's ideological rhetoric was too much for many Blacks to comprehend; his integrationist appeal was too much for many White workers to stomach.[13] (There is an ironic twist to all this. Du Bois shifted increasingly to the left in his later years and became a member of the Communist Party in Ghana where he had gone to live the remainder of his life and where he died at the age of 93. Randolph, still alive in the 1970s, found himself branded as a "handkerchief head" by militant young Blacks for holding to the notion of a unified—Black and White—attack on the system.)

Black Zionism

Randolph never reached the urban masses to which he appealed. Marcus Garvey did. The Jamaican founder of the Universal Negro Improvement Association (UNIA) in 1914, Garvey claimed that the integrationists were naïve for seeking to win concessions from a society that was and would always be racist.

Instead he favored the development of separate institutions in the United States and, in time, a return to Africa, the "Black Zion." He and his followers opposed miscegenation and extolled everything that was Black. The attractiveness of this movement was noted by one sociologist as follows:

The Garvey movement was based on good psychology. It made the downtrodden lower class Negro feel like somebody among white people who said they were nobody. It gave the crowd an opportunity to show off in colors, parades, and self-glorification.[14]

For a time the UNIA had great appeal, but neither Garvey nor his followers ever got to Africa. He was eventually denounced by prominent leaders of the Black community, barred from bringing his people to Liberia (which was seen as the African Zion), and finally indicted and sentenced to a prison term for using the mails to defraud in selling shares of stock for his "Black Star Ship Line." What had once been an important movement of Black nationalism ended when Garvey was deported in 1927 as an undesirable alien.

But Garvey left a rich legacy. In fact, his banner of red, green, and black is, once again, being seen in the United States. Many a young Black nationalist still proudly wears a button with the three colors—the first represents life's blood, the second is for hope, and the third is for the color of his skin.

The Civil Rights Movement

In the 1930s new organizations emerged, many of these seeking to find alliances with New Deal agencies that were more favorably inclined to the plight of Black citizens than their predecessors had been. Again criticism of the NAACP arose. Young leaders such as Ralph Bunche felt that the organization was not sufficiently radical to deal with the pressing needs created by the depression and the persistence of discrimination throughout the country.

During World War II two movements arose that presaged what was to come in the following decade. The first was A. Philip Randolph's "March on Washington" movement, which pressured President Roosevelt into issuing the famous Executive Order 8802, establishing the first federal Fair Employment Practices Commission. As Meier and Rudwick report:

> Even without enforcement powers, the FEPC set a precedent for treating fair employment practice as a civil right. The short-lived March on Washington Movement prefigured future trends in three ways: (1) It was an explicitly all-black organization; (2) it based its strategy on mass action by the urban slum dwellers; (3) it concentrated on economic problems.[15]

The second significant movement of the era was the Congress of Racial Equality (CORE), the first of several new civil rights organizations that gained prominence by their efforts to accelerate desegregation through nonviolent direct action. CORE began in 1942. James Farmer, then Race Relations Secretary of the Fellowship of Reconciliation, suggested the founding of an organization devoted to the use of "relentless non-cooperation, economic boycotts and civil disobedience," to fight for racial equality. A sit-in at a Chicago restaurant that same year led to the founding of the Chicago Committee on Racial Equality. Out of that organization CORE was born.

In the late 1940s radical-pacifist CORE was sponsoring sit-ins and freedom rides in the North and in Virginia, North Carolina, Kentucky, and Tennessee. And it was CORE that sponsored the integrated bus rides into Alabama in 1961 which ended in the beating of many of the participants. Those trips may have been a turning point, for, in the years to follow, CORE, an organization that had prided itself on its color-blindness, an organization whose membership was for a long time two-thirds White, turned away from the course of integration and toward the building of racial consciousness. In time its founder, Farmer, was succeeded by Floyd McKissick, who, in turn, was followed by the more nationalistic Roy Ennis, who completed the process of purging the membership of Whites and, in the process, lost considerable political and financial support. At present CORE is but a shadow of its former self, riven with dissensions and doing little to aid the cause of desegregation or ghetto improvement.

Its current leaders repeatedly have been charged with exploiting supporters to further narrow personal goals.

A third new civil rights organization arose from the highly successful bus boycott in Montgomery, Alabama, in 1956. A young minister named Martin Luther King, Jr., founded a group called the Southern Christian Leadership Conference (SCLC). Within a few years he became the leader and the symbol of nonviolent direct action in the United States. He and his followers, including Reverend Ralph David Abernathy (who became his successor) took their nonviolent campaign from community to community. People from many parts of the country joined in marches on the bastions of segregation, marches designed to prove Black people could walk with pride even in the face of "redneck" opposition. These committed young men and women followed their leader and turned the other cheek—and, all too often, got their skulls cracked open.

In 1960 a fourth organization informally began at a lunch counter in Greensboro, North Carolina, when a group of Black students decided to defy the proprietor who refused to serve them. The sit-ins of young people spread from town to town and, with the backing of the Reverend King, the Student Nonviolent Coordinating Committee (SNCC) was founded to coordinate such activities. Within a year, however, it severed ties with SCLC, claiming that the parent organization was too cautious. Within five years, the meaning of the letters in the acronym SNCC (pronounced "Snick") changed from Student Nonviolent Coordinating Committee to Student National Coordinating Committee, eschewing its previous stances of nonviolence and integration in favor of militant separation. It, too, was a portent.

But, in the late summer of 1963, before the break was complete, the old guard and the new—including A. Philip Randolph, Roy Wilkins of the NAACP, Whitney Young, Jr., of the Urban League, James Farmer of CORE, Martin Luther King, Jr., of SCLC, and some but not all of the SNCC leadership—joined forces to lead a massive march on Washington. To many, it was the culmination of years of struggle. To most of those who were there, it was a time of rededication, a time of hope, a time of dreams fulfilled—or about to be.

From the steps of the Lincoln Memorial, in a powerful and impressive voice, Martin Luther King, Jr., gave his oft-repeated speech:

I say to you today, my friends, that in spite of the difficulties and frustrations of the moment, I still have a dream. It is a dream deeply rooted in the American dream.

I have a dream that one day this nation will rise up and live out the true meaning of its creed: "We hold these truths to be self-evident; that all men are created equal."

I have a dream that one day on the red hills of Georgia that sons of former slaves and the sons of former slaveowners will be able to sit down together at the table of brotherhood.

I have a dream that one day even the state of Mississippi, a desert state sweltering with the heat of injustice and oppression, will be transformed into an oasis of freedom and justice.

I have a dream that my four little children will one day live in a nation where they will not be judged by the color of their skin but the content of their character. . . .

Dr. King concluded his oration with the following words:

When we let freedom ring, when we let it ring from every village and every hamlet, from every state and every city, we will be able to speed up that day when all of God's children, black men and white men, Jews and Gentiles, Protestants and Catholics, will be able to join hands and sing in the words of that old Negro spiritual, "Free at last! Free at last! Thank God Almighty, we are free at last!"[16]

Black Power

By the time of Emancipation's centennial (and, for some, before), it was becoming increasingly evident to many outside observers and to movement workers that neither ethnocentric backwardness nor soul-less militancy alone could turn the tide of racism, so deep did it flow.[17] Since there was little likelihood that they could really go it alone and even less that they could (or would) ever turn White, new Black leaders argued that their people had to learn (or relearn) to take pride in themselves *and* to become political activists. They had to hark to what Frederick Douglass had prescribed a hundred years before the Student Nonviolent Coordinating Committee was born:

Those who profess to favor freedom yet deprecate agitation are men who want crops without plowing up the ground; they want rain without thunder and lightning. They want the ocean without the awful roar of its many waters. . . . Power concedes nothing without demand. It never did and it never will. Find out just what any people will quietly submit to and you have found out the exact measure of injustice and wrong which will be imposed upon them, and these will continue till they are resisted with either words or blows, or with both. The limits of tyrants are prescribed by the endurance of those whom they oppress.[18]

Black Power did, in fact, begin as a movement of words, impassioned words, exhorting poor sharecroppers to exercise their franchise. But it was not enough. Intimidation and threats had raised the ire of the civil rights workers and turned many Black pacifists into soldiers while turning away many White allies. The code of Thoreau and Gandhi was replaced by the law of Hammurabi—much as Frederick Douglass had suggested.

For years, Black leaders and their White allies had counseled patience and fortitude. And for years their authority went unchallenged, for it was widely felt that the liberal integrationists (Black and White) were on the right path. The civil rights campaign in the late 1950s and the early 1960s and the bills passed by Congress in their wake seemed, to some at least, positive proof of the efficacy of nonviolent direct action. But as many of the victories proved hollow, as tensions mounted between Black civil rights workers who saw radical pacifism as a tactic and White integrationists to whom it was an ideology, as the Vietnam War syphoned off funds that (it was said) would have been earmarked for social programs, and, most of all, as the relative deprivation of Black people became more apparent, the climate shifted. The movement went sour and the old coalitions began to break apart.

Unquestionably, the urban riots in a dozen major cities were also an exacerbating factor. Many Whites in the general population who had begun to feel some sense of sympathy with the embattled civil rights workers or who, at least, were talking of "giving Negroes their due," grew increasingly fearful—and hostile—as they saw the flames of Harlem and Hough and Rochester and Watts and Detroit on their television sets or, in some cases, from their upstairs windows. There were charges and countercharges, cries of duplicity on one hand and of corruption on the other, shouts of "Burn, Baby, Burn" and "Get the Honkies" mixed with "Send them back to Africa."

Given the disillusionment, the uncertainty, and the persistence of institutionalized segregation, and, especially, given the fact that little was being done to satisfy those poorest Blacks whose expectations had suddenly begun to rise, it is not surprising that "We Shall Overcome" was replaced—literally and figuratively—with the call for "Black Power."

A new mood began to reach out and envelop the unorganized Black masses, particularly in the northern ghettos where few meaningful communal institutions existed around which people could rally and where even the oratory of Martin Luther King, Jr., had not been able to stir people into action. Now the focus began to shift away from integration and toward the more basic matter of "getting it together."

Half a century earlier the Black sociologist E. Franklin Frazier said that "if the masses of Negroes can save their self-respect and remain free of hate, so much the better. But . . . I believe, it would be better for the Negro's soul to be seared with hate than dwarfed by self-abasement. . . ."[19] Once again it was being argued that there was a psychosocial need for Black people to call the White society to task rather than to accept and internalize second-class status and all that it meant. As William H. Grier and Price Cobbs have suggested, among Blacks there had long been an almost desperate need to find a sense of both positive self-hood and of meaningful people-hood.[20]

To accomplish these goals meant that Black leadership would have to change. Whites had to be eased or pushed out of positions of dominance to make room for those who could more easily identify with, and be identified with, the Black masses. They were, moreover, the new leaders who sought to prove to their followers that *Black* was the symbol of "light" at the end of their tunnel.

As the Black Panthers gained notoriety, those in the traditional organizations changed too. SNCC became more militant. CORE turned away from its original stance of integration in favor of Black consciousness. The Urban League and the NAACP sounded more militant even while trying to assuage the anxiety of many White liberals. The Southern Christian Leadership Conference continued fighting its battles for jobs and freedom but also began forming uneasy coalitions with other embattled minority groups. Despite differences in symbol (the clenched fist or the double bar of equality), in slogan, and in style, pride and protest were joined and, for many, it had become a time to be Black.

The Second Reconstruction

Yet, even with the dramatic changes in the symbols and substance of the movement as Black Americans entered the decade of the 1970s, there was a real question as to whether the new turn of events would facilitate the growth of genuine and relevant organizations with power to effect both psychological and political changes in the Black communities and to make the need of those communities apparent to the rest of society, or whether the Second Reconstruction would end in tragic failure like the first. Those who took the former position were quick to invoke the model offered by other minority groups. They said that, in essence, Black Power was not an attempt to destroy society, but to provide a basis for pride and representation for those lacking it—the same kind of price and recognition that the English, the Italians, the Irish, the Jews, and other minority groups had had in themselves, using, among other tactics, a similar pattern of creatively distorting history, that is, building up the stature of minor figures, exaggerating the character of certain events, making the search for "roots" a quest for a Holy Grail of dignity and honor, even of nobility. (Historians of all colors, of course, have used such ethnocentric techniques of glorifying their own past ever since the days of Thucydides.) Black Power and Black Consciousness were also seen as the basis for the formation of institutions that could implement organized actions to aid in the ascent up the ladder. Those who held this view suggested that the ethnicity that already existed among black people had to be strengthened and embellished, and that once again ethnic power had to become a factor to reckon with. They said that it was really nothing new—it was "as American as apple pie." But there were others who argued that the zeal to expose everybody to released rage might well turn out to be self-defeating, for few Black leaders would be able to translate the language of estrangement into a meaningful remedy that would cure the disease of racism without killing the patient.[21]

There appeared to be no easy way out of the dilemma. Old techniques failed because they very rarely reached those who needed help most. New techniques (as advocated by the Black militants and others) would fail, it was said, because they would inevitably alienate the very people who were most needed in abetting the transition—concerned liberals in the schoolrooms and universities, on planning boards, in the government, and the like. Simon Lazarus went so far as to suggest that many well-meaning liberals, ignoring the innuendoes of a genuine separatist rebellion, often tended to give Black Power a familiar, pluralistic face and, believing their own propaganda, began to offer Black Power (or their version of Black Power) "both to whites on their right and to blacks on their left." He went on to say that " . . . convinced the black leaders should not adopt systematic violence as a tactic, liberals have assumed they will not adopt it."[22] The point was well taken, especially in view of the tensions extant in American society, on the campuses, and particularly in the ghettos. But it was easily exaggerated. The majority of Black Americans, including many in the slums, wished to join the society rather than to turn it upside down. And, for many, Black Power (read "bloc power") was seen as the best way *to get in.* How long Blacks would feel that way became a highly speculative issue. The potential for independence movements to break out of the colonized status, as Robert Blauner suggested, was always there.[23]

What happened in the 1970s was a confusing mixture of progress and stagnation, of increasing mobility for those who benefitted from certain successes of the 1960s—not least the implementation of "affirmative action" in employment and schooling—the persistent unemployment and despair among those sometimes referred to as "Black Lumpen," the urban poor. Even in celebrating the passage of the Civil Rights Acts of 1960, 1964, 1965, and even of 1968, it is now easy to forget that those victories were primarily the result of protest marches, boycotts, demonstrations, and threats of disruption. Such activities, it seems, did more to bring about changes in the status quo than all the pious platitudes from segregated pulpits or the admonitions of the specialists in urban affairs and poverty.

The federal government, dedicated to opening New Frontiers and making a Great Society and dedicated to waging war on poverty, became so bogged down in Vietnam that it could offer only monumental legislation and modest programs for carrying it out—programs offered to show good faith but construed by many as being proof of continued tokenism which contributed to the overall "minus-sum game."

Minus-sum games are those, as Aaron Wildavsky explains, in which *every* player leaves the contest worse off than when we entered:

Promise a lot; deliver a little. . . . Lead people to believe they will be much better off, but let there be no dramatic improvement. . . . Have middle-class civil servants hire upper-class student radicals to use lower-class Negroes as a battering ram against the existing political system; then complain that people are going around disrupting things and chastise local politicians for not cooperating with those out to do them in. . . . Feel guilty about what has happened to black people; tell them you are surprised they have not revolted before; express shock and dismay when they follow your advice.[24]

Those who warned about the dangers of such games were often told that the problem was being exaggerated or that they were "Nervous Nellies" inadvertently disrupting the cause of civil rights by trying to keep everybody's expectations within certain realistic bounds. In the Nixon-Ford Era many other voices were added to those who denounced certain sociologists and political scientists for their resistance to taking more radical stands.

The entry of large numbers of such spokepersons mounting the stumps from Harlem to Watts and the campus lecture halls from Boston to Berkeley—and writing in old Negro papers and the new Black ones—had brought about many changes in the Black mood and the Black movement. The crystal balls became far cloudier ("Whitey didn't know what we were going to do next"—and he didn't). In retrospect, the emergence of the Black Power movement appears to have been an almost inevitable next stage for those who were called " darker brethren" but were treated like hired hands by most Americans.

Entering the Eighties

During the 1970s, there seemed to be a growing realization that the grievances of Black Americans were legitimate: their schools were poorer, their neighborhoods were shabbier, their rents were higher than the value of the properties, their jobs were scarcer. More and more teachers, community leaders, landlords, and businessmen began to recognize that they had a critical role to play in abetting the transition from dependence to independence. They knew that the road was rocky and the risks were great. But failure to act meant even greater dangers in the future.

Second, opinion polls repeatedly show greater and greater understanding of the problems of Black—and other non-White minorities, empathy with their plight, and a measurable reduction in prejudice. This trend is indicated in Table 8, a summary of a Louis Harris survey conducted late in 1978.[25]

Not only were Whites more sympathetic to the needs of others, they had also altered many of their attitudes toward them. Such views were found to prevail in every area of the country although the most dramatic changes were found among young, white southerners.

By the mid-1970s there was also a growing recognition of the necessity of Black Americans to be allowed to assert their own dignity and to achieve full social recognition as members of the national community.

Table 8   What Whites Think of Blacks.

Here are some statements people sometimes make about black people. For each statement, please tell me whether you personally tend to agree or disagree with that statement.	PERCENT OF WHITES WHO AGREED					
	1963	1966	1967	1971	1976	1978
Blacks tend to have less ambition than whites	66	65	70	52	50	49
Blacks want to live off the handout	41	43	52	39	37	36
Blacks are more violent than whites	*	*	42	36	35	34
Blacks breed crime	35	33	32	27	31	29
Blacks have less native intelligence than whites	39	36	46	37	28	25
Blacks care less for the family than whites	31	33	34	26	22	18
Blacks are inferior to white people	31	26	29	22	15	15

*Not asked

Source: Polls by Louis Harris and Associates for the National Conference of Christians and Jews.

Presidential contender Jimmy Carter, White and Southern, seemed to understand. He based part of his 1977 come-from-nowhere campaign on an insider's perspective of the New South. Many have argued that his subsequent victory was in large measure due to the support he garnered from Black campaign workers and voters. In its wake he did make good on some of his promises to that constituency and appointed more Blacks to positions of prominence than had any of his predecessors. But other promises were more difficult to keep, in particular those dealing with the underlying problems of poverty in urban centers and rural districts.

As America entered the 1980s, schools, while far from being truly integrated in their student bodies, had curricula that more accurately reflected the true nature of America's checkered history and the plural character of the people. Factories, while not yet realizing parity of placement and achievement, were beginning to respond to the pressure of federal requirements and the moral suasion of Carter's minions and the more progressive labor leaders. Political parties and local organizations clearly showed the effects of the struggle for enfranchisement, recognition, and a share of the spoils. The gains in the political arena were the result of challenges to the old system, the growing strength of Black and other minority blocs, and anxiety among the once-dominant forces about their own vulnerability. The last factor undoubtedly led to many concessions to stave off disruption. As we shall see in the next chapter, it was not only the traditional "ruling" groups who were anxious about the changes that characterized race relations in the 1960s and 1970s.

In all, it is probably most accurate to say that, in the wake of rising Black consciousness, Black mobilization, and Black pressures—and similar developments among those in some other ethnic communities, gains were greatest in the areas of mental health and political clout. Psychologically, those who had been seen, and often saw themselves, as second class, increasingly rejected such imagery and took pride in who they were. That pride undoubtedly gave impetus to the outward expressions of a collective sense of selfhood, which I previously called "peoplehood." As members of a group, an *ethnic* group, not just a social category, more and more Black Americans sought to use their collective strength to get their piece of the action. In this they were also somewhat successful. But in two other arenas, the economic and the social, the record is less impressive.

On the one hand, many Blacks with sound educational credentials— and many with rather marginal ones, as critics of certain new policies were quick to point out—benefitted dramatically from efforts to improve employment opportunities. Not a few came from the already well established Black segment of the working class (an often neglected part of the population). But, as William J. Wilson shows, by the early 1970s it was apparent that there was an ever-widening gap in Black America. Those who were "eligible" to make it, were ready and willing and often able to move; and move they did.[26] By 1978 a far larger percentage of college students, graduate students, foremen (and women), junior managers, and local, state, and federal government officials were members of minority groups than ever before. But as the decade of the seventies ended, the country entered a period of stagflation, a time when recession and inflation simultaneously threatened all Americans, taking a heavy toll on those in the precarious position of having just entered the middle-class technocracy. Moreover, as Department of Labor statistics revealed, those in the lower class had even less hope of breaking out of their dependency. They remained as unemployed and as unemployable as did so many of their older siblings and parents 10, 20 and 30 years before.

One of the lasting ideological effects of the movements of the 1960s and early 1970s was to highlight the disproportionate percentage of minorities in the ranks of the poor. (As noted elsewhere, it became almost axiomatic to stress that "While most poor are white, most Blacks are poor.") Yet, other voices began to articulate a different slogan, "If you're poor, you're poor." If poverty is colorless, there must be more to it than racial exploitation—or less. Perhaps it was exploitation, period. The last point is important, for the arguments of those who made it in 1980 sounded like a reprive of Randolph's (and others') clarion call for a socialist alternative to capitalist oppression. Such a message was to be directed toward the Black "lumpen." More often than not, those who heeded the call were not the poorest, the nonworkers, but the victims of economic hard times, the redundant employees of the auto giants, the superfluous workers in the steel mills of the north central states and the cotton mills of the south, White as well as Black. Their members were few but more and more seemed ready to listen.

Finally, despite the court victories and the new government regulations, the demonstrable reduction in prejudicial attitudes, the growing political power of Blacks, the educational gains of the many and the economic gains of the few, and some evidence of issue-oriented coalitions of White and Black workers, the "Five O'Clock Shadow" still prevailed. Those called minorities, particularly non-Whites, tended to live and play in separate social worlds no matter how much they interacted in school and at work. In 1980, as before, most primary relations were within their own communities and within their particular segment of it (what Gordon called the "ethclass"). Moreover, even while more and more Blacks moved to the suburbs, often for the same reasons others had done so (including the desire to live in presumably healthier and safe environs), they tended to recapitulate that old pattern of forming what some have called "gilded ghettoes," ethnically homogeneous neighborhoods with more expensive homes than those left behind. This is not to say that there was no housing integration in the revitalized (and often "gentrified") central city or the suburbs. There was, and there was more of it than ever before. Still, for most Blacks, social separation remained the prevalent pattern.

As in the case of immigrants from eastern and central Europe and those from Asia, the Caribbean, and Mexico, discrimination was not the only factor leading to this lack of integration at the level of intimate socializing. The sense of being happiest "with one's own kind" is the answer most often given to those who say there should be no barrier to prevent them from doing whatever they want or being with whomever they choose—and choosing to be with those most like themselves.

NOTES

1. See Ruby Jo Kennedy Reeves, "Single or Triple Melting Pot: Intermarriage Trends in New Haven, 1870–1940," *American Journal of Sociology*, 49 (January 1944), 331–339; and Will Herberg, *Protestant–Catholic–Jew* (New York: Doubleday, 1955).
2. James Baldwin, *Nobody Knows My Name: More Notes of a Native Son* (New York: Dial Press, 1961).
3. See, for example, James Baldwin, *Go Tell It on the Mountain* (New York: Knopf, 1952).
4. *The Autobiography of Malcolm X* (New York: Grove Press, 1964), pp. 169–190.
5. See, for example, Eldridge Cleaver, *Soul on Ice* (New York: McGraw-Hill, 1968), p. 46.
6. Norman Podhoretz, "My Negro Problem—and Ours," *Commentary* (February 1963), pp. 93–101.

7. This sentiment was expressed by Ron Karenga at a Human Rights Conference at Brotherhood-in-Action, New York City, May 5, 1967. He made similar statements in Los Angeles and elsewhere.

8. Booker T. Washington, "The Atlantic Exposition Address, September 1895," from *Up from Slavery* (New York: Doubleday, Page and Company, 1901), pp. 218–225.

9. As reprinted in August Meier, Elliott Rudwick, and F. L. Broderick (eds.), *Black Protest Thought in the Twentieth Century*, 2nd ed. (Indianapolis: Bobbs-Merrill, 1971), p. 6.

10. *Ibid.*, p. 7.

11. August Meier and Elliott Rudwick, "Radicals and Conservatives: Black Protest in Twentieth-Century America," in Peter I. Rose (ed.), *Old Memories, New Moods* (New York: Atherton, 1970), p. 124.

12. *Ibid.*, p. 125.

13. *Ibid.*, p. 127.

14. Maurice Davie, *Negroes in American Society* (New York: McGraw-Hill, 1949), p. 440.

15. Meier and Rudwick, *op. cit.*, p. 130.

16. Martin Luther King, Jr., "I Have a Dream," *SCLC Newsletter*, 12 (September 1963), 5, 8.

17. See, for example, James Farmer, *Freedom, When?* (New York: Random House, 1965); and Stokely Carmichael and Charles V. Hamilton, *Black Power: The Politics of Liberation in America* (New York: Vintage, 1967).

18. The quotation is from a West Indian emancipation speech delivered by Douglass in 1857. It appears in Carmichael and Hamilton, *op. cit.*, p. x.

19. This is also expressed most poignantly by Richard Wright. See his "Foreword," in St. Clair Drake and Horace Clayton, *Black Metropolis* (New York: Harcourt, Brace, 1945).

20. William H. Grier and Price M. Cobbs, *Black Rage* (New York: Basic Books, 1968), esp. pp. 152–167.

21. See, for example, Lewis M. Killian, *The Impossible Revolution?: Black Power and the American Dream* (New York: Random House, 1968), esp. Chap. 7.

22. Simon Lazarus, "Domesticating Black Power," *New Republic* (June 8, 1968), pp. 37–38.

23. Robert Blauner, "Internal Colonialism and Ghetto Revolt," *Social Problems*, 16 (Spring 1969), pp. 393–408.

24. Aaron Wildavsky, "Recipe for Violence," *New York*, 1 (May 1968), 28–36.

25. *Newsweek* (February 26, 1979), p. 48.

26. See William J. Wilson, *The Declining Significance of Race* (Chicago: University of Chicago Press, 1978).

8

THE RESURGENCE
OF ETHNICITY

Social Physics

One of the basic laws of physics is that every action has an equal and opposite reaction. The laws of society are not that simple. Yet, it is safe to say that in "Social Physics" (a label Auguste Comte, the "father" of sociology, wanted to use for his new discipline) there are numerous examples of changes provoking reactions. This is certainly the case in the area of racial and ethnic relations. It was evident in the responses of American nativists to the increasing flow of immigrants into "their" country. It was also expressed in the growing militancy among the ranks of minority groups who had grown restive as they waited for the nation's institutions to uphold its own ideals.

In previous chapters we have looked at some of the principal sources of opposition that members of minority categories faced as they sought to deal with those who set the rules and often served as "gate-keepers." Much of their opposition was reinforced by that sector of society Seymour Martin Lipset refers to as the "once-hads," that is, persons in positions of power who feared or felt that they were losing it.[1] In the present chapter I will concentrate on reactions to such movements as Black Power by those once removed from the centers of power, the so-called "white ethnics." The latter are not all "never-hads," although many make such claims; but they are people who have known subordination themselves. Many even consider that they, too, are minorities.

Feeding the Backlash

Placing Black people in a different light, giving them new models to admire and to emulate, offering them the opportunity to say, "We're somebodies, too," certainly helped to change the self-conceptions of many Black Americans. Richard Wright once wrote, "White man, listen!" In recent years Whites were made to listen; and what they heard and saw and felt greatly affected both attitudes and behavior.

Some welcomed the fact that the Black Power advocates and Third World allies began seriously to challenge the system they felt kept many in servitude, perpetuated racism, and took a. horrendous toll in human costs. Some were delighted that the assertion of Blacks resulted in the foreseeable end of old stereotypes and of deference. Some were confused because they thought the struggle was for integration (or, as noted in Chapter Three, for assimilation) and began to see that goal thwarted by changed tactics and strategies advocated by many leaders. They could not understand why other Blacks did not call a halt to the drift apart. (Many Blacks were similarly confused.) Some were frightened because they simply could not predict what would happen next. ("Do they *really* mean guerrilla warfare?") Many became increasingly angry—angry because they felt that they were being asked or told to pay for the damage they believed was caused by others.

There are many indications of the changes to which those in each of the categories described above responded. All clearly recognized the profound differences between Blacks in the days before the shift in orientation and after. They had known about protest; they had known about Black Nationalism; but, as discussed in Chapter Seven, the issues had not been joined until the mid-1960s. Suddenly White Americans began to hear demands for a general reexamination of American history to put the Black experience in a more balanced light, to get rid of caricatured portrayal of Black people, to prove to others—and to themselves—that Black is also beautiful. They saw a new swagger in the step, a new assurance in the swagger. They saw personal changes, both cosmetic and sartorial. "Processed" hair was replaced by the "Afro"; clothes associated with whitey or with the ghetto were replaced by dashikis and other garb from Africa. (Ten years later shorter hair or corn-row braids were the style and few were wearing African-style clothing.)

The radio blared soul music at prime time. Television networks scrambled for more Black actors and actresses and presented more programs on "The Problem." The Black trend was evident elsewhere: on the streets, on the campuses, in Black Studies Departments, in Black Cultural Centers, in political organizations, both local and national. The first Black Political Convention was held in Gary, Indiana, in the spring of 1972, foreshadowing the implementation of the McGovern reforms during the Democratic Party's Miami convention the following summer. "Blacks," said one observer, "were suddenly everywhere." They got there, it should be stressed, through hard work, concerted pressure, and sometimes by demanding special and categorical treatment.

These developments, most especially the last, had a profound effect, sometimes bringing about what appeared to be "an equal and opposite reaction." The new ground rules set up in response to the demands of

Blacks, and the demands of other non-White minorities, significantly changed the basic premise that many liberals had fought long to establish and to which many other Americans, especially those of immigrant stock, subscribed: the idea that every individual must be judged on his or her merits "regardless of race, creed, color, or national origin."

In point of fact, as sociologist Michael Lewis has stated, this "individual-as-central" meritocratic creed had always been undercut by structural factors which inhibited genuine and open mobility. But, as Lewis suggests, this is not a phenomenon limited to any single group. All have been affected by the endemic ideological contradictions. What is interesting is that many seem unaware of this fact of American life and continue to blame themselves (or those called "the victims") for failure.[2] Many of those who began to recognize the significance of cultural and systemic barriers were members of the non-White categories or (often as not) their supporters. It was they, in particular, who began to demand "group rights" as recompense for past injustices. Equality of placement was sought to replace the idealized equality of opportunity for that placement. That the issue is exceedingly complicated—involving, for example, the serious question of whether an altogether equal race is possible in the face of structurally guaranteed cultural, social, and political handicaps—did not lessen the important fact that the rules of the game had been changed. And this change, at bottom, is where much of the backlash focused.

Black Studies

It has been noted that one of the principal arenas of debate and conflict over the newly expressed sense of racial identity was the college campus. Indeed, one of the most tangible signs of victory after the battles of the mid- and late 1960s was the establishment of Black Studies programs at many universities across the country and Chicano, Puerto Rican, and Native American programs in appropriate geographic areas. These were staffed by a mixture of highly trained academics who specialized in the study of ethnicity, race relations, history, and literature; militant activists whose professional skills were more often organizational rather than analytical; and assorted minority instructors whose main claim to expertise was their status as members of the group being studied and whose main staying power depended on the support of student claques. Not surprisingly, the arguments over whether or not Black Studies had a place in the academy gave way (once it was a *fait accompli*) to debates over what was being taught and by whom. Several studies were conducted which examined these questions. One of the most comprehensive was that carried out by C. Wilson Record.

With grants from the Metropolitan Applied Research Center and the

American Philosophical Society, in 1972, Record moved around the country visiting 70 campuses and interviewing 209 Black and White sociologists who "at the time or in the previous few years considered race and ethnicity as a teaching or research field."[3] Among this admittedly select sample, Wilson found that reactors to his questions could be grouped under four rubrics: (1) the *Embracers*, those who welcomed the innovation of ethnically-specific courses and programs (although they were rather sharply divided as to the rationales for doing so); (2) the *Antagonists*, those who openly opposed Black Studies as a separate field and resented the tendency of its supporters to exclude *them* from participation or dismiss their prior contributions; (3) the *Accommodators*, those who reluctantly accepted what they saw as inevitable and tried to make the best of a dubious situation; and (4) the *Dropouts*, those who withdrew from the field under the fire of Black militants.

Each group had a rather motley array of members. The first, the "Embracers," was dominated by critics of the Establishment and included a number of Marxists. But also in the ranks were some conservatives who saw Black Studies as a device of both containment and decompression (much in the way that urban police forces had set up "human relations units" in the wake of the riots of the previous decade, and then went about business as usual). And there were those who saw Black Studies courses as a needed challenge to the traditional ways sociologists and others had addressed themselves to the Black experience.

The "Antagonists" were also a heterogeneous group, but at its core were a number of White integrationists (and some Blacks) who saw themselves as part of the solution not the problem. It was this subgroup more than any other that was caught between the rock and the hard place. For years, many had studied race relations and tried to implement policies that would serve to make society more sensitive to discrimination and more open in all its aspects. Many had been civil rights activists who were also frustrated by the slowness of change and saw the necessity for Blacks and other minorities to become more assertive. What they didn't expect was that they would become targets and, in many cases, scapegoats for those who saw them as establishment-types themselves. Some reacted with traditional academic arguments, thereby confirming the suspicions of their critics. Said one "antagonist" interviewed by Record, "They read Fanon but not Rustin; Malcolm X but not Kenneth Clark; Angela Davis and LeRoi Jones but not Roy Wilkins; the latter-day Du Bois but not Booker T. Washington; Marcus Garvey but not the mature Frederick Douglass. And a lot of time they don't read anything."[4] (Such statements played right into the hands of Black critics who would see them as positive proof of the reactionary character of certain old-line liberals.)

The third category, of "Accommodators," seemed better able to ride the tide, many undoubtedly thinking that, in due course, it would ebb. Some seemed to agree with the one who said "Of course it isn't academically respectable, but there are a lot of things around here that aren't—physical education, home economics, social work, business administration."[5] In other words, Black Studies was something that had to be tolerated and even legitimated as part of the general offerings of a multiversity.

"Dropouts," roughly 20 percent of the sample, were older and more bitter than most of the others including the "Antagonists." Unlike the "Antagonists" whose members dug in their heels to fight against the separatist bent of the Black Studies supporters, those in this last category threw in the towel. Like all the others, this cohort included Black as well as White sociologists, individuals who were often accused of being "Uncle Toms" whatever their skills or prior commitments. In fact, most seemed to have dropped out only after having had a series of confrontations with militant nationalists or cultural revolutionaries who publicly denounced them or barred them from speaking or blocked access to classrooms and offices. Included in this last group were a disproportionate number of old leftists (many of them Jewish) who were particularly troubled by two aspects of the protest. As Record explained:

The direct or indirect challenge to academic standards that black studies programs posed, as they developed on most campuses, was particularly abrasive to the scholarly tradition of Jews. Denigration of the cognitive skills and insistence that nonblackness is an insurmountable barrier to understanding black experience clashed head-on with the Jew's esteem for the traditional intellectual tools, in the use of which he had excelled, and with the classical academic perception of human experience as essentially universal. Black assault upon individual merit, traditionally defined, as the single criterion for entry and achievement rattled the age-old Jewish fear of quotas. Furthermore, the separatist thrust of the black studies movement offended a heavy Jewish commitment to integrationist ideology.

Perhaps more pointedly, the rhetoric of the black militants who typically promoted the black studies movement was often openly anti-Jew and anti-Israeli. The identification of some black militants with Africa bridged them emotionally to Muslims, to Arabs, and hence to oral attacks upon Israel. Moreover, the focus of many black studies programs upon the black ghetto as subject matter as well as action arena has brought the old tension between the Jewish shopkeeper/landlord and the black consumer/renter into the classroom and onto the campus podium for fresh examination. Attempts to apply colonial theories to black-white historical experience in the United States leave little doubt that the "colonizers" include Jews.[6]

Of course, demands for and the establishment of Black Studies programs were not the only manifestations of conflict between conservatives and radicals, integrationists and separatists, or Whites and Blacks. Campuses also came under increasing pressure to alter traditional standards for admission to facilitate the entry of more minority students. Sometimes the pressure took the form of demands for "Affirmative Action" and racial quotas.

Affirmative Action

Responding to the change of strategy and, in turn, of policy as it was responded to by sympathetic power brokers or vulnerable governmental agencies and frightened managers, principals, union leaders, politicians, and college admission boards, historian Daniel Boorstin wrote a facetious essay. Zeroing in on college admission boards, Boorstin suggested that if the trend were to be followed to its logical conclusion, the I.Q. and other such tests would be abandoned as criteria for academic admission and would be replaced by an "E.Q.," an Ethnic Quotient.[7] This would mean that students and eventually teachers and their subject matter would have to be apportioned strictly according to background. There would be so many Blacks and so many Whites; so many Jews and so many Catholics—these to be further subdivided according to whether they were children or grandchildren of Italians or Irishmen, Slavs or Slovaks. (Fractional men, as Vance Bourjaily once called people like himself,[8] would prove difficult to judge. What, for example, would one do with an application from a modern-day Fiorello La Guardia, that half-Italian, half-Jewish Protestant mayor of New York? Boorstin offers an answer: give him so many points for each of his traits in proportion to their representativeness in the overall population and make sure, of course, that his curriculum is balanced in similar fashion!)

What Boorstin lampooned a few years ago was soon to become a very real issue and it went far beyond the campus. Indeed many of the strongest advocates of *affirmative action*, the phrase used to denote weighting the balance in favor of the minority applicant, found it increasingly difficult to implement their new policies without exacerbating resistance by those who felt that special treatment and open enrollment and the establishment of minima (often called "targets" and "goals") were designed only for certain segments of the population—which, for obvious reasons, they were. Even if what some call "benign quotas" were applied across the board, it was argued that certain groups would have to lose. Many Jews were especially sensitive on this issue as well. They were overrepresented in university teaching, law, and medicine, professions in which, ironically, not long ago they were often constrained by restrictive quotas that tried to limit how many Jews would be permitted to enter. (To gain admission to college or university they frequently had to have higher qualifications than other applicants.) They began to fear that in forcing institutions of higher learning to accept at least a minimum percentage of the members of all groups in the overall population, their own numbers would be severely cut. Many saw this trend as racism in reverse.[9] And some brought suit. In the Spring of 1973 complaints were filed against several schools and universities.

The most celebrated case at the time was that of Marco DeFunis, a white Jewish applicant to the University of Washington Law School who

was twice denied admission and brought suit claiming that his constitutional guarantee of equal protection of the laws under the Fourteenth
Amendment had been violated. DeFunis charged that the Law School
used racial categories to admit less qualified minority students on a pref-
erential basis. In time his claim was rejected by the highest court in the
State but, in many ways, the die was cast. A quite similar case, brought
by Allan Bakke, a twice rejected applicant to a University of California
Medical School, eventually made it to the Supreme Court where, in an
ambiguous decision, the Court ordered Bakke admitted since it appeared
that the only grounds for his denial were racial. Yet, it also upheld the
use of affirmative action measures in which the race of the applicant was
to be one of a number of criteria admission boards might use in recruiting
and selecting candidates.[10] Here is what was actually said in the Brief
filed by the Office of the Attorney General of the United States as *amicus
curiae* in October 1977.

... the judgment of the Supreme Court of California [which upheld the University's exclusion of Bakke] should be reversed to the extent that it forbids the
Medical School to operate any minority-sensitive admissions.

The remaining question is whether respondent is entitled to admission to the
Medical School. We have argued that it is constitutional in making admissions
decisions to take race into account in order fairly to compare minority and non-
minority applicants, but it is not clear from the record whether the Medical School's
program, as applied to respondent in 1973 and 1974, operated in this manner.

The trial court found, and the University does not contest, that 16 places in
the class were reserved for special admitees. The record does not establish, however, how this number was chosen, whether the number was inflexible or was
used simply as a measure for assessing the program's operation, and how the
number pertains to the objects of the special admission program. ...

The deficiencies in the evidence and findings—which pertain to both the details
of the program and the justifications that support it—may have been caused by
the approach both parties, and both courts below, took to this case. They asked
only whether it was permissible to make minority-sensitive decisions but that it
is necessary to address, as well, questions concerning *how* race was used, and for
what reasons. The findings with respect to these latter, critical questions are in-
sufficient to allow the Court to address them.

Accordingly, the judgment of the Supreme Court of California should be vacated
to the extent that it orders respondent's admission and the case should be remanded
for further appropriate proceedings to address the questions that remain open. In
all other respects the judgment should be reversed.[11]

In its arguments the majority made the following points which, to many,
served as guidelines for future action:

A. This Court has held that minority-sensitive decisions are essential to eliminate the effects of discrimination;
B. Both the legislative and executive branches of the federal government have

adopted minority-sensitive programs for the purpose of eliminating the effects of past discrimination;

    C. Minority-sensitive relief is not limited to correction of discrimination perpetrated by the institution offering admission; and,

    D. Discrimination against minority groups has hindered their participation in the medical profession.[12]

    Then stating that "The central issue on judicial review of a minority-sensitive program is whether it is tailored to remedy the effects of past discrimination,"[13] citing numerous cases, the Court concluded:

    A. A program is tailored to remedy the effects of past discrimination if it uses race to enhance the fairness of the admissions process; and,

    B. There is no adequate alternative to the use of minority-sensitive admissions criteria.[14]

All told, knowledge of racial group affiliation could be considered a necessary criterion, but it could not be the only one.

    Many people followed these cases with considerable interest. Not a few were uneasy about the pressure to right recognized wrongs by accepting a change in the ground rules for "making it" into the university, onto public school faculties, or entering a profession. Many others felt a different sort of pinch. They worried more about jobs and neighborhoods than quotas in college placement, although, here too, there were White working-class parents who began to ask why their children could not obtain special scholarships to elite schools for which, like many Blacks, Puerto Ricans, Mexican-Americans and other non-Whites, they realized that their children were, as one put it, "equally unqualified" (at least according to traditional criteria).

    The problem, as Allan Sindler has pointed out, is partially the differing perspectives (and understandings) of what "Affirmative Action" or "Equal Opportunity" actually means. Sindler summed up the traditional view by asserting that

    The traditional concept of equal opportunity, when applied, say, to jobs, emphasized a fair process of evaluation among the applicants competing to be hired. This involved assessment of applicants on an individual basis by use of nongroup criteria relevant to satisfactory handling of the job in question. The result of such a meritocratic process was the selection of the persons best qualified to do the job, judged in terms of the current performance abilities of the competitors. By definition, a genuinely meritocratic process was fair and, therefore, both guaranteed and defined a fair outcome and equality of opportunity. The elimination of racial discrimination in hiring thus represented a belated purification of the traditional concept, not a challenge to it. Hence both nondiscrimination and government enforcement of nondiscrimination have become comfortably incorporated within the prevailing notion of equal opportunity. . . . [15]

At least one justification embodied an alternative view of equality. In contrast to the traditional concept, it stressed groups and outcomes, not individuals and process. If all other things were truly equal, asserted this view, a genuinely fair and meritocratic process would result in roughly the same proportion of nonminorities and minorities gaining the school admissions, the jobs, or whatever the competition. Where disparate group proportions were the outcome, that indicated the existence of unfairness and unequal opportunity for the underrepresented groups, for which the selection process had acted simply as a "pass-through" rather than a corrective. The proper measure of fair process and equal opportunity was, then, proportional group results.[16]

Many poor and working-class Whites were wont to accept the first view, feeling (as suggested earlier) that their failures could be explained by being unlucky or not having tried hard enough. Most likely they would not accept the second argument. They would doubtless say that no one ever gave them special treatment just because they were poor even though they, too, knew the meaning and effects of discrimination.[17]

Looking Backward

It is sometimes forgotten that like non-White minorities, Jewish and Catholic ethnics also had to deal with special problems in this society. Many of them were among the "wretched refuse" Emma Lazarus described in her famous poem cited earlier.[18] As noted in Chapter Two, these people were not always welcomed with equanimity. And many Americans, far from sympathetic, agreed with the sentiments of Madison Grant, who in his racist tract *The Passing of the Great Race* (1916) wrote:

These new immigrants were no longer exclusively members of the Nordic race as were the earlier ones who came of their own impulse to improve their social conditions. The transportation lines advertised America as a land flowing with milk and honey and the European governments took the opportunity to unload upon careless, wealthy and hospitable America the sweepings of their jails and asylums. The result was that the new immigration . . . contained a large and increasing number of the weak, the broken and the mentally crippled of all races drawn from the lowest stratum of the Mediterranean basin and the Balkans, together with hordes of the wretched, submerged populations of the Polish Ghettos. Our jails, insane asylums and alms-houses are filled with this human flotsam and the whole tone of American life, social, moral and political has been lowered and vulgarized by them.[19]

Thus the newcomers found that many were hostile to them. They suffered from discrimination, often based upon erroneous notions about their mysterious ways or their allegedly undemocratic tendencies. Even after the Immigration Laws of 1921 and 1924 had closed the Golden Door (largely in response to widespread antiforeign sentiment), the prejudices remained. "Old stock Americans have become restless," announced a Ku Klux Klan pamphlet in 1924, " . . . They are dissatisfied with the denaturalizing forces at work in the country. There is something wrong and the American people know there is something wrong, and they are talking among themselves as to where the trouble is."[20] The tract continued:

> They know the arrogant claims of the Papacy to temporal power and that the Romish church is not in sympathy with American ideals and institutions. They know that Rome is in politics, and that she often drives the thin edge of her wedge with a muffled hammer; they have seen the results of her activities in other lands.
>
> • • •
>
> These old stock Americans are coming to believe that Jews dominate the economic life of the nation, while the Catholics are determined to dominate the political and religious life. And they have apprehensions that the vast alien immigration is at the root an attack upon Protestant religion with its freedom of conscience, and is therefore a menace to American liberties. . . . [21]

Even those who were themselves anathema to the Klan sometimes echoed their anti-Catholic sentiments. The Black educator Booker T. Washington is reported to have considered Sicilian sulfur miners deserving of their fate as human beasts of toil—"They are superstitious Catholics who eat garlic." According to Everett and Helen Hughes, "Mr. Washington passed upon them the judgment of a middle-class American Protestant; quite naturally so, for that is what he was."[22]

We are again reminded that the European immigrants were often victims of discrimination and subjects of prejudicial thoughts and sentiments that set them apart from the "WASPs" and sometimes, as one wag once put it, from certain "BASPs" (Black Anglo-Saxon Protestants) as well. (It is well to note that, of late, White Anglo-Saxon Protestants have found themselves victims of sorts, verbal targets of "ethnics" or, as Irving Lewis Allen suggests, of their intellectual or academic spokesmen who "perceive and perhaps reprove White Protestants as a category.")[23]

On Being an Ethnic

Hegel once said that "the eyes of others are the mirrors in which we learn our identities." A student of the author once put it even more pointedly: "I am," she said, "what others think I am." For many decades the eyes of others looked down not only upon Blacks and Chicanos and the American Indians, but also upon Jews and Irish and those other ethnics whom Michael Novak sardonically has referred to as "PIGS": Poles, Italians, Greeks, and Slavs.[24]

Novak claimed to speak for many children and grandchildren of eastern and southern Europe whose relatives left the Old Country to seek a better life in the new and often found it. They also found that they were outsiders and, in many ways, were to remain so despite the fervor of their patriotism and their willingness to prove it. They were, to many, "peasants," looked down upon not only by White Protestants who saw them as socially, religiously, even racially inferior, but also by more than a few intellectuals of varying backgrounds themselves who depicted them as unwashed, uneducated, uncouth—in general, culturally inferior.

The legacy of this kind of attitude still lingers; sometimes it is expressed in far from subtle terms. To Novak and many of those about whom he writes, there is more than a kernel of truth in former Vice President Spiro Agnew's remark about that "effete corps of impudent snobs." The latter are the kind of people about whom Ralph Levine writes:

> Those who appear most willing to sacrifice time and effort in a "good" cause, whatever the cause, prove invariably to be those who can retreat to upper middle class sanctuary and rejoin the "establishment" whenever the need arises. Such [individuals] seem either unable or unwilling to recognize a simple truth; that people considerably lower (although not the lowest) in the class structure, lack a similar sense of mastery and freedom, but rather are fighting desperately to achieve the sense of economic and social security which these [people] accept as their birthright.[25]

David Riesman summed up this sentiment when he wrote that some intellectuals "espouse a snobbery of topic which makes the interests of the semi-educated wholly alien to them—*more alien than the interests of the lower class.*"[26]

Riesman's words are italicized here because they underscore one of the main points made by those who look with some skepticism at the seemingly selective sensitivity of some of those intellectuals and pundits who write about America in general and intergroup relations in particular. White as well as Black, they often appear to be unaware of differences in ethnic values, class-based orientations, and political concerns, especially of those who have not so long ago left the ghettos themselves.

The fact is that, while many white ethnics have been more sympathetic to Black aspirations than the controversy over equal opportunities might suggest, they have been primarily concerned with their own survival and success, concerns shared by most other Americans. What other Americans, at least those who lived in middle-class neighborhoods or suburban communities, did not share with many ethnics was the proximity to the Black ghettos, a situation that, in time, was to place the latter in a difficult double-bind. They often found themselves forced to choose between staying in the changing neighborhood or leaving what were, in effect, their urban villages. They had to face the fact that others in similar situations had become victims themselves in places where old neighborhoods, even stable slums, deteriorated into disaster areas marked by anomie and despair, by internal confusion and pent-up frustration, where the old-timers found themselves ready targets and convenient scapegoats for the newcomers.[27]

In corner bars and coffee shops the ethnics remonstrated about "the squeeze," about the insensitivity of the people uptown. They also complained about those whom they saw as threats to their safety and security. But for a long time even what was said was voiced within the confines of the community itself.

In the 1970s and 1980s, however, after decades of public silence, spokespersons for increasing numbers of angry, frightened, frustrated, and seemingly abandoned people did begin to express their feelings. They did so by supporting conservative candidates for local and national political offices, by organizing neighborhood associations, which some observers saw as northern equivalents of White citizens' councils, by playing on the growing resentment that others were feeling. Not only did all Americans hear what was being said, they began to read about the sentiments in a spate of articles and books on ethnic Americans.[28]

Common themes ran through many of these writings: The earlier immigrants faced great difficulties and obstacles, but they accepted the challenges and internalized the values of the wider society, values that were often quite alien to their own heritages. They knew camaraderie with kin and countrymen, their own people who understood them, respected them, and stood by them when others failed to do so. Indeed many had become more pridefully Irish or Polish or Italian or Greek than they had been "back home."[29] They knew what it meant to be helped by others in similar straits and how to use certain public institutions to advantage—especially the schools, political machines, and, eventually, the civil service. But what they also knew, and this is perhaps the most persistent theme, was that one could not ask for special favors because of background or by pleading "special conditions."

Given these sentiments, it is not surprising that many white ethnics reacted with astonishment at the seeming capitulation being made to demands by Blacks and other non-Whites for group rights and privileges. "Who in hell do they think they are?" They began to say, "Why can't they be like us?" A growing resolve to get their own share arose. A sense of righteous indignation at being put down by those above them to satisfy the demands from below became more and more apparent, and more and more annoying. Many argued that they were loyal, decent, hardworking, God-fearing, and patriotic Americans who had had nothing to do with slavery or with segregation but were being forced to pay for the sins of other peoples' fathers.

The Challenge of the "Unmeltables"

The new situation provided many examples of the feelings of members of white ethnic groups. Let one illustration suffice. In San Francisco a new word entered into the glossary of bureaucratic newspeak in the early part of the 1970s—"deselection." To meet new government guidelines, certain school supervisors were removed from their positions and placed elsewhere in the system, to be replaced by members of "minorities"— that is, in this case, such non-Whites as Black, Mexican-, Japanese-, and Chinese-Americans. In the first month of the program many administrators, all white, were deselected. The merits of this new system are debatable and one can argue that somebody has to begin to pay. But the furor created is also quite understandable.

Episodes of this kind encouraged one group after another to assume a position of *defensive pluralism* in which they began to reassert their old ties, stress their own earlier deprivations, and demand their own hearings and their own affirmative action plans. One of the many results of the ethnic protest was the establishment of campus centers for Irish Studies, Jewish Studies, Polish Studies, and so on. Another was the increased attention paid to ethnic programs on radio and television.

It often led to a gnawing sense of frustration and bitterness among many Americans who had been, at best, only moderately successful and had received no special aid. Many were especially upset by the fact that authorities seemed too willing to buy urban peace at their expense. They grew to resent the "kneejerk" liberal response of those who seemed to love the poor (often at a distance) and champion the underdog but condemn the average white ethnic or middle American for his complacency, his ignorance, his lack of compassion, even for living in a "ticky-tacky" house and liking it; those who proclaimed support for such gangs like the Blackstone Rangers but had no sympathy for their victims, Black or White.[30] They grew equally impatient with the "radical chic" displayed by many celebrities who appeared to kowtow to militants, especially when the latter, in their view, were satisfying their own needs to appear magnanimous at relatively little cost to themselves. The comments of a steelworker, Mike Fitzgerald of Cicero, Illinois, reported by Studs Terkel, are illustrative:

Terkel: Does anger get you, bitterness?
Fitzgerald: No, not really. Somebody has to do it. If my kid ever goes to college, I just want him to realize that when I tell him somebody has to do it, I just want him to have a little bit of respect, to realize that his dad is one of those somebodies. This is why even on (muses)—yes, I guess, sure—on the black thing . . . (Sighs heavily) I can't really hate the colored fella that's working with me all day. The black intellectual I got no respect for. The white intellectual I got no use for. I got no use for the black militant who's gonna scream about 300 years of slavery to me while I'm busting my back. You know what I mean? I have one answer for that guy, Go see Rockefeller. See Harriman. See the people who've got the money. Don't bother me. We're in the same cotton field. So just don't bug me. . . .

It's very funny. It's always the rich white people who are screaming about racism. They're pretty well safe from the backlash. You ever notice it's always: go get the Klansman, go get the Hunkies, go get that Polack. But don't touch me, baby, 'cause my name is Prince John Lindsay. Park Avenue, Lake Shore Drive. They're never gonna get at 'em, baby, uh-uh.[31]

People like Mike Fitzgerald feel and express a backlash sentiment most strongly. They are old ethnics who, for a time, had begun to move up and away from seeing themselves solely in terms of their hyphenation. Since such people were often the first to be affected by the new policies, we began to witness a forceful reassertion of ethnicity in many white communities, even at the expense of class-based allegiances. As Glazer and Moynihan noted:

> . . . ethnic identities have taken over some of the task of self-definition and in definition by others that occupational identities, particularly working-class identities, have generally played. The status of the worker has been downgraded; as a result, apparently, the status of being an ethnic, a member of an ethnic group, has been upgraded . . . . *Today, it may be better to be an Italian than a worker. Twenty years ago, it was the other way around.*[32]

The New Pluralism

Andrew Greeley has written that "the new consciousness of ethnicity [among white ethnics] is in part based on the fact that the Blacks have legitimated cultural pluralism as it has perhaps never been legitimated before.[33] This legitimation significantly altered a number of other aspects of American life. Not least is the fact that, once again, the issue of assimilation versus pluralism was being hotly debated in the universities, in the journals of opinion, in government circles, and, in some communities, in the streets.

There were those like Andrew Greeley and Murray Friedman who, despite certain misgivings, believed that the resurgence of ethnicity was highly functional for our society—because, in the end, America must remain what it has always been: a tissue of primordial ties.[34] Some writers, such as Peter Schrag and Michael Novak, went further. They argued that not only would Blacks benefit from their newfound sense of consciousness but so too would the White ethnics, those who had suffered far too long under the cultural hegemony of "the WASP Establishment."[35]

Still, other observers contended that reality was simply catching up with the dreamers, especially those who see things in class terms. Thus, Irving Levine and Judith Herman suggested that there had not been much important change, save for the fact that the strains and divisions that have always existed began to be acknowledged both by social scientists and ethnics themselves.[36]

In most of the cities where the white working class is ethnic—in the Northeast and Midwest particularly—common origin is reflected in distinctive neighborhoods. People tend to live near one another according to ethnic background, even "unto the fourth generation." For some, the choice is a conscious one, influenced by the presence of such institutions as the church. For others, the ethnic neighborhood is a convenience, maintaining some features of the extended family, lost (but yearned for) in more heterogeneous neighborhoods.

Even suburbanization has not diminished the intensity of many ethnic neighborhoods. In many cases, what looks like an economics-based blue-collar suburb is in reality a community consisting of several ethnic enclaves. For instance, Long Beach, a Long Island town, has been described as "three worlds," Italian, Black, and Jewish—though to the outsider it may seem a "typical lower income suburban community."[37]

Before accepting these views, we should note two—quite different—disclaimers, both dealing less with the substances of the analysis and more with the sympathy expressed for the tendency to advocate further mobilization or separation along ethnic lines. The first is that alluded to by both Glazer and Moynihan and Levine and Herman, that is, the extent to which ethnicity may have become a mask to hide greater differences based upon social class.[38] Many sociologists believe that too much attention is given to ethnic feelings and too little to the sense of alienation of all who are relatively powerless in the context of the larger society. Their argument is that fostering ethnicity—of Blacks or White—serves mainly to keep them from uniting into a coalition of opponents to a repressive system. Foremost in the ranks of those who take this stand was the late Bayard Rustin, who opposed both Black nationalism and White ethnicity. Rustin wanted the people to have power and believed that they would not achieve it by putting their special ethnic interests above more basic social and economic needs.[39] In a sense, this is also the position of William J. Wilson, whose recent book, *The Declining Significance of Race*, puts forth a forceful (and highly controversial) thesis that there is a widening gap in Black America. Middle-class Blacks (or those who have crossed the threshold from poverty to affluence or, at least, have steady employment and respectability) often align themselves more with those they seek to emulate than those whose racial identity they share. The Black poor are left behind to find for themselves or to become putative wards of the welfare state. While Black consciousness may help them, Black separatist ideas may only add to the misery of their plight.[40] They need others who share their *other* identity, the identity of the "have-nothings."

The second critique came from those liberal integrationists who had long stood firm against the winds of change, challenging the Black militants and the new pluralists alike, if for somewhat different reasons than those of Bayard Rustin. Most notable among them was Harold Isaacs who condemned what he saw as a "retribalization."[41] Reviewing Murray Friedman's volume *Overcoming Middle Class Rage*, which sought to explain backlash politics and ethnic insularity, Isaacs wrote:

The two themes—on the Middle American as a harassed man and as an ethnic—are presented . . . as if they harmonize. They are in fact tunes beaten out by separate drummers who march down quite different roads. In effect, the appeal here to the Middle American is to depolarize on social issues and to repolarize ethnically.[42]

Referring to the older pluralists, particularly Horace Kallen and Randolph Bourne and their imagery of symphonic harmony, Isaacs warned against too high expectations. Modern symphonies often sound cacophonous! Thus: "This [repolarization along ethnic lines] may make beautiful music in the heads of some of these composers, but it has to be played out loud to hear what it actually sounds like."[43]

NOTES

1. Seymour Martin Lipset, "Prejudice and Politics in the American Past and Present," in Charles Y. Glock and Ellen Siegelman (eds.), *Prejudice U.S.A.* (New York: Praeger, 1969), pp. 17–69.
2. See Michael Lewis, *The Culture of Inequality* (Amherst: The University of Massachusetts Press, 1978).
3. C. Wilson Record, "Responses of Sociologists to Black Studies," in *Black Sociologists: Historical and Contemporary Perspectives*, James Blackwell and Morris Janowitz (eds.) (Chicago: University of Chicago Press, 1974), pp. 368–401.
4. *Ibid.*, p. 381.
5. *Ibid.*, p. 386.
6. *Ibid.*, p. 398.
7. Daniel Boorstin, "Ethnic Proportionalism: The 'E.Q.' and Its Uses," from *The Sociology of the Absurd* (New York: Simon and Schuster, 1970), pp. 25–35. See also Martin Mayer, "Higher Education for All? The Case of Open Admissions," *Commentary*, 45 (February 1973), 37–47; and, "An Exchange on Open Admissions," *Commentary*, 45 (May 1973), 4–24.
8. Vance Bourjaily, *Confessions of a Spent Youth* (New York: Dial Press, 1952). See, especially, the chapter, "The Fractional Man."
9. See, for example, Pierre van den Berghe, "The Benign Quota: Panacea or Pandora's Box?" *The American Sociologist,* 6 (June 1971). Murray N. Rothbard, "The Quota System, in Short, Must Be Repudiated," *Intellectual Digest* (February 1973), pp. 78, 80. See also Earl Raab, "Quotas by Any Other Name," *Commentary* (January 1972), pp; 41–45; Bart Barnes, "Reverse Bias Alleged in College Hiring," *The Washington Post* (March 5, 1973). See also Nathan Glazer, *Affirmative Discrimination* (New York: Basic Books, 1978).
10. See Allan P. Sindler, *Bakke, De Funis and Minority Admissions: The Quest for Equal Opportunity* (New York: Longmans, 1978).
11. *The Regents of the University of California, Petitioner v. Allan Bakke,* Brief for the United States as *Amicus Curiae,* 76–811 October Term, 1977, pp. 28–29.
12. *Ibid.*, pp. 30, 33, 38, 41.

13. *Ibid.*, p. 50.
14. *Ibid.*, p. 55, 63.
15. Sindler, *op cit.*, p. 12.
16. *Ibid.*, pp. 14–15.
17. See Ralph Levine, "Left Behind in Brooklyn," in Peter I. Rose (ed.), *Nation of Nations* (New York: Random House, 1973), pp. 335–346.
18. Emma Lazarus, "The New Colossus," in *Poems* (Boston: Houghton Mifflin, 1889), pp. 202–203.
19. Madison Grant, *The Passing of the Great Race* (New York: Scribner, 1916). (Quoted from the 3rd ed., published in 1944, pp. 88–92, *passim.*)
20. *The Fiery Cross* (February 8, 1924).
21. *Idem.*
22. The statement attributed to Washington was made by his friend and associate Robert E. Park. See Everett and Helen Hughes, *Where Peoples Meet* (New York: The Free Press, 1952), p. 10.
23. Irving Lewis Allen, "WASP—From Sociological Concept to Epithet," *Ethnicity*, 2 (June 1975), 153–162.
24. Michael Novak, *The Rise of the Unmeltable Ethnics* (New York: Macmillan, 1971).
25. Levine, *op cit.*, p. 342.
26. As cited in Novak, *op. cit.*, p. 149.
27. See, for example, Winston Moore, Charles P. Livermore, and George F. Galland, Jr., "Woodlawn: The Zone of Destruction," *The Public Interest* (Winter 1973), 41–59; Norman Podhoretz, "My Negro Problem—and Ours," *Commentary*, 35 (February 1963), 93–101; and Paul Wilkes, "As the Blacks Move In, the Ethnics Move Out," *The New York Times Magazine* (January 24, 1971), pp. 9–11, 48–50, 57.
28. See, for example, Ben Halpern, "The Ethnic Revolt," *Midstream* (January 1971), pp. 3–16.
29. Nathan Glazer and Daniel Patrick Moynihan have pointed out that, in many ways, the American ethnic groups are a new social form, having no counterpart anywhere. See *Beyond the Melting Pot*, 2nd ed. (Cambridge: M.I.T. Press, 1970), p. 16.
30. Michael Lerner, "Respectable Bigotry," *The American Scholar*, 38 (Autumn 1969), 606–617.
31. Studs Terkel, "A Steelworker Speaks," *Dissent* (Winter 1972), pp. 12–13.
32. Glazer and Moynihan, *op. cit.*, pp. xxxiv–xxxv.
33. Andrew Greeley, *Why Can't They Be Like Us?* (New York: Dutton, 1971), pp. 13–19.
34. Greeley, *op. cit.*, and Murray Friedman (ed.), *Overcoming Middle Class Rage* (Philadelphia: Westminster, 1971).
35. See Peter Schrag, *Out of Place in America* (New York: Random House, 1970); and Michael Novak, *op. cit.*
36. Irving M. Levine and Judith Herman, "The Life of White Ethnics," *Dissent* (Winter 1972), p. 290.
37. *Ibid.*, p. 290. The reference is to Bob Wyrick, "The Three Worlds of Long Beach," *Newsday* (October 18, 1969), p. 6w.
38. See Dennis H. Wrong, "How Important Is Social Class," *Dissent* (Winter 1972), pp. 278–285.

39. See, for example, Bayard Rustin, "'Black Power' and Coalition Politics," *Commentary*, 42 (September 1966), 35–40; and "The Failure of Black Separatism," *Harpers*, 240 (January 1970), 25–34. See also Orlando Patterson, *Ethnic Chauvinism: The Reactionary Impulse* (New York: Stein and Day, 1977).

40. William J. Wilson, *The Declining Significance of Race* (Chicago: University of Chicago Press, 1977). For a critique of this view see Charles V. Willie, "The Inclining Significance of Race," *Society* (July–August 1978).

41. Harold Isaacs, "The New Pluralists," *Commentary*, 53 (March 1972), 75–79. See also Robert Alter, "A Fever of Ethnicity," *Commentary*, 53 (June 1972), 68–73.

42. *Ibid.*, p. 75.

43. *Ibid.*

9

THE REAGAN YEARS
AND BEYOND

Watershed

In 1980, the election of Ronald Reagan over incumbent President Jimmy Carter shifted many national priorities, especially in the realm of civil rights. It dramatically put the brakes on a course of action that was begun in the 1940s (with the Fair Employment Practice Act and the desegregation of the military); accelerated in the 1950s (particularly after the Brown decision of the Supreme Court outlawing school segregation); took significant leaps forward in the early 1960s (the civil rights and Black Power movements being among the most notable generators of changes such as the Civil Rights Act of 1964); and with all the concerns about new directives demanding the implementation of "affirmative action" in schools and workplaces, persisted through the 1970s. That course was characterized by, perhaps more than any other single factor, ever greater governmental involvement in the redress of minority grievances.

During the years of the Carter administration, the president from the Deep South had rekindled the spirit of "welfare-minded" Democrats from the New Deal days of Franklin Delano Roosevelt through the Kennedy–Johnson Era; lent his weight to a variety of programs to assist the poor, especially those in racial minorities; and vigorously advocated human rights at home and abroad. But Carter, an outsider to the Washington establishment, had difficulty in a variety of spheres. Not least was his inability to curb mounting inflation (which reached double-digit heights before he left office) or to quell the feeling of serious malaise throughout the country, a sentiment which he sometimes expressed himself. By the time of the presidential election of 1980, it seemed to many that America was in deep trouble and needed a change.

Carter's opponent, Ronald Reagan, campaigned on a "Get-America-Moving-Again" and "Get-the-Government-Out-of-Private-Life" ticket and won handily. Once in control, he moved to keep the promises made

195

during the campaign. Through a variety of economic strategies, including a massive increase in spending for defense, inflation was reduced as was the percentage of Americans unemployed. In addition to those on the right (both political and religious), many middle Americans—including numerous white ethnics—felt that at last there was someone in the White House who understood their plight and was not only willing to articulate it but was acting to stop the drift of the "welfare state."

Under the first Reagan Administration hundreds of programs designed to aid the poor were disbanded, thousands of conservative judges were appointed to federal courts, and millions of dollars were diverted to matters other than human services. The early replacement of Mary Berry with Clarence Pendleton as chair of the U.S. Civil Rights Commission and the curtailment of its role as both arbiter of interracial conflict and as a dynamic force for the advocacy of fairer practices sent a very clear message across the land: activists for group rights, beware!

In many ways the representatives of the Reagan administration and their sympathizers were returning to the "individual-as-central sensibility,"[1] which, as noted in the last chapter, argues that responsibility for success and failure is highly personal, not collective. They contended that, in America, one must always be encouraged to strive to be the master of his or her own fate—that too much reliance on others, particularly on the institutions of government, threatens the moral fiber and weakens the whole conception of a true meritocracy.

While emphasizing the work ethic and praising individual initiative, the proponents of Reagan policies also stressed the importance of patriotism and the idea that "We are all Americans." Not inconsistently, given the interplay of individualistic and nationalistic themes, many opposed (openly in some cases, more circumspectly in others) "affirmative action" policies. These, it was argued, were not only unfair and, perhaps unconstitutional—because they gave special advantage to certain designated groups (Blacks, Hispanics, Asians, and Native Americans)—but aggravated the tendency toward polarization along racial and ethnic lines.

All told, those in positions of the greatest power seemed determined to move minority issues low down on their list of priorities—and did.

Many civil rights advocates were troubled but not surprised. They had seen the handwriting on the wall. Still, not a few predicted that the anticipated retrenchment would trigger new outbursts of protests from the quarters of those who seemed to be losing the most from new federal action as well as inaction. Curiously, the response was not as explosive as many had expected. When it came, very late in the decade, it took rather unexpected forms.

For almost a decade those still concerned about continued discrimination against racial and ethnic minorities watched in sadness but did little to attempt to stem the erosion of the federal commitment to redress legitimate grievances. There is little doubt that the lack of vigorous response was related, at least in part, to the failure of the civil rights movement's aging leadership to replace itself. There were far fewer spokespersons, and those who were there were hardly the firebrands of the earlier era.

Renewed Debates

Within the ranks of what was left of the old race relations community—which still included the remnants of the civil rights movement, a number of mainstream politicians, and several prominent social scientists—an old issue much discussed in the turbulent 1930s (and again in the 1960s) became the focus of deliberation once again. Some called it the "Race versus Class Debate."

In its earlier manifestations, it tended to be an either/or matter. Some argued that racial oppression was a unique phenomenon, relating to particular attitudes toward those viewed and treated as different from themselves ("the White man's burden"), and was therefore almost immutable. Others contended that racial oppression was hardly unique but was instead a clear example of capitalist exploitation and that "difference" was being used as a mask for privilege.

The more recent debate is more complex. The sociologist William Julius Wilson attempted to put it in perspective. In his 1977 book, *The Declining Significance of Race*,[2] briefly mentioned in the previous chapter, Wilson argued that, as traditional barriers were removed or lowered as a result of the political, social, and economic activities of the civil rights era, they were replaced with a new set of problems, problems that "may prove to be even more formidable for certain segments of the black population."[3] Among the most significant are the lessening need for unskilled workers (the traditional road to stabilization if not instant success), extreme poverty and deprivation of the basic amenities of living, the anomic conditions of home environments and decaying neighborhoods, the lack of middle-class role models, diversion from conventional paths by drugs and other means of escape (most of which give but short-term gratification), and increasing dependence on a welfare system that, many feel, undercuts incentives.

Wilson noted that " . . . whereas the old barriers bore the pervasive features of racial oppression, the new barriers indicate an important and emerging form of class subordination."[4] Those being left behind are what he and others have come to refer to as "the truly disadvantaged."[5]

Wilson's claim of a widening gap in Black America, and, by extension, in other minority communities, was widely acknowledged, but his seeming unwillingness to place all the fault for problems faced by Blacks and other non-White members of the underclass in one basket labeled "Racial Discrimination" rankled many critics. Indeed, the Association of Black

Sociologists, a group to which Wilson had belonged, attacked him for downplaying what, to them, remained the principal issue: institutional racism.[6] They contended that, despite the changes in law and practice, it remained true that, while most poor people in the United States were (and are) white, most Blacks and Hispanics in the country were (and continue to remain) poor—and that unemployment rates among such cohorts have hardly changed in the past four decades. Moreover, they pointed to the resegregation of society (usually citing the increasing number of all or mostly Black schools in northern cities, a function, in large part, of "white flight" to the suburbs) as evidence of the shallowness of Wilson's arguments.[7]

Still others linked the Race/Class Debate to another issue, the matter of "ethnic background and social values." Writers like Thomas Sowell[8] suggested that the real issue is culture not race, pointing to the differential success of those who—having themselves faced severe discrimination, including clearly race-based discrimination—were able to rise and even flourish in the system. Citing Jews and various Asian groups, Sowell also singled out fellow Blacks, namely, West Indians, as exemplars of what others have called, in a related context, "model minorities."

In addition to race, class, *and* culture, other closely related matters were also up for serious reassessment. Among them was a questioning of traditional, and Democratic, approaches to welfare. Increasing numbers of liberals began to rethink the efficacy of programs that seemed to ensure rather than eliminate dependency, programs their more conservative critics had always claimed, "paid people more not to work than to get a job." While such claims were generally off-target, since they failed to allow for the special needs of many who were not only unemployed but also unemployable, they did raise questions about the overall system. More and more people came to espouse "workfare," a program where the able-bodied poor would be required to do community service in order to earn their allotments.

In actual practice, the workfare programs that were instigated varied widely. Most effective seemed to be those most sensitive to the conditions under which those in need came to be dependent. Understanding both the problems and the "culture" of poverty, the programs altered outmoded and outrageous stipulations that limited access to certain programs [for example, accepting a family into the program with the father present even when it was almost necessary to be husbandless to obtain AFDC (Aid to Families with Dependent Children) benefits] and provided two very necessary services: childcare and training.

The "Welfare versus Workfare Debate" symbolized in concrete terms the more widespread reassessment of various long-entrenched social policies and practices, many of which focused on services for racial and ethnic minorities. It also led to the realignment of advocates, contributing to—and accelerating in a number of dramatic ways—a process that had already begun to take shape in the late 1960s and throughout the 1970s when many liberals, who in the aggregate were consistently the staunchest supporters of minority causes, became critical of certain trends that deeply disturbed them.

For example, the long-established, mutually-reinforcing relationship between the Jewish and Black leadership was under increasing strain. This was a result of continuing disagreements over both the meaning and the usefulness of special programs designed to rectify past discrimination as well as certain political stances, such as those relating to the Middle East, which further reduced the effectiveness of united campaigns to consolidate gains already made. The conflicts between certain members of the Black and Jewish communities were not the only strains in old alliances.

Labor movement leadership, often at the forefront of the struggle for human and civil rights, found itself under increasing pressure from rank and file members to resist the kind of categorical imperative required by the advocates of "affirmative action" programs. Those in small businesses also raised questions about the fairness of policies that seemed to be discrimination-in-reverse.

In 1980, the very beginning of the Reagan Era, the Warren Court had upheld a congressional plan that required 10 percent of federal work contracts to be set aside for businesses controlled by minorities. While opposed by many conservatives in the new administration, such set-asides were viewed as a victory for civil rights forces who felt that without special consideration it would remain very difficult for Blacks and others long excluded from full participation in all aspects of the economy to break the pattern. The opponents saw the set-asides, and other schemes to increase minority participation, as "affirmative discrimination."[9] Many scholars and lawyers debated the morality and legality of programs that were based not on a specific company's acts but as general ways to redress past grievances. (The arguments echoed those heard surrounding the De Funis and Bakke cases discussed in the previous chapter.)

In a landmark 6–3 decision, early in 1989, the Supreme Court (still known to many as "The Reagan Court," owing to the conservative justices appointed by Reagan) ruled that the Richmond (Va.) City Council unconstitutionally discriminated against Whites by demanding (presumably in compliance with the earlier ruling) that a contractor with any city building contract must give at least 30 percent of the value of the project to firms which are at least one-half minority-owned. Speaking for the majority, Associate Justice Sandra Day O'Connor claimed that the city had violated the Constitution because it had relied on past societal discrimination to justify the quota. "Since none of the evidence presented by the city points to a..y identified discrimination in the Richmond construction industry . . . , the dream of a nation of equal citizens, in a society where race is irrelevant to personal opportunity and achievement, would be lost in a mosaic of shifting preferences based on unmeasurable claims of past wrongs."[10]

Associate Justice Thurgood Marshall, one of the three dissenters and the only Black member of the high court, bitterly stated that the new ruling "sounds a full-scale retreat from the Court's longstanding solicitude to race-conscious remedial efforts." He continued by claiming that "[the] decision masks a deliberate and giant step backward in the court's affirmative action jurisprudence."[11]

Within several weeks the Supreme Court followed its Richmond decision with two other related reversals of prior policy. In the first, the Court set new limits on measures minorities could use to attempt to prove that they had been relegated to less desirable jobs. In the other, *Martin v. Wilks*, a case involving white firefighters in Birmingham, Alabama, who contended that they were being discriminated against because of affirmative action policies, the Court ruled in their favor.

President George Bush, viewed by many as more sensitive to minority concerns than his predecessor, while claiming he believed in fairness and the protection of civil rights, did not challenge the Court's decisions in these critical cases. Many Americans were troubled by this, particularly in view of the very strong stance he took *against* the Court when, but a few weeks later, he expressed outrage at the failure of the judicial body to rule against the burning of the American flag in a civil liberties case. Indeed, on hearing of the 5–4 decision to uphold the right under protection of the First Amendment guaranteeing freedom of expression, the President immediately called for an amendment to make the desecration of Old Glory unconstitutional.

Campus Trends

The widespread public debate over the flag burning case, and several other instances of this now-protected form of symbolic protest, brought back memories of antiwar and civil rights activities on college campuses in the 1960s. Some commentators predicted that the flag issue might portend new demonstrations on campus in the 1990s. If so, it would be one of the first matters to stir students to widespread political action since the beginning of the 1980s.

Two decades after the tumultuous 1960s, campuses that had reeled under the constant strain of political polarization and confrontation seemed rather oblivious to these real-world debates. In fact, across the country, the onset of the Reagan Era seemed to have signaled a redux of the 1950s—and a final break from the 1960s—as aspiring "Yuppies" (young, urban, professionals) replaced the somewhat sanitized but still committed "Yippies" (Youth for International Peace) as the quintessential representatives of the coming generation. For a time, group-based activism gave way to self-centered personalism. The change was noticeable in course enrollments and the choice of majors, especially in the social sciences: Sociology, which had flourished in the heyday of civil rights and antiwar protest, lost students; economics gained them; and business administration thrived with a new respectability.

Ironically, it was on some of these same campuses that things began to change yet again in the latter years of the Reagan presidency. According to Shelby Steele,[12] two phenomena led to a heightening of tension and, in many places, repolarization along racial and ethnic lines. The first, he claims, was the result of the *successes* of the group rights campaigns of the 1960s and 1970s which had made even the most elite of universities far more open to the enrollment of individuals from very different backgrounds, and, thus, far more diverse in student composition than ever before. The second was the result of the additional measures taken to further ensure that the trend toward the integration of the schools did not abate even when those minorities best qualified to compete were able to go where they wanted. It was not enough to remove the color bar; affirmative action policies on college and university campuses, though increasingly under attack, were in fact expanded and more carefully monitored.

But in spite of the significant increase in the presence of non-Whites (now including many Asians) on campuses—or perhaps because of it—in the middle of the decade "race" again became an issue. In some places it was a positive phenomenon, most dramatically characterized by coalitional campaigns to demand that regents of public institutions and members of boards of trustees of private ones divest themselves of stockholdings in companies doing business in South Africa. But in many places it was not apartheid abroad or segregation at home that brought out the protesters: it was structural pluralism on the campus and challenges to long-lived traditions and the "Eurocentric" curriculum. (A similar charge was made regarding "sexist biases" and parallel demands were made to revamp courses and programs to address the contributions and roles of women.)

Beginning in 1986, on campuses from New England to California there were ugly racial incidents ranging from name calling and graffiti writing ("Niggers, Spics, and Chinks: If You Don't Like It Here, Go Back To Where You Came From") to cross burnings and direct physical violence. Minority students, especially Blacks (who were most often the targets) responded with petitions, marches, rallies, sit-ins, and sieges of administrative offices. According to Shelby Steele, " . . . much of what they were marching and rallying about seemed less a response to specific racial incidents than a call for broader action on the part of the colleges and universities they were attending."[13] Many "over-forty" observers viewed the incidents with a sense of *déjà vu*, a seeming replay of an earlier scenario. Black students were again making demands: more African-

American faculty members, more Black courses, more attention to the issue of diversity. (In many places across the country, most notably on the west coast, these demands were matched by those of Asian and Hispanic students.) Yet, for all the similarity, there were differences between the protests of the sixties and the more recent ones.

> Today's undergraduates were born after the passage of the 1964 Civil Rights Act. They grew up in an age when racial equality was for the first time enforceable by law. This too was a time when blacks suddenly appeared on television, as mayors of big cities, as icons of popular culture, as teachers, and in some cases even as neighbors. Today's black and white college students, veterans of *Sesame Street* and often of integrated grammar and high schools, have had more opportunities to know each other—whites and blacks—than any previous generation in American history. Not enough opportunities, perhaps, but enough to make the notion of racial tension on campus something of a mystery.... "[14]

Steele suggests that the mystery may be partly explained by the recognition that the new problem became how to live in an atmosphere of guaranteed equality instead of the old context of accepted, if sometimes challenged, inequality. "On a campus where members of all races are [now] gathered, mixed together in the classroom as well as socially, differences are more exposed than ever."[15]

Henry Louis Gates, in a forceful essay on the debate over the demands to make core curricula less "Eurocentric" and to include in the basic canon the works of minority writers and women, suggested that much of the conflict has arisen as new voices with significant representation on the campuses have challenged what he calls the " 'antebellum esthetic position' when men were men and men were white, when scholar-critics were white men and when women and people of color were voiceless, faceless servants and laborers, pouring tea and filling brandy snifters in the boardrooms of old boys' clubs."[16] Those leading the campaign to reshape the character of traditional education, challenging the assertions of the new cultural right, have used the collective strength of newly present groups to assert their critical theories.

Many observers noted that, even over issues unrelated to race, individuals seek solace with those who share their "label" (be it politically- or gender- or race-based), leading to what some call the increasing balkanization of the campus. Such politics of diversity is viewed by many as giving further support to those siding with Harold Isaacs who, as noted in the last chapter, worried about too much emphasis on "the idols of the tribe" and too little on integration.

The Election of 1988

In many ways the presidential campaign of 1988 was expected to provide a series of forums for the contending parties to put forth their ideological positions on such issues as the character and direction of intergroup relations in America. Race, class, and gender were thought to be prominent among them. In a sense they were—but, save for the powerful voice of Democratic candidate Jesse Jackson, they were among the most significant issues *buried* under Republican rhetoric about good times brought on by peace and prosperity and Democratic rhetoric about helping the little guy access the system. When race was raised, it was by innuendo— such as the Bush campaign's celebrated exploitation of the decision of Governor Michael Dukakis's administration to furlough the Black convicted murderer Willie Horton, who committed violent crimes while on leave. The Democrats' counterattack was weakened by a reluctance, until the waning days of the campaign, to take strong, identifiably *liberal* stands.

Both parties used patriotism to rally support, with American flags being more common icons of the 1988 election than bumper stickers or lapel buttons. The Republicans claimed that things had never been better; the Democrats promised (with clear echoes of the campaigns of Adlai Stevenson in the 1950s) greater tomorrows. Although acknowledging that there were still unsolved social problems, neither of the chosen candidates seemed willing or able to specify how he would address the needs of millions of Americans who had not only failed to benefit from the vaunted boom of the Reagan Era but had fallen farther and farther behind. Nor were either specific in speaking to the realities of homelessness, teenage pregnancy, drug trafficking and substance abuse, the ills of the elderly, and continued racial unrest in our cities.

The election itself proved to be a mandate for continuity as the majority of Americans appeared to be more willing to rally to a team that, to them, had brought stability than to the vague promises of the Democrats. And, in the beginning, stability seemed to be what they got.

However, almost immediately upon his inauguration, George Bush began to send out signals that, in favoring what he called "a kinder, gentler nation," he would be reaching out to those generally ignored, including the members of racial minorities. His words were applauded by many Democrats, including a number who had supported the unsuccessful candidacy of Jesse Jackson in the primaries and who now suggested the possibility of some shifting of party allegiances if Bush began to deliver on his newly proclaimed promises. Still, many advocates of minority rights remained skeptical of the new administration's ability to do so, particularly with its continued commitment to avoiding the imposition of new taxes or other means of revenue enhancement—as well as its position on those previously mentioned Supreme Court decisions that signaled a continued erosion of hard-won gains relating to improving opportunities for minorities to gain access to the social, political, and economic systems.

The new administration inherited a number of old, unresolved foreign policy problems, some of which have indirect if not direct bearing on ethnicity—and ethnic politics—in this country. Most critical were relations with the Soviet Union and the matter of the opportunities for emigration for Jews, Armenians, Pentacostalists, and ethnic Germans; the 40-year-old Arab-Israeli conflict and the effects of the Palestinian uprising in the occupied territories on the future of the area, its people, and those who supported them here; the much older civil and religious war in Northern Ireland, fought in the streets of Belfast and Londonderry but also the source of tension in the homes and community centers of Irish Americans; the powerful impact of the Japanese on the American economy and the growing resentment it engendered in many parts of the country, especially in the industrial sector; the continuing conflict with Iran, greatly exacerbated in the winter of 1989 by the violent reaction throughout the Muslim world to the publication of Salman Rushdie's controversial novel *The Satanic Verses* and the leadership's order to kill its author for blaspheming against Islam; the persisting conflicts in Central America and the outflow of persons from Nicaragua, Guatemala, and El Salvador who seek asylum as refugees—the same status which is more easily obtained by those fleeing Indochina, Cuba, the U.S.S.R., and (after the violent suppression of the pro-democratic demonstrations in the late spring of 1989 in Beijing) China; and the general matter of immigration, both legal and illegal, from Latin America and from across the Pacific.

The Newest Americans

In addition to the debate about class versus race, the realignment of confederates in various civil rights struggles, the matter of the legality and significance of "affirmative action" and "set-asides" off the campuses and on them, or the meaning of foreign policy matters for those in various interest groups in the United States, the ever-smoldering immigration debate had been fanned afresh by the increasing presence of "foreign elements" on American soil, which made many American workers uneasy. The general reaction sometimes manifest itself in a resurgence of com"nativism" sometimes even within the ranks of certain non-White minorities.

In the 1980s, many Americans, concerned about those most disadvantaged in the society, found themselves in an ironic situation. All around them there were signs that things were improving—for all, it seemed, except for those they cared about most! Some worried about the increasing presence of outsiders, who, they argued, seemed bent on taking a large share of the hard-won entitlements set aside for the American poor. General impressions were corroborated time and again in opinion surveys which showed that, in general, the majority of those polled at random felt that immigrants get more from the United States through social services and unemployment benefits than they contribute. This sentiment was often expressed most strongly within lower socio-economic groups.

Many of the newcomers, particularly those from Latin America and Asian countries, have been beneficiaries of the 1965 Immigration Act which did away with the infamous quota system (discussed in Chapter Two), raised the number of persons to be admitted from any country to 20,000 per annum, and established seven preference categories, four of which dealt with family reunion. Some two million others, known as refugees (people who had been forced to flee their homelands because of "a well-grounded fear of persecution"), were admitted under the special parole authority of the Attorney General, the "seventh preference" of the 1965 Act, or according to the terms of the Refugee Act of 1980. Many of the recent refugees were able to receive special federal assistance through entitlements specified in the 1980 Act.

Since the abolition of slavery, the vast majority of those who entered the United States were White and of European origin. Today well over 90 percent of recent arrivals (legal and illegal) are non-White and non-

Table 9 Legal Immigrants Admitted to the United States, by Region of Birth: 1931–1984

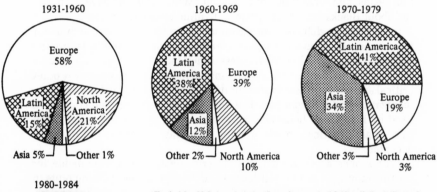

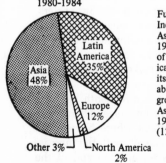

Fueled by U.S. immigration law changes in 1965 and the influx of Indochinese refugees after the Vietnam War ended in 1975, the Asian share of U.S. legal immigration soared from 12 percent in 1960-69 to 48 percent in 1980-84, when it surpassed the 35 percent of legal immigrants from Latin America. As of 1985, the Asian American population—originating from Pakistan and Asian countries to its east but excluding Soviet Asia and the Pacific Islands—numbers about 5.1 million, 2.1 percent of the total U.S. population, and is growing far faster than the Black and Hispanic minorities. The major Asian American groups are Chinese (21 percent of the total in 1985), Filipinos (20 percent), Japanese (15 percent), Vietnamese (12 percent), Koreans (11 percent), and Asian Indians (10 percent).

Source: *Population Bulletin*, Population Reference Bureau, Inc.; Washington, D.C., Vol. 40, No. 4, October 1985, page 2.

European. In many ways they are (or seem) more different from those already here than were those who came from Southern, Eastern, and Central Europe in the late nineteenth and early twentieth centuries. Old nativist sentiments began to resurface. There was talk, once again, of the influx of "alien elements." This time, however, others' views were added, those of so-called neo-nativists. They argued that, until American society takes care of its own, it should not allow others to enter. Some of the neo-nativists were white ethnics; others were members of American minority groups: Blacks, Puerto Ricans, Native Americans, and Chicanos. Sometimes their leaders and spokespersons expressed the view that it is they who would have to pay the highest price for assistance to immigrants and for refugee relief. They claimed that whatever scarce government funds there are they were likely to be diverted to more appealing causes. They also contended that their constituents were at a disadvantage in the job market since "immigrants will do anything" and will often do it for well below minimum wage. Both points sounded strikingly similar to what was said by Anglo-Americans in the mid-nineteenth century about the Irish; what the Irish said about the Italians and Southern and Eastern Europeans; and what those now-labeled "White Ethnics" have been saying about Blacks and other "preferred" minorities more recently.

In addition to debates over entitlements and allowances (such as for the reunion of immediate family members, which currently favors the recently naturalized like Vietnamese-Americans over those who became citizens long ago like Irish-Americans or Italian-Americans), two other critical areas of controversy surrounding immigration were those of Americanization and bilingualism. The former is, of course, an old code word used by many who believed firmly in the idea that forced assimilation into Anglo-American molds was the only way outsiders could ever be accepted.

Critics once again argued that Americanization was responsible for turning ethnic pride into self-hatred and for leaving many immigrants in the unenviable position of being cast adrift on an alien sea. Supporters, by contrast, echoing the ideas of early assimilationists, voiced the opinion that only when foreigners cast off their alien skins and forget the customs of the past can they *really* be absorbed. To be sure, they admitted, the immigrants would have to give up a great deal, make tremendous sacrifices; but, they argued, "Think of what they are getting."

Bilingualism is a more modern concept. In the nineteenth century, many European immigrants retained their native language. There were areas where German was the *lingua franca*, others where Norwegian, Swedish, and other languages predominated. However, with the increasing influx of Southern and Eastern Europeans toward the end of the century, a campaign was mounted to see that everyone spoke English. It became a part of the Americanization process.

Despite ambivalences and insecurities, most newcomers accepted the idea that learning English was critical in order to move into society. Their children learned it in school "sink-or-swim" style and, highly motivated, many swam. Some of the adults also attended night schools where they studied English, sometimes with those who knew nothing of their culture or native languages, sometimes with those who, in perhaps the first instance of bilingual education, taught them English *as a foreign language.* In order to prevent their offspring from being totally immersed in the new language and culture, some immigrants set up and maintained private language after-school schools. Some of these still exist.

The migration of large numbers of Spanish-speaking Puerto Rican Americans to the New York area in the late 1940s and early 1950s, prompted by the economic boom of the post-World-War II period and the availability of cheap and fast air service, changed the culture and the character of the city, brought about vigorous resistance to assimilation, and more formally introduced the idea of bilingualism. As indicated previously, some sociologists have speculated that clinging to their Hispanic heritage was one way Puerto Ricans could separate themselves from Black Americans with whom they were often being grouped. Others say that easy access to Puerto Rico made acculturation less necessary or desirable.

The latter argument also came to be used to explain the reluctance of many Mexican immigrants to Americanization. The closeness of the motherland meant that one could be *in* one world (that of the United States) while in a sense *living* in another (Mexican). Whatever the reason, the result was that many Mexican-Americans, like many Puerto Ricans, felt they should be allowed to retain their ways and their language. Some argued that their children should have instruction in Spanish and that their home language should be used as a transitional vehicle for moving along the road to learning to use English in everyday life. (In 1974, in the case of *Lau v. Nichols,* the Supreme Court ruled that Chinese-speaking students of San Francisco were being discriminated against by being taught in a language they did not understand. Schools were required to find bilingual teachers to work with these students.) Others claimed that even such a strategy was too "assimilationist," that they—and other non-English speakers—ought to be encouraged to maintain their own language, even to the extent of having it as an recognized option to English in all public matters, following the pattern in Francophone Quebec.

Because Hispanics make up the largest linguistic minority in the United States, debates about bilingualism have revolved around the teaching of Spanish and the provisions for bicultural as well as bilingual programs for them. However, Hispanics were not alone in this controversy. Other groups began pressing for similar opportunities. (The Lau case, cited above, is a clear example.)

The reaction against the pressures for bilingualism grew apace in the 1980s, culminating in a campaign to establish the rule of "English Only," not only proclaiming but mandating that Americans have a single official language: English. The effort soon led to the passage of laws in 15 states, and more battles are expected in the years ahead. One ironic twist in the controversy is that some of the most fervent supporters of English Only—the result of whose campaign imposes severe hardships on those who must fill out forms for medical assistance, welfare, further schooling, and employment—also argued that once the singularity of "our" language is established in law, we can then encourage the teaching of other languages to "enhance the understanding of others."

Americanization and bilingualism are not the only policy debates with respect to new Americans. Others include questions about how assistance is offered and given to newcomers and the extent of control service-providers should have on their settlement in this country, especially refugees who receive support from federally funded programs. Should Soviet Jews, Khmer Buddhists (from Cambodia), or Cubans be allowed to cluster, to form and maintain enclaves where they might find security through familiarity, or should they be scattered to encourage their early absorption into the mainstream?

If past history is any indication, it would seem most logical to allow people (indeed, to assist them) to form ethnic communities, thereby easing the transition into the American scene from often totally alien cultural milieus. While some immigrants and refugees, especially those with higher education and familiarity with the language and customs of this country, have successfully moved into dominant communities with little difficulty, the evidence suggests that, for many, the acculturation process is painful and often prolonged. The support of compatriots who have traveled the difficult road from "foreigner" to "American ethnic" has always been a boon to newcomers.

Finally, the most difficult question of all: If everyone who wants to come to the United States for whatever reason cannot be allowed to do so, who should be admitted? At a conference on "The Acculturation of New Americans," sponsored by the Institute on Pluralism and Group Identity of the American Jewish Committee held in the late 1980s, one participant, an economist, asked the assembled corps of policy makers—representatives of major volunteer agencies that work with immigrants and refugees, members of several ethnic organizations, and some foundation personnel and academics—a similar question: How many would favor unlimited immigration to the United States?[17] Not one said he or she would. But the experts could not, or would not, say whom they would admit and whom they would exclude.

Some members of minority groups who were at the meeting later commented that most Americans would probably be willing to continue to welcome as many Indochinese as wanted to come, as well as any number of anti-Communists from Europe, including Soviet Jews and Pentacostalists, but would balk at large-scale requests from Africans or Latin Americans. They called this "racism," pure and simple. Others, also speaking off the record, argued that it was not racial prejudice *per se* but political and cultural bias, a preference for those fleeing left-wing dictatorships and those thought to have the skills or the "potential" for developing skills necessary for a modern industrial society.

The issue reached the halls of Congress when, in the last year of the Reagan Administration, the Kennedy-Simpson Immigration Bill was introduced. (It was passed overwhelmingly in the Senate, failed in the House, and was resubmitted a year later.) The bill sought to alter certain provisions of the 1965 Immigration Act by including reductions in the family reunion system (there were no such limit under the terms of the 1965 Act) and the addition of an independent category of some 50,000 visas allocated on the basis of a point system that favored those with high educational levels, professionals over unskilled workers, and English language ability. The bill was denounced by many Hispanic and Asian representatives because of the favoritism shown to English speakers. They also opposed it because it would eliminate visas for married brothers and sisters under what is known the "fifth preference," used mostly by Hispanics and Asians to bring in relatives. Others from all over the world objected to the proposed elimination of "sixth preference" visas, those issued to unskilled workers who are in demand in the U.S. labor market.

Much of the controversy over the proposed legislation reflected deeply felt sentiments in our society. For some it was continuing concern about the changing character of American culture (being directly linked to debates about Americanization and bilingualism), a feeling that "they" are so different from "we" that things will never be the same, and that a limit has to be imposed on what seems like a threat of inundation. For others, the threat was not that the newcomers were so different but that, whatever they are today, tomorrow they will be too similar: skilled competitors in a society in which ethnic ties remain a primary basis for group cohesion and for social action. The latter sentiment seemed especially to underlie the concerns of those who object to the high rate of emigration from Asia.

Variations on Some Old Themes

In Nathan Glazer's essay "The Politics of a Multiethnic Society,"[18] he begins by summarizing what he and Daniel Patrick Moynihan wrote in the revised edition of *Beyond the Melting Pot*. Their view was of two alternative paradigms of intergroup relations in the United States circa 1970. One was southern (and rural); the other, northern (and urban). Not only the locales but the patterns were seen as quite different.

The "Southern Alternative" was, essentially, a dichotomous Black-White model in which "'separate but equal' [was] an ideology if not a reality"— and the ways of overcoming what was in fact separation and inequality was to campaign for a removal of the color bar, for protection of civil rights, for redress of past wrongs.[19] The Northern Scheme was closer to the old notion of the multiethnic spectrum and the idea of *E pluribus unum* (Out of many, one). The northern pattern was one of adaptation and acculturation, with the principal debates being those discussed in Chapter Three: the efficacy of assimilation or amalgamation versus the (generally preferred) pattern of accommodation.

While one could quibble with some of their specific predictions about what would happen in the next decade, Glazer and Moynihan proved quite prescient. Some critics thought their major failing was that they did not see or acknowledge *other* possibilities based on other circumstances. Their views seemed circumscribed by a limited (and limiting) historical and geographic perspective, a bias that long characterized many sociologists who have written about racial and ethnic relations in the United States while actually relying on observations of what went on in cities and hamlets on the east side of the Mississippi River!

Perhaps it was because it was an extension of their own study of New York's ethnic minorities that their perspective was so limited. Glazer clearly acknowledges this in *Ethnic Dilemmas: 1964-1982* and proposes consideration of a third alternative, a Western one. This, he suggests, would take into account the experiences and encounters of those large minority groups whose heritage is neither African nor European, whose "ports of entry" were along the Mexican border or the Pacific coast, and whose settlements tended to be in the western and southwestern states.

Aside from those from Mexico who were "here" before they were incorporated or who came (and continue to come) across the Rio Grande to settle in the United States, Glazer reiterates a point already made:

[The] newer groups are more distant in culture, language and religion from White Americans, whether of the old or new immigration, than these were from each other. We now have groups that are in American terms more exotic than any before. Added to the Chinese and Japanese are now Filipinos, Koreans, Asian Indians, Vietnamese, Cambodians, Laotians, Pacific Islanders, many of them speaking languages unconnected to the languages of Europe, many practicing religions that have very few representatives in this country (though there are many Christians among them), and most [are] of racial or ethnic stocks distant from European.[20]

Glazer's idea to provide another model is a good one. However, his proposed "Western Alternative" is too broad and, perhaps, misleading—being based mainly on geographic considerations rather than sociopolitical ones.[21]

A careful review of what is already known about the new immigrants and their patterns of adaptation and integration, and the reception of others, leads to the conclusion that there is no truly Western Alternative but, instead, variants on the other—Southern and Northern—patterns taken by those who enter the United States from Latin America and Asia, respectively. Thus those in the first cohort, the Hispanics, focus much of their attention on the problems of living in a formerly segregated society. Attempts to improve their collective status are signposted with phrases like "Down with Internal Colonialism," "Oppose Institutional Racism," and "We Shall Overcome," and by demands that Whites (or "Anglos") be made to relinquish their unacceptable hegemony over what is ostensibly a bicultural (meaning, in this instance, Latino-Anglo) society and to give deprived individuals their just due. With the notable exception of Cubans, Hispanics—a broad category of persons that includes Puerto Ricans, Mexicans who speak of *La Raza* (the race), Central Americans, and many other "Spanish-surnamed" persons—tend to place greater emphasis on power politics, voter registration, and direct appeals for governmental assistance than do persons from Asia.

With the notable exception of Filipinos, in the aggregate Asian-Americans, despite their own continuing encounters with discrimination in various forms (one of the most recent being that they do not deserve special treatment but, instead, ought to be limited because they are "too smart" and "too hard working"), are more apt to follow the other, more Northern path. They will do what they have generally done in the past: use communal action less for raising the consciences of their own peoples or those in the controlling sectors than for the aggrandizement of kin and clansmen within the different and distinctive ethnic groups. As Ronald Takaki says, while they have a history that bursts with telling and an increasing willingness to break the silence which has kept others from knowing them,[22] in many ways they seem bent on moving down a repaved road toward "northern-style" European-type integration. Many Asians, newcomers as well as oldtimers, have expressed ambivalent attitudes about capitalizing on inherited "disadvantages." To most, meritocratic principles are the norms by which their lives in the United States have been organized in the past and ought to be in the future. It is this ethos—and the publicity their achievements have received—that causes many outsiders to look to them (rather than Hispanics) as archetypes of successful adaptation, as "model minorities."

While more and more Asian-Americans have come to represent the best of what those who promulgate modern Americanization would like to create, they are not and will not be fully assimilated, at least not in the foreseeable future. And, though they may increasingly use the blanket term "Asian" for political purposes, it is more likely that, along with the separable groups of European ethnic—Irish-, Italian-, Polish-, and especially Jewish-Americans—they will seek to retain their hyphenated status, while being increasingly accepted as full, not junior, partners in a viably pluralistic social system.

NOTES

1. See Michael Lewis, *The Culture Inequality* (Amherst, Mass.: University of Massachusetts Press, 1978).

2. William J. Wilson, *The Declining Significance of Race* (Chicago: University of Chicago Press, 2d ed., 1980).
3. *Ibid.*, p. 1.
4. *Ibid.*, p. 2.
5. See William Julius Wilson, *The Truly Disadvantaged* (Chicago: University of Chicago Press, 1987).
6. See Anthony Gary Dworkin and Rosalind J. Dworkin, *The Minority Report* (eds.) (New York: Holt Rinehart & Winston, 2d ed., 1928), p. 125.
7. *Idem.*
8. Thomas Sowell, *Ethnic America: A History* (N.Y. Basic Books, 1983).
9. See Nathan Glazer, *Affirmative Discrimination* (New York: Basic Books, 1975).
10. This quotation appeared in *The New York Times* and in Associated Press releases on January 24, 1989.
11. *Idem.*
12. Shelby Steele, "The Recoloring of Campus Life," *The Atlantic*, February 1989, pp. 47–55.
13. *Ibid*, p. 47.
14. *Ibid*, p. 48.
15. *Idem.*
16. Henry Louis Gates, "Whose Canon Is It, Anyway?" *The New York Times Magazine*, February 26, 1989, pp. 44–45.
17. See *The Newest Americans*, a report of the American Jewish Committee's Task Force on the Acculturation of Immigrants to American Life, New York: American Jewish Committee, 1987.
18. Nathan Glazer, *Ethnic Dilemmas: 1964–1982* (Cambridge: Harvard University Press, 1983), pp. 315–336.
19. *Ibid*, pp. 315–316, 320–321.
20. *Ibid*, p. 331.
21. The argument that follows was first developed in the author's essay, "Asian Americans: From Pariahs to Paragons," in Nathan Glazer, *Clamor at the Gates*, (ed.) (San Francisco: Institute for Contemporary Studies, 1987). See especially pp. 210–240; Notes, pp. 324–331.
22. Ronald Takaki, *Strangers From a Different Shore* (Boston: Little, Brown & Co., 1989).

10

INSIDERS AND OUTSIDERS

A Case in Point

Several years ago, with a lightbulb flash of recognition, I realized that I was witnessing one of those events secretly dreaded by ethnographers. The natives were challenging the outsiders' description of themselves.

The challenge was not very dramatic or even very vocal. It consisted of whispers and the ultimate putdown, shrugs of dismissal. To those who belonged to the group in question, it was just one more piece of evidence to confirm the fact that acquaintance with something is very different from true understanding, that there is a wide chasm between *kennen* (knowing) and *verstehen* (understanding). Outsiders might know a bit of another person's history and some cold facts; but, it seems it was much more difficult for them to feel the undertones, to get the vibes.

It wasn't the Australian Aborigines or the Bushmen of the Kalahari or Thai peasants being discussed, but some fellow Americans who, it turned out, were middle-class Jews. Those who described them were students who had spent several weeks culling through the literature to present summary papers on the American Jewish community.

What I experienced really wasn't surprising. As a sociologist who had studied and written about cultural prisms, I was sensitive to the differing perspectives of outsiders and insiders, of "them" and "us." But, somehow, I found myself troubled and rather uncomfortable.

This chapter is based in large measure on the discomfort experienced, a discomfort felt, I daresay, by many teachers and students who are reading this book. It is offered as a personal epilogue to *They and We*. As such it differs somewhat from earlier sections. First, it is written in the first-person singular, a device mostly avoided earlier. Second, the chapter is filled with thoughts and reflections on 35 years of thinking, teaching, researching, and writing about racial and ethnic relations, especially in the United States. This is not to say the essay is nonanalytical. Indeed, it tries to wrestle with the interaction of personal and professional concerns, of matters of heart and mind, as well as the challenges to outsider-experts and insider-members. But, let me turn to the setting of the afore-mentioned discomfort.

The setting was a small seminar of 15 junior and senior students who had come together to study four ethnic groups—Jews, Italians, Blacks, and Puerto Ricans—as they related to their own "brothers and sisters" and to each other in one American city—New York. Together the students and I were embarking on an examination of the backgrounds and experiences of the four critical groups in an attempt to understand better such specific issues as the debate over community control of schools and other crises which were then current.

The seminar roster included four Jews, four Blacks, and one Irish Catholic. The rest were white Protestants, two of them from the south. Ordinarily their ethnic, religious, racial, and regional connections would have had little classroom relevance. The mix was not uncommon. But, it turned out that in this particular setting, it made a world of difference.

During the first part of the semester the students were asked to decide on which of the four groups they wanted to concentrate and then to give me a preference list indicating their choices. They were to develop whatever expertise they could in a short period of time. To assure adequate breadth of coverage, not more than four were to be permitted to deal with a single one of the chosen minorities. For whatever reason, none of those whose first choice was New York's Jews was Jewish. It was the report of one of them that triggered the shrugs and sighs and the unsaid message that "They just don't get it."

At the time I let the looks pass. I wasn't even sure that everybody saw them or, if they did, understood what was happening. But I did, and so did the speaker. He shuddered a bit and pushed on with it, further confounding his credibility by innocuous but telling evidence of seeming insensitivity. For example, to make an important point about the Reconstructionist Movement in contemporary Jewish life, he began by saying that, "To most people, the Jewish church in America has but three divisions, Orthodox, Conservative, and Reform . . ." Apparently he didn't realize that despite its functional similarity to other religious bodies, no Jew would ever describe his ecclesia as a church. (I doubt he would say "ecclesia" either!)

To help out a bit, this fact of Jewish life was pointed out to the smiles of the "all-knowing" Jews in the room and to the blank stares of some of their classmates. Eventually we got back to the more general subject of Jewish settlement and mobility presented in the student reports. Discussion followed that day and on into subsequent meetings.

Several times the somewhat embarrassed presenters bested the too smug insiders in arguments over points of fact. Feelings, they found, they could hardly touch.

Several weeks later, three hours were spent on New York's Italians and the differing viewpoints of sociologists and historians who wrote about them were debated. We discussed migration patterns, religious beliefs, and the nature of life for those often referred to as "birds of passage." We discussed the character of Little Italy and the role of family, church, and workplace. We discussed stereotypes and reactions to them. It was a lively session.

As I left the seminar, I asked myself why it was so different from the previous ones. Then it hit me. No shrugs this time. No sighs. No Italians either!

I was reminded of the several classes on "The Negro in America" I had taught not so long before when no Black faces were in evidence and everyone enthusiastically discussed interpretations of what we now call "the Black Experience." Commenting on this to a colleague, he said, in utter seriousness, that it was easier to be objective in those days. Perhaps. Maybe our debates about the writings and researches of sociologists and historians with names like Campisi, Nelli, Lopreato, Panunzio, Tomasi and the others were better than they might have been had one or more of the students been named Carbone or Marselli. Maybe there were advantages in being unchallenged assessors, playing the role of dispassionate observers. From discussions during the preceding weeks, we had all become sensitive to the fact that there are obvious risks to including the subject of one's research in the discussion of it. Several years before, a Jules Feiffer cartoon character made the point with righteous simplicity. His button-down, grey-flanneled liberal character stated, "Civil rights used to be so much more tolerable until the Negroes got into it."

And what about those "Negroes"?

In the third set of sessions we came to New York's Blacks. This time two of the reporters were Black, two were White. Though they had read the same material, general studies of urban Blacks including parts of St. Clair Drake and Horace Cayton's *Black Metropolis*, Karl and Alma Taeuber's *Negroes in Cities*, and Kenneth Clark's *Dark Ghetto* and specific studies of New York City including James Weldon Johnson's *Black Manhattan* and Gilbert Osofsky's *Harlem: The Making of a Ghetto*, it was clearly apparent that the White students constantly deferred to the Black students. Moreover, whenever the Black students presented their ideas, the White students tended to take them down with little or no challenge. Neither they nor the remaining Blacks did the same when the White students gave their part of the report. On those few occasions when questions were asked about behavior or attitude or social conditions, the tension was palpable. If a straightforward answer was given, everyone seemed relieved. If the speaker, almost invariably one of the Black students, seemed annoyed, tensions mounted again. Part of the problem was that everyone was playing out their appropriate roles circa 1970, the Black students playing the "insiders" game and saying, in the words of the old Negro spiritual, " 'Nobody knows the trouble I've seen'—and nobody can."

Lastly came the Puerto Ricans. Again, with no representatives present and little general knowledge save for the "I-want-to-be-in-Amer-i-ca" imagery portrayed in *West Side Story*, we reverted to academic oneupmanship. We reviewed and debated what some of the experts, including Oscar Lewis, Elena Padilla, Eduardo Seda-Bonilla, Clarence Senior, and Melvin Tumin described. For example, considering the role of race in Puerto Rican society, one reported began with the contention that, "There is a difference between people raised in a racially continuous society, one where there are people in all walks of life of varying shades, and those who grow up in a racially dichotomous one, where there are whites and nonwhites, like ours."

"True," said another, "Clarence Senior makes the same point. But do you really think race is the main basis of difference?"

"I do," said the first speaker, " 'though I note that it is not such an important factor in the writing of Oscar Lewis. His use of the idea of the 'culture of poverty' would suggest that things are not very different on the island or here, at least for those who are poor. And *he* knows!"

I end my description of the events that led up to this discussion with that last, almost verbatim comment of the white southern Amherst College student who wrote and spoke about Puerto Ricans, people he had admittedly never met, and about the late Oscar Lewis. It seems fitting because it was Lewis himself who, perhaps more than anyone, tried to get outsiders inside the experience of others, who tried to convey the true meaning of culture "in their own words," who provided nonmembers with a vision of what it was like to be poor and Puerto Rican—and Mexican and East Indian. As is well known, even Lewis had difficulty convincing some that he was telling it like it really was and even more difficulty convincing others that he had the right to attempt it.

A Personal Reflection

In all, that seminar set me to thinking again about a problem that has long plagued all of us who study and teach about ethnic experiences. I say "again" for the seminar I described was not the first time I had encountered these issues or tried to deal with them.

The first large scale study I ever conducted was on the meaning of isolation to minority-group members who were strangers in the midst of alien territory. In 1957, I began to explore the character of Jewish life in rural towns and to test certain thoughts I had about the nature of a process sociologists have come to call "the exemption mechanism" and laymen know as the " 'some-of-my-best-friends-are . . .' syndrome."

As I got the small-town Jews to help me tell their stories, I became increasingly intrigued by two phenomena: the first was their incredible allegiance to a group they could "feel" though they could not "touch." They were Jews and they reported, almost to a man and woman, that they constantly felt obligated to play the role of ambassador to the Gentiles. Moving from village to village and gathering life-histories and attitudes and opinions about how they were faring and how successful they were in their ambassadorial roles, I had a growing sense that they might have rather distorted notions about how they were actually being received. That second concern led to a parallel study of some 20 rural communities with less than 5,000 inhabitants, half of which had one to three Jewish families in residence (and about whom I already had information) and half of which had no Jews. I learned that stereotypes persisted in both sets of communities, the only difference being that, in the communities with Jews, exemptions took place.

"Oh, the Cohens are not like other Jews. They're different."

And what of those other Jews? They fulfilled the then-commonly held images to a "T"—or to a "P," for prejudice.[1]

Ten years later, a group of Smith College students and I sought to learn what other social scientists were doing about conveying the meaning of ethnicity through a nationwide survey of university-level courses on racial and ethnic relations. From the study, conducted in the mid-1960s, it was learned that most courses on the subject, despite their different titles, were quite similar. Most teachers concentrated on prejudice but rarely dealt with the issue of power (White or Black); most described in detail the attitudes of dominant group members and the patterns of discrimination which they imposed but, too often, skimmed over the nature of minority reactions and even more rarely attempted to deal with ethnic experiences themselves. Focusing on Black-White tensions, most instructors firmly pronounced that color-blind integration was the answer when, it seemed, they really meant white-washed assimilation.[2] Using a single standard for judging others, they appeared to reflect exactly what James Farmer said so eloquently in his book, *Freedom—When?* published around the time of our study. There (we will remember) he wrote:

> We have found the cult of color-blindness not only quaintly irrelevant but seriously flawed. For we learned that America simply couldn't be colorblind. It would have to become color-blind and it would only become color-blind when we gave up our color.[3]

Looking at the data on over 800 different courses we felt that Farmer's charge, leveled at many of his friends and colleagues and comrades in arms, including a number of sociologists, rang true. Many seemed to interpret most things from the perspective Richard Schermerhorn once labeled as "victimology"—the view that each and every experience must be seen in terms of deprivation, suffering, and attendant social pathologies; that all known as "minorities" are, somehow, rather pathetic specimens to be pitied and cared for.[4] (The implication is, of course, that the resolution of the problem was to facilitate assimilation of those who were deprived.) That many were victims is not to be disputed; that they were *only* victims without culture or character is quite another matter. But few had bothered to listen to what *they* were trying to say.

As many social scientists came, belatedly perhaps, to appreciate the significance of the assertion of ethnic pride, fierce arguments arose about who really knew what was going on. Tensions mounted between the now-skittish professors and the now-assertive and often self-appointed spokespersons as various issues began to be seriously debated regarding the nature of minority experiences and, particularly, those of Black Americans. Among the issues were those focussing on the retention of or loss of "Africanisms," the impact of slavery on personality (the famous "Elkins Debate"), the origins of rebellion and the meaning of revolt, the nature of the Black family (the "Moynihan Controversy"), the northward migration, the civil rights movement, Black Power, and the question of identity itself.

I addressed myself to some of these matters in several lectures and in a lengthy essay in the *Social Science Quarterly* (that turned out to be the basis for Chapter Seven in this book).[5] The essay was a sort of gamble, for I was trying personally to cross the barrier mentioned previously, attempting to deal in some detail with someone else's experiences. That I was partially successful was poignantly conveyed at a conference where I was presenting a paper. A Black conferee came up and said that he felt betrayed. He had read and liked my essay, but was disappointed to find that I was not a "brother." Somebody, he said, must have helped me. The assumption was, once again, that nonmembers could never really cross the threshold. Another conferee was disturbed because he claimed that I said some things that, he felt, were best left unsaid or should be discussed only within "the family."

These views, while troubling, were not unfamiliar. In fact, just about that time, I addressed myself to these very issues in a "Foreword" to Marshall Sklare's excellent little book, *America's Jews*. There I wrote:

   Most of what is written about American Jews comes from the pens of Jewish specialists—novelists and playwrights, journalists and yiddishists, many outside the formal academic community (some within) whose primary concern is to contribute to continuing deliberations with fellow Jews about themselves and their problems. Too frequently it appears that the *sine qua non* for understanding interpretations of Jewish history, the nuances of religious practice, or even contemporary problems is that the reader already be *au courant*. ("If you don't know what I'm talking about, you will never be able to understand.")[6]

The last line sounds quite similar to that of Louis Armstrong who said "If they don't know, you can't tell them." Still, despite the argument that "it isn't the job of the oppressed to educate the oppressor, but simply get him off their backs,"[7] there is a price to pay for such smug insulation and chauvinism. Playing "We've Got a Secret" is no way to help others alter erroneous views. But then there is that other side as the non-Jewish sociologist Ernest van den Haag discovered after he published his book, *The Jewish Mystique*. "Show and Tell" isn't appreciated either—at least not by those written about. In fact, in recent years, as we well know, various "minority" writers, politicians, and professors have decried what they claim are the unwitting as well as intentional distortions by so-called experts on race relations. Whether the criticisms are justified or not, there is no question but that a major part of the effort of those promoting a new ethnic consciousness has been to question the right of *any* outsider to attempt to explain what it means to be something they are not.

The Epistemological Debate

In a very real sense, the problems I discussed above fall within the general realm of the sociology of knowledge and in that part of it popularly referred to as the "Insider-Outsider Debate." As Robert K. Merton has stated, "the sociology of knowledge has long been regarded as a complex and esoteric subject, remote from urgent problems of contemporary life."[8] But, as he indicates, that is certainly not true in the present instance. The Insider-Outsider Debate is complex but it is far from esoteric. Everyone, it seems, has gotten into it. It reaches far beyond the groves of academe, although, to be sure, it is on the campuses where some of the fiercest arguments and confrontations about "who speaks for whom—and who can?" have taken place.

That question has obvious ramifications in all current attempts to understand the nature of dominant-minority relations, the structure and character of plural societies, and ethnic identity itself. It always has. But, in the present temper, it is not surprising that scholarly and dispassionate discourse about sources of knowledge, means of discovering truth, methods of inquiry, and questions of freedom of expression and the control of ideas get embroiled in and often overwhelmed by ideological considerations, the *political* aspects of the old epistemological controversy.

Since the beginning of modern sociology, there have been two contending views about which is the better way to assess social phenomena, through observation or through participation. Histories of sociology and textbooks on social research usually describe the two ideal types: the spectator position, which claims the advantages of distance and detachment, and the participant position, which claims that only through intimacy and involvement—but, note well, not necessarily actual membership—can one ever get to know the subtleties of rules and roles and social relationships.[9]

While these approaches have been discussed and debated by Emile Durkheim, Max Weber, and countless others, and have been variously labeled, for our purposes the former might well be called the "Walter Cronkite Approach," the latter the "Walter Mitty Approach." In the first case the idea is that the researcher looks at society or some segment of it as if through a one-way screen (like watching a battle or a sports event from the sidelines, being able to see how all combatants act, interact, and react from afar). The second type, in its ideal form, is one in which the participant takes on all the characteristics of the object of his or her concern, blending into the scene in order to partake of the activities at first hand. Sometimes he or she has the added advantage of membership but this is rarely discussed and when it is, it is passed over lightly for the assumption is that Walter Mitty can learn to play anybody's role.

In actual fact, many empirically-oriented sociologists have long found themselves hedging their bets. Recognizing the difficulties of both total detachment and full involvement has led to various compromises. One of the most popular techniques taught to American graduate students is that of "participant observation," where investigators are trained to go into the field to record the doings of one group or another not as one of them (a most difficult task in most instances) but by playing roles that give apparent legitimacy to their presence such as claiming to be historians trying to learn about the background of communal life or journalists trying to get a fix on a particular issue. Key informants become critical sources of information in order "to get a point of view of the natives." But there are inevitable limits to what gets reported and what gets left out because of what is told to whom and what is withheld by the real insiders. Many social scientists have become increasingly concerned about such limitations in trying to "get behind the masks." Others have abandoned any efforts to do so, retreating into quantophrenia claiming that "if you can't count it, it doesn't count." Still there are those who continue to pursue their traditional goals, probing and prodding their human subjects in the hope of finding out not only the nature of life among the Cantonese or the Cheyenne or the Chicano (to the best of their limited ability) but also to better understand the broader implications of what they find to the understanding of social interaction, social stratification, and social change. This, they will argue, is, after all, what it is really all about.

If the sociologists in this group were to accept the damnation of those who claim no Outsider can know another's character, then they, along with historians and ethnographers, would have to resign themselves to seeking new careers! Like much of sociology, history and ethnography are also based on the assumption that the Outsider *can* know and *can* understand.

In the essay referred to earlier, Merton spoke to this issue, saying,

If direct engagement in the life of a group is essential to understand it, then the only authentic history is contemporary history, written in fragments by those most fully involved in making inevitably limited portions of it. Rather than constituting only the raw materials of history, the documents prepared by engaged Insiders become all there is to history. But once the historian elects to write the history of a time other than his own, even the most dedicated Insider, of the national, sex, age, racial, ethnic, or religious variety, becomes the Outsider, condemned to error and misunderstanding.[10]

The ethnographer, as Merton reminds us, is very like the historian. Both may be concerned with societies other than those in which they live. Merton quotes Levi-Strauss to illustrate the point.

Whether the *otherness* [or "Outsiderism," in our terms] is due to remoteness in time (however slight) or to remoteness in space, or even to cultural heterogeneity, is of secondary importance compared to the basic similarity of perspective. All that the historian or ethnographer can do, and all that we can expect of either of them, is to enlarge a specific experience to the dimensions of a more general one, which thereby becomes accessible *as experience* to men of another country or another epoch. And in order to succeed, both historian and ethnographer must have the same qualities: skill, precision, a sympathetic approach and objectivity.[11]

We must take note of four key words: skill, precision, sympathy, and objectivity. The assumption remains that one can be properly trained to use the latest in data-gathering techniques—ranging these days from one-way mirrors to interviewing to camouflaged entry; that one can learn to separate the important from the trivial and know the difference; that one can be sympathetic and understanding; that one can hold one's own values in abeyance being the true cultural relativist. The question is, of course, not whether these directives are reasonable goals for a social scientist to strive for but whether they are possible to attain. That is the rub.

I once facetiously defined an ethnographer as "a social scientist who faithfully records his biased view of somebody else." Kidding aside, I believe that some bias is endemic and inevitable in the sort of work we do. What is important, as noted in the quotation of Robert MacIver in Chapter One, is to seek ways to minimize its intrusion.

But bias is not the only problem that confronts the reflective investigator. His or her very presence is often enough to alter the social system itself and to cause various changes, some immediate, some longer ranging.

When I was a graduate student in anthropology, we used to describe the Navaho nuclear family as "mother, father, children, and anthropologist." It wasn't really so funny. Numerous commentators on social change in the Southwest have attested to the impact of the fieldworker. And others have mentioned their own disruptive effects on those they sought to study with sensitivity and compassion. Oscar Lewis, for example, was greatly concerned when the real "children of Sanchez" gained worldwide recognition and celebrity and were, in his words, never able to be themselves again.

So intrusion in and of itself is an issue and it cannot be dismissed. (I will have more to say about it further along.)

Before going on, however, it should be remembered that Walter Cronkite and Walter Mitty, the nonparticipant and the full participant, are both Outsiders. Though they may claim expertise, they are not (or rarely are) part of that which they are studying.

Insiders are different. In general, they are not methodologists but members; they share not a set of professional tools but what many claim is a sort of "privileged access" to that which only they say they can know and feel.[12] Their concern about themselves is not abstract but immediate; it is not intellectual but visceral; it is not objective but highly subjective. In the broadest sense, whether corporate executives, college professors, guest workers, Pakistani villagers, Blacks in Bedford-Stuyvesant, or small-town Jews, they are united (as noted in earlier chapters) by an interdependence of fate and a fellowfeeling that, most argue, cannot be penetrated. Monopolists of culture, they are the "We," as Kipling said, and "everyone else is They."[13] They belong, in the words of William Graham Sumner, to "in-groups" and few would deny their own ethnocentrism.

After defining "ethnocentrism" (discussed in Chapter Four) Sumner continued, explaining that,

Folkways correspond to it [ethnocentrism] to cover both the inner and outer relation. Each group nourishes its own pride and vanity, boasts itself superior, exalts its own divinities, and looks with contempt on outsiders . . . the most important fact is that ethnocentrism leads a people to exaggerate and intensify everything in their own folkways which is peculiar and which differentiates them from others. . . .[14]

Insiders, the subjects of many of our researches, dubious about the premise that Outsiders are value-free or ethnically-neutral, rarely make such claims for themselves. Most, if asked—and until recently, rarely have they been asked—to explain their lives, would stress that it is in the very values and biases and nuances of personal existence, that is, in the folkways and the mores, that the true warp and weft of the social fabric is to be comprehended. Further, those who speak for them would argue that only they and a few enlightened souls who share their outlooks, if not always their statuses or appearances, have access to their *sanctum sanctorum*, whether village or neighborhood, barrio, ghetto or psychological turf.

Black versus Mainstream Sociology

In recent years, this point of view has been most explicitly articulated by certain Black intellectuals, including those who contend "that only Black historians can truly understand Black history, only Black ethnologists can understand Black culture, only Black sociologists can understand the social life of Blacks and so on."[15] Typical of the views reflecting this stance are Joyce Ladner's remarks in the introduction to her edited volume *The Death of White Sociology*.

> Why a book on "Black sociology"? Is there such a discipline? Many readers, indeed, will argue that sociology, like physics, is without color and can validly apply the same methodology and theoretical framework, regardless of the ethnic, racial and other backgrounds of the group under investigation.
>
> But sociology, like history, economics, and psychology, exists in a domain where color, ethnicity, and social class are of primary importance. And, as long as this holds true, it is impossible for sociology to claim that it maintains value neutrality in its approach.[16]

This bold statement is supported by a selective review of the writings of some of the most prominent sociologists whom generations of students and scholars came to believe had some objective understanding of Black life. Ladner suggests that many of them misrepresented what they were purportedly trying to describe. Robert Park, for example, former newspaperman, advisor to Booker T. Washington, and founder of the famed Chicago School of Sociology, and his collaborator Ernest W. Burgess, described Negro character as follows:

> The temperament of the Negro as [we] conceive of it consists in a few elementary but distinctive characteristics, determined by physical organizations and transmitted biologically. These characteristics manifest themselves in a genial, sunny, and social disposition, in an interest in and attachment to external, physical things rather than to subjective states and objects of introspection, in a disposition for expression rather than enterprise and action.[17]

And Edward B. Reuter, author of *The American Race Problem*, one of the first textbooks in the sociology of race relations, boldly asserted:

> [The Negroes] were without ancestral pride or family tradition. They had no distinctive language or religion. These, like their folkways and moral customs, were but recently acquired from the whites and furnished no nucleus for a racial unity. The group was without even a tradition of historical unity or racial achievements. There were no historic names, no great achievements, no body of literature, no artistic productions. The whole record of the race was one of servile or barbarian status apparently without a point about which a sentimental complex could be formed.[18]

Ladner says that "one could argue that the doctrines of racial inferiority which these men sought to document scientifically have been disposed of."[19] In fairness, she might have pointed out that Park and many of his colleagues repudiated some of their earlier contentions in view of what they learned. And what they learned often came from the researches and writings of a number of Black commentators, including W. E. B. Du Bois, James Weldon Johnson, Bertram W. Doyle, Charles S. Johnson, Arna Bontemps to name but a few of the better known figures.

Despite the backing-off of some of the harsher judgments about the lack of a meaningful past or of a significant culture, certain themes have persisted. Not surprisingly, many prominent historians and sociologists continue to be cited as reflecting an incredible lack of sensitivity about the ambiguous meaning of being Black in White America. Consider again the following statement by Nathan Glazer and Daniel Patrick Moynihan, made in the first edition of *Beyond the Melting Pot* (and mentioned in Chapter Seven):

... It is not possible for Negroes to view themselves as other ethnic groups viewed themselves because—and this the key to much in the Negro world—the Negro is only an American and nothing else. He has no values and culture to guard and protect.[20]

Not only Black critics have charged the mainstream sociologists with bias, ignorance, or naivety. In 1972 Stanford Lyman presented a rather devastating critique of the way in which many prominent experts failed in their efforts to deal with Black ethnicity. His argument is an interesting one. He contends that neither Park nor John Dollard nor Gunnar Myrdal nor Gordon Allport nor T. W. Adorno nor Talcott Parsons (who edited a large *Daedalus* volume on *The Negro American*) ever really understood "the American dilemma."

Condemning the proclivity of these and other social scientists to follow the Aristotelian view "that science could only study that which behaved in accordance with slow, orderly, continuous, and teleological movement," Lyman argued that they were led "to make radical separation of events from processes."[21] As legatees of evolutionary anthropology and nineteenth century functionalism, many sociologists seemed to have been wedded to notions of unilinear development, set stages, fixed trends. In chapter after chapter, Lyman attempts to explain what is wrong with such assumptions and then offers a back-handed compliment to those he criticized, saying, "Despite the contradicting arguments of these studies, they have supplied valuable insights on the race issue, sensitized many readers to hitherto unnoticed features of American life, and, with widely varying degrees of optimism, suggested that a resolution to the black problem might be found."[22] In other words, the sociologists of race relations reflected, in many ways, one of the most significant *leitmotifs* of the discipline itself, a kind of liberal conservatism, a faith in the system which many believed was capable of righting historic wrongs inflicted on the victims of past injustices, of dealing with but never solving the dilemma.

To Lyman, and increasing numbers of other commentators, the proper sociology of Black people (and others in similar straits) has to address itself to existential matters and deal with the disjunctive, marginal, and often absurd position of those caught between two worlds. For too long, Lyman claimed, the mainstream sociologist's view of the Black has, in Camus' terms, "divorced him from his [real] life, removed the actor from his setting, denied that he has any existence at all—no past, no future. . ."[23] and though Camus might not have used such words, I would add, "no soul."

Ladner in her way and Lyman in his—and a host of others—argue that Blacks have always been measured against an alien set of norms. As Ladner puts it:

Mainstream sociology . . . reflects the ideology of the larger society, which has always excluded Black life-styles, values, behavior, attitudes, and so forth from the body of data that is used to define, describe, conceptualize and theorize about the structure and functions of American society. Sociology has in a similar manner excluded the totality of Black existence from its major theories, except insofar as it has deviated from the so-called norms.[24]

The generalization is sweeping, but, from my experience, bears more than a kernel of truth. Blacks have too frequently been seen as a residual category or deviant group, not as part of the general cross-section. One simple example is the tendency of statisticians and survey analysts to use the White/non-White dichotomy as a critical one, often dropping the latter from analysis because they are *assumed* to be so different, even when close examination would indicate that such other variables, as gender, level of education, and social class are more critical in distinguishing people on many issues than race or ethnic group membership.

There is a strange paradox in all this. As was evident in discussions of affirmative action and set-aside policies in Chapters Seven, Eight, and Nine, these days school administrators, government officials, and social scientists find themselves damned when they fail to draw distinctions based on race or ethnicity after having been berated for making such "discriminating distinctions." The charge is, once again, that outsiders fail to recognize the uniqueness of those who are different.

A growing number of "minority" social scientists and even more lay people have begun to echo the sentiment. The argument is that old and familiar cry of insiders mentioned in my introduction. Not only can no outsider comprehend what others experience, they have no adequate frame of reference with which to assess it. Lerone Bennett spoke for many Blacks when he wrote:

It is necessary for us to develop a new frame of reference which transcends the limits of white concepts. It is necessary for us to develop and maintain a total intellectual offensive against the false universality of white concepts, whether they are expressed by William Styron or Daniel Patrick Moynihan. By and large, reality has been conceptualized in terms of the small minority of white men who live in Europe and in North America. We must abandon the partial frame of reference of our oppressors and create new concepts which will release our reality, which is also the reality of the overwhelming majority of men and women on this globe. We must say to the white world that there are things in the world that are not dreamt of in your history and your sociology and your philosophy. . . .[25]

Bennett carried the argument to the extreme by advocating not a universalistic model but one which looks at the world from *his* rather than someone else's perspective. William J. Wilson has pointed out that, in reality, this is quite intentional for many "black Insiders . . . [argue] that the ultimate aim of black social science should not be to achieve scientific adequacy but to conduct research and produce writing that aids in black liberation."[26] He does not object to the use of social science findings for political purposes but does take exception to the politicization of social science itself.

The political scientist Martin Kilson, among others, has been even more forceful in warning against the tendency to exchange a White perspective for a Black one. Referring to early debates over Afro-American Studies, where these issues were emotionally discussed, he wrote,

> . . . we must be frank about this, what this amounts to is racism in reverse— black racism. I am certainly convinced that it is important for the Negro to know of his past—of his ancestors, of their strengths and weaknesses—and they should respect this knowledge, when it warrants respect, and they should question it and criticize it when it deserves criticism. But it is of no advantage to a mature and critical understanding or appreciation of one's heritage if you approach that heritage with the assumption that it is intrinsically good and noble, and intrinsically superior to the heritage of other peoples. That is, after all, what the white racists have done; and none of my militant friends in the black studies movement have convinced me that racist thought is any less vulgar and degenerate because it is used by black men. . . .[27]

Kilson did two things in his essay. He challenged the assumption that only the Insider has access to truth (and beauty) and he did so as a member of the very group in question. As a Black political scientist he is a sort of "Insider Without," the equivalent, in this particular context, to the "Outsider Within," the person who has successfully penetrated the veil of suspicion.

"Insiders Without" are called by many names. "Tom" is one. But it is not the only one, as many who labeled Kilson "courageous" will attest.

"Outsiders Within" are also called different things, the two most common are "friend" and "foe." Friends are those acceptable strangers who are exempted from the rule that claims that membership is the key to understanding. The *bona fides* of Friends depend in large measure on their ability to reflect the current ideological stance regarding the position of those they study. This is not to denigrate their efforts but one cannot help but point out that even the fortune of friends is fickle.

If, for example, William Styron had published his version of *The Confessions of Nat Turner* ten years earlier, it is conceivable that he would have been praised rather than damned for making the protagonist a religious-type leader rather than a revolutionary; and even Senator Moynihan, that *bête blanche* of so many critics, might have been applauded instead of excoriated for saying what a number of Black scholars, including Kenneth Clark, had already said, had he presented *The Negro Family: A Case for National Action* a decade before he did.[28] And, by contrast, a decade before, Robert Blauner might have been attacked for turning the race problem into a class problem, which, of course, many feel it is.

But Styron and Moynihan, as Joyce Ladner stated in the essay quoted earlier, were not to be viewed as Friends in the 1960s. They were Foes or "Ofays." Foes are seen as members of the enemy camp who pretend to be your friend but are really engaging in exploitation. They are not there to learn from you, goes the argument, but to take from you. And they often engage in surreptitious entry.

Indeed, it may well be that there is in fact great suspicion of Outsiders not because they cannot ever learn the Insider's problems (á la Louis Armstrong's contention) but because in fact they've got his number. This, I contend, underlays much of what is objected to by those who see the Outsider—whether social scientist or politician or simply as an agent of The Man—as able to expose their innermost thoughts and exploit their weaknesses.

This view, the last I shall discuss, is expressed with brutal clarity not only in the writings of some Black (and other minority) sociologists but also by many essayists and novelists and poets and playwrights like Ishmael Reed, Maya Angelou, Toni Morrison, and LeRoi Jones. Take Jones for a moment and his bitter play, *Dutchman*.

The setting is a subway in New York. Two characters, Lula, a White woman (the symbolic Outsider), and Clay, a Black man, are engaged in a heated conversation. Lula taunts Clay, "You're afraid of white people. And your father was. Uncle Tom Big Lip!"

Clay slaps her as hard as he can across the mouth and Lula's head bangs against the back of the seat. When she raises it again, Clay slaps her again.

"Now shut up and let me talk," he says. And then, with rising anger he begins to berate her.

As the argument continues, Clay pushes Lula back into her seat. "I'm not telling you again, Tallulah Bankhead! Luxury. In your face and your fingers. You telling me what I ought to do. Well don't! Don't you tell me anything! If I'm a middle class fake white man . . . let me be. And let me be in the way I want."[29]

He lets loose a tirade of vituperation and venom, mocking Lula and all she stands for. But beneath the surface one feels a tension, a tension between being found out and of losing control because somehow Lula/Outsider seems to know Clay's vulnerability.

Clay is an Insider whose psychic space has been invaded by Lula, the embodiment of White power and White intrusion. But when she realizes that Clay knows she knows, she must destroy him and she does. She stabs him and he dies. The circle is closed and the oppressor remains in control.

New Sources of Data

So, where are we?

It is apparent that the understandable suspicions of Insiders are as inhibiting to any attempts to understand the meaning of ethnicity and to reduce intergroup tensions as are the alleged and real biases of Outsiders. Is there any way out of the dilemma? How does one answer the following sets of questions?

1. Can Outsiders ever become expert enough to know the right questions to ask, to obtain meaningful information about others, and be able to interpret them? Even if this is possible, is it right? Who is to define the boundaries between acceptable inquiry on the one hand and unacceptable intrusion on the other? The investigator? The subjects of research? If the latter, how does one seek and obtain permission to enter their physical domain or cultural space?

2. Insiders may know themselves but do they fully understand why they are the way they are? Does it matter? If it does, who is to help them? An Outsider? If Insiders accept that there is some merit in having others enter, especially as Friends, will they be willing to lower their guards enough to let those Outsiders have access to personal information and innermost thoughts? Or will the acceptable strangers invariably have to be on guard against the pontification of "inside dopesters" who tell only what they think the others want to hear or what they think others should hear rather than what they truly believe and actually feel?

3. Finally, recognizing the limits of both distance and intimacy, of detachment and involvement, accepting that there are and will always be competing claims to truth and insight, and being mindful of the very real political aspects of the whole debate, can we ever comprehend the full meaning of ethnicity and get inside someone else's world?

Given my personal concerns and the circumstances that led to interest in the whole subject, I would like to end by addressing myself to the last set of questions in particular.

There are things that I still believe a well-trained social scientist brings to any situation, not least framework of inquiry (discussed in many parts of this book), a comparative focus, and an interest in the particular mainly (though I can hardly say exclusively) to better understand the more general. There are things that must remain at more than arm's length, things that can never be directly experienced. As a white person, I will never be Black; as a man, I will never be a woman. But, in addition to the obvious fact that there are Black social scientists and female ones (who may have my problems in reverse), it is also possible to experience things vicariously, through careful study of the acts and art and artifacts of others, through what they do and say and produce for themselves *and* for others. I am referring not only to the materials based on formal interviews or field studies or answers to questionnaires but also to the commentaries and polemics of "members" and to portraits painted in the lofty and lowly literature of a given group. I am referring not only to what my colleagues and I can gather as we stand on the outside peering in but also to what people say to and for each other.

The fact is that too many sociologists have often overlooked or avoided dealing with one of the richest lodes of empirical data there is for understanding cultural phenomena in modern societies, the personal histories, novels and poems and plays and essays and letters home that, long ago, such masters as Florian Znaniecki, co-author of *The Polish Peasant in America*, warned us not to ignore.[30]

While it neither rejects Functionalist-Consensus Theory (which stresses integration and pluralism) or Marxist-Conflict Theory (which emphasizes power struggles and polarization), the approach I am suggesting incorporates the tradition of the symbolic interactionists and some of the ethnomethodologists. This perspective is as concerned with posturing and posing, with fronts and masks, as with what underlies them. It is as important to be as concerned with perceptions of reality as reality itself.

The scholarly and political and literary and personal works of Insiders offer special insights into the character of societies and communities and the minds of those within them. The writers and their subjects—and their characters—are, in a very real sense, key informants, better ones in many cases than the sycophants we have often had to rely on in our scientific surveys. Lerone Bennett is thus a key informant; so is LeRoi Jones or Imira Baraka (the name Jones adopted after writing *Dutchman*). So, too, are Lula and Clay. Richard Wright is such a key informant as are his characters Bigger Thomas and "The Man who Lived Underground." Maya Angelou is one; so is her "Momma." And the same can be said for Jewish commentators real and fictitious from Abraham Cahan and David Levinsky to Philip Roth and Nathan Zuckerman; it can be said for James T.

Farrell, Studs Lonigan, and Danny O'Neill; for Mario Puzo and his "fortunate pilgrims"; for Oscar Lewis and for Cruz; for Harry Petrakis and the descendents of Pericles. In fact, it can be said of hundreds of writers whose descriptions and characterizations allow readers to be temporarily transported into another world, to feel what it is like to have another *Weltanschauung*, to sense the tension of marginality so simply but poignantly portrayed over 50 years ago in Countee Cullen's brief poem, "Incident."

> Once riding in old Baltimore,
> Heart-filled, head-filled with glee,
> I saw a Baltimorean
> Keep looking straight at me.
>
> Now I was eight and very small,
> And he was no whit bigger,
> And so I smiled, but he poked out
> His tongue and called me, "Nigger."
>
> I saw the whole of Baltimore
> From May until December:
> Of all the things that happened there
> That's all that I remember.[31]

Cullen helps us to feel what it means to be a Black child in White America. His words are a part of what I see as an expanded data bank, to be included in our analyses alongside the facts and figures and technical assessments. They add substantive gristle to the theoretical bones and to the cold statistics.

Reading real literature along with what we are wont to call the literature, looking at cultural material not conventionally considered as "data" may have the latent function for social scientists of reconnecting us with our humanistic brothers and sisters. It does not mean abandoning the sociological perspective. That orientation still offers to provide the framework within which to understand what is being read, the larger picture of the systems in which people live and work and play and suffer, the context in which to indicate and test the variables that relate to human affairs everywhere.

After all, Blacks like Whites, Jews like Gentiles, Chicanos like Anglos, Irish Protestants and Irish Catholics institutionalize their behavior patterns, set criteria for the conferring or denying of status, indicate the tolerance limits of accepted and expected behavior, and maintain social systems of great intricacy even when they, themselves, have difficulty articulating their character. To explain these things is and should remain the primary role of the sociologist.

Postscript

Beyond the last thought there is no real conclusion to this series of ruminations save for the fact that I now feel very strongly that the work of the sociologist is like that of the Japanese judge in *Rashomon*, the one who asks various witnesses and participants to describe a particular event as seen through their own eyes. Like the judge, neither teachers of sociology nor students can be allowed to get off the hook. We must analyze the disparate pieces of evidence and then try to figure out how they fit together. If we use the suggested approach of broadening what in the trade we call our data base, then, perhaps, we *will* be better able to know the troubles others have seen and be better able to understand them.

NOTES

1. See Peter I. Rose, *Strangers in their Midst: Small-Town Jews and Their Neighbors* (Merrick, N.Y.: Richwood Publishing Co., 1977).
2. See Peter I. Rose, *The Subject Is Race: Traditional Ideologies and the Teaching of Race Relations* (New York: Oxford University Press, 1968).
3. James Farmer, *Freedom—When?* (New York: Random House, 1965), p. 87.
4. Richard A. Schermerhorn, *Comparative Ethnic Relations* (New York: Random House, 1970), pp. 8–9.
5. See Peter I. Rose, "The Black Experience: Issues and Images," *Social Science Quarterly* 15, No. 2 (September 1969), 286–297; and Peter I. Rose (ed.), *Slavery and Its Aftermath*, Vol. I and *Old Memories, New Moods*, Vol. II of *Americans from Africa* (New York: Atherton, 1970).
6. Peter I. Rose, Foreword to Marshall Sklare, *America's Jews* (New York: Random House, 1971), p. ix.
7. Jules Chametsky, "Race in American Life: A Personal View," *Fresh Ink* (October 20, 1977), p. 3.
8. Robert K. Merton, "Insiders and Outsiders: A Chapter in the Sociology of Knowledge," *American Journal of Sociology*, 24 (July 1972), p. 9.
9. See, e.g., Norbert Elias, "Problems of Involvement and Detachment," *British Journal of Sociology* (1956), pp. 226–252; and Johan Goudsblom, *Sociology in the Balance* (Oxford: Basil Blackwell, 1977), especially pp. 180–186.
10. Merton, *op. cit.*, p. 32.
11. Claude Levi-Strauss, *Structural Anthropology* (New York: Basic Books, 1963), p. 16 (Originally published in 1949).
12. Merton, *op. cit.*, pp. 11–12.
13. Rudyard Kipling, "We and They," in *Debits and Credits* (London: Macmillan, 1926), pp. 327–328.
14. William Graham Sumner, *Folkways* (Boston: Ginn and Company, 1906), p. 13.
15. Merton, *op. cit.*, p. 13.
16. Joyce A. Ladner, "Introduction," *The Death of White Sociology* (New York: Random House, 1973), p. xix.

17. Robert E. Park and Ernest W. Burgess, *Introduction to the Science of Sociology* (Chicago: University of Chicago Press, 1924), pp. 138–139.
18. Edward B. Reuter, *The American Race Problem* (New York: T. Y. Crowell, 1970), p. 365 (originally published in 1927).
19. Ladner, *op. cit.*, p. xxii.
20. Nathan Glazer and Daniel P. Moynihan, *Beyond the Melting Pot* (Cambridge, Mass.: M.I.T. Press, 1965), p. 53.
21. Stanford M. Lyman, *The Black American in Sociological Thought* (New York: Capricorn Books, 1972), p. 24. See also pp. 28–31, 166–168.
22. *Ibid.*, p. 175.
23. *Ibid.*, p. 183.
24. Ladner, *op. cit.*, p. xxiii.
25. Lerone Bennett, "The Challenge of Blackness," (as quoted in Ladner, p. xiii).
26. See William J. Wilson, "The New Black Sociology: Reflections on the 'Insiders' and 'Outsiders' Controversy," in James E. Blackwell and Morris Janowitz, (eds.) *Black Sociologists: Historical and Contemporary Perspectives* (Chicago: University of Chicago Press, 1974), p. 328.
27. Martin Kilson, "Black Studies Movement: A Plea for Perspective," *Crisis*, 76 (October 1969), 329–330 (as quoted in Merton, *op. cit.*, p. 26).
28. Many Black leaders have returned to the very themes that Moynihan wrote about—and was criticized for—25 years ago.
29. LeRoi Jones, *Dutchman* (New York: William Morrow and Company 1964), p. 33–34.
30. Florian Znaniecki, *The Method of Sociology* (New York: Farrar and Rinehart, 1934).
31. Countee Cullen, "Incident," from *On These I Stand* (New York: Harper & Brothers, 1925).

PERMISSIONS ACKNOWLEDGMENTS

SELECTED BIBLIOGRAPHY

Nearly 200 books are listed here. Included are histories, textbooks, studies, essays, anthologies, and works of fiction. These volumes are a fraction of the many sources available to those who wish to study racial and ethnic relations in the United States—or any of its aspects—more closely. They represent the breadth of work in the field and the variety of approaches used to explore racial and ethnic relations in the United States.

Abrams, Charles. *Forbidden Neighbors*. New York: Harper & Row, 1955.
One of a number of studies of discrimination in housing in post-World War II America.

Adorno, T. W. et al. *The Authoritarian Personality*. New York: Harper & Row, 1950.
A study of prejudice and personality. The "F Scale" and others are introduced and used here.

Alba, Richard D., editor. *Ethnicity and Race in the U.S.A.* New York: Routledge, 1988.
Eight sociological analyses of key issues facing white and non-white American minorities at the end of the 20th century.

Allport, Gordon W. *The Nature of Prejudice*. Cambridge: Addison-Wesley, 1954.
One of the most comprehensive and best known early texts on the social psychology of prejudice.

Anderson, Charles H. *White Protestant Americans*. Englewood, N.J.: Prentice-Hall, 1970.
A socio-historical analysis, "from national origin to religious group."

Archdeacon, Thomas S. *Becoming American*, New York: The Free Press, 1983.
An ethnic history of the U.S.

Asch, Sholem. *East River*. New York: Putnam, 1946.
Ghetto life in New York during the early part of this century is the subject of this work.

Bahr, Howard M., Bruce A. Chadwick, and Joseph H. Strauss, *America's Ethnicity*. Lexington, Mass.: D. C. Heath, 1979.
A collection of essays on minority experiences. Especially useful are essays on Native-Americans and Mexican-Americans.

Baldwin, James. *The Fire Next Time*. New York: Dial Press, 1963.
A prophetic essay about White oppression and Black response.

————. *Go Tell It on the Mountain.* New York: Knopf, 1952.

Baldwin's first novel. A story based on his early life as a preacher's son living in Harlem.

————. *Nobody Knows My Name: More Notes of a Native Son.* New York: Dial Press, 1961.

Essays on his Black experience by the famous novelist.

Baltzell, E. Digby. *The Protestant Establishment.* New York: Random House, 1964.

A study of the caste-line of privilege maintained by certain members of society which keeps others from access to power. Baltzell's special concern is with anti-Semitism.

Banton, Michael. *Race Relations.* New York: Basic Books, 1967.

Written by an English anthropologist, this volume offers a variety of approaches to the study of race relations. It includes analyses of the American scene.

Bash, Harry H. *Sociology, Race and Ethnicity.* New York: Gordon and Bream, 1979.

A detailed critique of American ideological influences on theories about race relations.

Bellow, Saul. *Mister Sammler's Planet.* New York: Viking, 1970.

A novel about a European-Jewish refugee in America and his attempts to understand racial conflict in the 1960s.

Bentz, Thomas. *New Immigrants: Portraits in Passage,* New York: Pilgrim Press, 1981.

Glimpses into the lives of 13 New Americans.

Bettelheim, Bruno and Morris Janowitz. *Social Change and Prejudice.* New York: Free Press, 1965.

Two books in one, the authors include the full text of their earlier study "The Dynamics of Prejudice" and a reassessment of that study two decades later.

Blackwell, James and Morris Janowitz, eds. *Black Sociologists: Historical and Contemporary Perspectives.* Chicago: University of Chicago Press, 1974.

A series of essays.

Blalock, Hubert M., Jr. *Toward a Theory of Minority-Group Relations.* New York: Wiley, 1967.

An attempt to systematize theory in the study of racial and ethnic relations. Special attention to socio-economic factors, competition, and power.

Blauner, Bob. *Black Lives, White Lives,* Berkeley: University of California Press, 1989.

A longitudinal study of three decades of race relations in America.

Bloom, Leonard and Ruth Riemer. *Removal and Return.* Berkeley: University of California Press, 1949.

A study of the relocation of Japanese-Americans during World War II and of their experiences after being released from internment camps.

Branch, Taylor. *Parting the Waters*. New York: Simon and Schuster, 1989. American society in the age of Martin Luther King, Jr. and his critical role in the civil rights movement.

Burma, John, ed. *Mexican-Americans in the United States*. New York: Schenkman, 1970. A collection of readings.

Cade, Tony, ed. *The Black Woman*. New York: New America Library, 1970. An anthology of commentaries on the Black Power movement and the women's liberation movement from the perspectives of Black women.

Carmichael, Stokely and Charles V. Hamilton. *Black Power: The Politics of Liberation*. New York: Vintage, 1967. The former director of the Student Nonviolent Coordinating Committee and a political scientist examine the meaning of Black Power and the role it could play in American society.

Christie, Richard, and Marie Jahoda, eds. *Studies in Scope and Method of "The Authoritarian Personality."* Glencoe, Ill.: Free Press, 1954. An examination and critique of the studies of "The Authoritarian Personality."

Clark, Kenneth. *Dark Ghetto: Dilemmas of Social Power*. New York: Harper & Row, 1965. The results of the famous Harlem Youth Opportunities Unlimited (HARYOU) program and a commentary on life in the ghetto by a noted social psychologist.

Cox, Oliver C. *Caste, Class and Race: A Study of Social Dynamics*. New York: Doubleday, 1948. An examination of the economic basis of prejudice and racial oppression.

Cronin, E.D. *Black Moses*. Madison: University of Wisconsin Press, 1957. A biography of Marcus Garvey and commentary on his Universal Negro Improvement Association.

Cruse, Harold. *The Crisis of the Negro Intellectual*. New York: William Morrow, 1967. A cultural history and commentary on Black writing, politics, and artistic involvement.

Cullen, Countee. *Color*. New York: Harper, 1925. A book of poems on Black life by a great Black poet.

Dean, John P. and Alex Rosen. *A Manual of Intergroup Relations*. Chicago: The University of Chicago Press. 1955. A short book on prejudice, discrimination, and suggested ways for resolving intergroup tensions.

DiDonato, Pietro. *Christ in Concrete.* New York: Bobbs Merrill, 1939. A poignant story about Italians in the building trades in the 1930s.

Dinnerstein, Leonard, ed. *Anti-Semitism in the U.S.* New York: Harper & Row, 1971.
An edited collection of historical essays.

———— and David Reimers. *Ethnic America.* New York: Harper & Row, 3rd ed., 1988.
A concise history of "the ethnic experience" of many Americans.

Dissent. Winter 1972.
The entire issue is devoted to the working class. Of particular interest are papers on class and ethnicity.

Dixon, Vernon J. and Badi Foster, eds. *Beyond Black and White.* Boston: Little, Brown, 1971.
A collection of papers on the conflict between Black and White Americans and a discussion of the concept of a di-unital approach to help to understand, then deal with it.

Dollard, John. *Caste and Class in a Southern Town.* New Haven: Yale University Press, 1937.
The famous study which examines the bases for prejudice in a southern community. Noted for the combination of Marxian and Freudian perspectives.

————, et al. *Frustration and Aggression.* New Haven: Yale University Press, 1939.
Psychological determinants of behavior are considered in this series of essays.

Drake, St. Clair and Horace Cayton. *Black Metropolis.* New York: Harcourt, Brace, 1945.
A study of the Black community of Chicago.

Du Bois, W. E. B. *The Souls of Black Folks,* 1903. (Reprinted in many editions.)
A classic portrait of Negro life by an important sociologist and famous Black leader.

Duff, John B. *The Irish in the United States.* Belmont, Calif.: Wadsworth, 1971.
A socio-historical analysis.

Duran, Livie Isauro and H. Russell Bernard, eds. *Introduction to Chicano Studies.* New York: Macmillan, 1973.
A reader on the past, present, and future status of Mexican-Americans.

Dworkin, Anthony Gary and Rosalind, J., eds. *The Minority Report.* New York: Holt Rinehart Winston, 2d ed. 1982.
Sociological analyses of the state of racial and ethnic relations in the United States.

Easterlin, Richard A. et al. *Immigration.* Cambridge, Mass.: Belknap Press of Harvard University Press, 1982.

Four essays on the economic and social characteristics of immigrations to the United States, their settlement patterns and spatial distribution, American immigration policy, and the process of "naturalization."

Ellis, John Tracy. *American Catholicism.* Chicago: University of Chicago Press, 1956.

Ellis discusses Catholics in colonial America during the nineteenth century (with particular emphasis on mass immigration and Protestant reaction) and in more recent times.

Ellison, Ralph. *Invisible Man.* New York: Random House, 1962.

A symbolic novel about the Black man's search for identity in America.

Essien-Udom, E. U. *Black Nationalism.* Chicago: University of Chicago, 1962.

An African's assessment of the Black Muslim movement and its appeal.

Farmer, James. *Freedom, When?* New York: Random House, 1966.

The co-founder of CORE, the now almost defunct Congress of Racial Equality, looks back at his and others' experiences in the civil rights movement.

Foner, Philip S., ed. *The Black Panthers Speak.* Philadelphia: J. B. Lippincott, 1970.

A collection of essays including the Black Panther Party's noted platform and excerpts from the writings of Huey P. Newton, Bobby Seale, Eldridge Cleaver, and others.

Francis, E. K. *Interethnic Relations.* New York: Elsevier, 1976.

A series of essays by one of the first sociologists to use the term "ethnicity."

Franklin, John Hope. *From Slavery to Freedom,* 3rd ed. New York: Knopf, 1967.

A historian's portrayal of the Black experience in Africa and the United States.

Frazier, E. Franklin. *Black Bourgeoisie.* Glencoe, Ill.: Free Press, 1957.

A controversial study of the Negro middle class.

Frederickson, George M. *The Arrogance of Race,* Middletown: Wesleylan University Press, 1988.

A historical perspective on slavery, racism, and racial inequality by one of America's leading historians.

Friedman, Murray, ed. *Overcoming Middle Class Rage.* Philadelphia: Westminster Press, 1971.

A series of papers dealing with the views and relations of White working- and middle-class Americans to the changes wrought by Black consciousness and the Black Power movement.

Gans, Herbert. *The Urban Villagers.* New York: Free Press, 1962.

A study of social interaction and social class in an Italian-American neighborhood in Boston.

Glazer, Nathan, ed. *Clamor at the Gates.* San Francisco: Institute for

Contemporary Studies, 1985.

A series of original papers on the character of the post-1965 immigration to the United States.

———. *Ethnic Dilemmas: 1964–1982.* Cambridge, Mass.: Harvard University Press, 1983.

A collection of papers on Blacks, Jews, and others; on pluralism and bilingualism; and on affirmative action.

———. *Affirmative Discrimination.* New York: Basic Books, 1978.

A critical look at recent social policies which, the author claims, are as discriminatory as the norms they are intended to redress.

———. *Remembering the Answers.* New York: Basic Books, 1970.

Glazer's essays on the student revolt of the 1960s and related matters.

——— and Daniel Patrick Moynihan. *Beyond the Melting Pot,* 2nd ed. Cambridge: MIT Press, 1970.

An examination of New York City's five major minorities: Black, Puerto Rican, Jewish, Italian, and Irish. The book is concerned with the meaning of cultural pluralism and the tenacity of identity. The introduction to this revised edition is particularly important for here the authors review the profound changes that occurred in New York—and elsewhere—since 1963, when the first edition was published.

Glock, Charles Y. and Ellen Siegelman, eds. *Prejudice, U.S.A.* New York: Praeger, 1969.

A collection of essays reporting on recent studies of prejudice in America.

Gomez, Rudolph, Clement Cottingham, Jr., Russell Endo, and Kathleen Jackson, eds. *The Social Realities of Ethnic America.* Lexington, Mass.: D. C. Heath, 1975.

A collection of essays on Native Americans, Blacks, Mexican-Americans, and Japanese-Americans, intended as an introductory textbook.

Gordon, Milton M. and Richard Lambert, eds. *America as a Multicultural Society.* Philadelphia: The Annals of the Academy of Political and Social Science, 1981.

Essays on the American people with a particular focus on minorities and intergroup relations.

Gordon, Milton M. *Assimilation in American Life.* New York: Oxford University Press, 1964.

An analysis of varying patterns of "assimilation" in the United States. Of particular note is Gordon's typology of assimilation and his discussion of the relationship betwen social class and ethnicity.

———. *Human Nature, Class and Ethnicity.* New York: Oxford, 1978.

A collection of the author's most important essays.

Greeley, Andrew M. *That Most Distressful Nation.* New York: Quadrangle Books, 1972.

A study of Irish America.

———. *Ethnicity in the United States.* New York: Wiley, 1974.

An examination of the demography of ethnic identification, the religio-ethnic composition and distribution of the American population, and the educational and social differences among various social and ethnic groups.

——. *Why Can't They Be Like Us?* New York: Dutton, 1971.

Reports on research and the attitudes of "white ethnics" to Blacks and others and a series of commentaries on the resurgence of ethnicity in recent years.

Grier, William H. and Price M. Cobbs. *Black Rage.* New York: Basic Books, 1968.

Two psychiatrists explore personality problems which, they claim, are attributable to racial oppression.

Grodzins, Morton. *The Metropolitan Area as a Racial Problem.* Pittsburgh: University of Pittsburgh Press, 1958.

A prophetic booklet which describes the character of discrimination in the American city of the 1950s.

Gurin, Patricia et al. *Black Consciousness, Identity and Achievement.* New York: Wiley, 1975.

A study of Black colleges conducted in the late 1960s.

Gutman, Herbert. *The Black Family in Slavery and Freedom, 1950–1975.* New York: Random House, 1976.

One of the best studies of family life among Black Americans. The book challenges the myth of the inevitable "problem home."

Haley, Alex. *Roots.* New York: Dell, 1977.

A widely read and often criticized historical novel about slavery and its legacy as seen through the experiences of the members of a single family.

Handlin, Oscar. *The Newcomers: Negroes and Puerto Ricans in A Changing Metropolis.* Cambridge: Harvard University Press, 1959.

A short volume which compares the history of New York's earlier immigrants with that of southern Blacks and Puerto Ricans.

——. *Race and Nationality in American Life.* Garden City, N.Y.: Doubleday, 1957.

Essays on race, racism, and American society.

——. *The Uprooted.* Boston: Little, Brown, 1951.

A Pulitzer Prize-winning history, this book is "the epic story of the great migrations that made the American people." Of special interest are Chapters 4, 6, and 7, which deal with the creation of ethnic communities in the United States.

Hannerz, Ulf. *Soulside.* New York: Columbia University Press, 1970.

An ethnographic examination of a ghetto culture and communal life in one part of Washington, D.C., by a Swedish anthropologist.

Hansberry, Lorraine. *Raisin in the Sun.* New York: Random House, 1959.

A play about a Black family living in Chicago in the 1950s.

Hansen, Marcus Lee. *The Atlantic Migration: 1607–1860.* Cambridge:

Harvard University Press, 1940.

A classic study of immigration. It also won a Pulitzer Prize.

———. *The Immigrant in American History*. Cambridge: Harvard University Press, 1940.

A series of essays by the Harvard historian. The book includes material that was to have been used in later volumes on immigration.

Haring, Douglas C. *Racial Differences and Human Resemblances*. Syracuse: Syracuse University, 1947.

An anthropologist's view of "race."

Herberg, Will. *Protestant-Catholic-Jew*. New York: Doubleday, rev. ed., 1983.

A study in the sociology of American religion. Herberg contends that the United States is a "triple-melting pot."

Herskovits, Melville. *The Myth of the Negro Past*. New York: Harper & Row, 1941.

The most famous of Herskovits' many examinations of the retention of Africanisms by Black Americans.

Hertzberg, Arthur. *The Jews in America*, New York: Simon and Schuster, 1989.

A new history of four centuries of Jewish life in America.

Higham, John. *Strangers in the Land*. New Brunswick, N.J.: Rutgers University Press, 1955.

An examination of American nativism from 1860 to 1925 and an analysis of the forces which led to the enactment of legislation against unrestricted immigration in the 1920s.

Hirsch, Herbert and Gutierrez Aronando. *Learning to Be Militant*. San Francisco: R and E. Research Associates, 1977.

A monograph describing a study of the development of political militarism in a Chicago community in the 1960s.

Hobson, Laura. *Gentleman's Agreement*. New York: Simon and Schuster, 1947.

A magazine writer poses as a Jew in this best-selling novel about anti-Semitism.

Hoetink, Harry. *The Two Variants on Caribbean Race Relations*. New York: Oxford University Press, 1967.

A critical essay which describes the author's idea of a "somatic norm image."

Howe, Irving. *World of Our Fathers*. New York: Simon and Schuster, 1976.

A comprehensive and highly readable social history of the journey of East European Jews to America and the life they found there.

Hsu, Francis L. K. *Challenge of the American Dream*. Belmont, Calif.: Wadsworth, 1971.

An introduction to Chinese-American.

Jensen, Arthur. *Bias in Mental Testing*. New York: Free Press, 1980.

Jensen's latest salvo in the continuing debate over the relationships between genetic background and intelligence as measured by I.Q. tests administered to Black and White youngsters.

Kallen, Horace M. *Cultural Pluralism and the American Idea*. Philadelphia: University of Pennsylvania Press, 1956.
An elaboration on an idea, "cultural pluralism," about which Kallen first wrote in 1915.

Kelley, Gail Paradise. *From Vietnam to America*. Boulder, Colo.: Westview Press, 1977.
A description of the experience of Indochinese refugees in the 1970s.

Kennedy, John F. *A Nation of Immigrants*, rev. ed. New York: Harper & Row, 1964.
A posthumously published edition of President Kennedy's brief history of the American people.

Kessner, Thomas and Betty Boyd Caroli. *Today's Immigrants: Their Stories*. New York: Oxford University Press, 1982.
A description of the lives of a number of new Americans from all over the world.

Killian, Lewis M. *The Impossible Revolution? Black Power and the American Dream, Phase II*. New York: Random House, 1975.
A critical study of the civil rights movement, of Black Power, and the future of race relations in America.

———. *White Southerners*. Amherst, Mass.: University of Massachusetts Press, 1985.
The author views White southerners as an ethnic group and a "quasi" minority in this sociological analysis.

Kinloch, Graham C. *The Sociology of Minority Groups*. Englewood Cliffs, N.J.: Prentice-Hall, 1979.
A recent textbook which contains several useful paradigms for analyzing race relations in the U.S.

Kitano, Harry H. L. *Japanese Americans*. New York: Chelsea House, 1987.
A brief introduction to the experiences of Japanese-Americans in the United States with special attention to the World War II period.

Kovel, Joel. *White Racism*. New York: Pantheon, 1970.
One of the first psycho-histories of the phenomenon of institutionalized racism in the United States.

Kramer, Judith K. and Seymour Leventman. *Children of the Gilded Ghetto*. New Haven: Yale University Press, 1961.
A study of second- and third-generation Jews in America.

Kurokawa, Minako, ed. *Minority Responses*. New York: Random House, 1970.
Various reaction patterns are considered here including *submission, withdrawal, separation,* and *revitalization.*

Ladner, Joyce, ed. *The Death of White Sociology*. New York: Random House, 1973.

A hardhitting and controversial critique of "mainstream sociology" by a variety of Black sociologists.

Lee, Alfred McClung. *Fraternities Without Brotherhood*. Boston: Beacon, 1955.
One of the few full-scale reports of discriminatory practices in private organizations on the college campus.

Lee, Rose Hum. *The Chinese in the United States of America*. New York: Oxford University Press, 1960.
A classic study of immigration, settlement, and intergroup relations.

Lerner, Max. *America as a Civilization*. New York: Simon and Schuster, 1958.
An extensive study of American society. Of special interest is Lerner's discussion of "People and Place."

Levine, Robert A. and Donald T. Campbell. *Ethnocentrism*. New York: Wiley, 1972.
A comprehensive review of theories of conflict, ethnic attitudes, and group behavior.

Levy, Mark R. and Michael S. Kramer. *The Ethnic Factor*. New York: Simon and Schuster, 1972.
The results of a comprehensive study of the significant role of minority-group membership in American elections.

Lewin, Kurt, ed. *Resolving Social Conflicts*. New York: Harper & Row, 1948.
A social psychological treatment of racial and ethnic problems.

Lewis, Michael. *The Culture of Inequality*. Amherst, Mass.: University of Massachusetts Press, 1978.
An important contribution to the study of social stratification and American values.

Liebow, Elliott. *Tally's Corner*. Boston: Little, Brown, 1967.
An anthropologist's portrait of "Negro Streetcorner Men."

Lincoln, C. Eric. *The Black Muslims in America*. Boston: Beacon Press, 1968.
One of the first detailed studies of those Black Americans who joined the Muslim faith.

Lipset, Seymour Martin and Earl Raab. *The Politics of Unreason*. New York: Harper & Row, 1969.
A social history of right-wing movements in the United States and a commentary on those to whom such movements appeal. One should pay particular attention to discussions of the "once-hads" and the "never-hads."

Loescher, Gil and John A. Scanlan. *Calculated Kindness*. New York: Free Press, 1986.
A critical assessment of the making and implementing of United States refugee policy from 1945–1985.

Lopata, Helen Znaniecki. *Polish Americans*. Englewood Cliffs, N.J.: Prentice-Hall, 1976.
A brief sociohistorical analysis.

Lopreato, Joseph. *Italian Americans*. New York: Random House, 1970.
In this volume, one of a series of "Ethnic Groups in Comparative Perspectives," the author presents an insightful portrait of Italian Americans as a model immigrant group.

Lowenthal, Leo and Norbert Guterman. *Prophets of Deceit*. New York: Harper & Row, 1949.
An examination of the language of prejudice and the nature of demagoguery.

Lyford, Joseph P. *The Airtight Cage*. New York: Harper & Row, 1966.
A study of New York City's multi-ethnic west side.

Lyman, Stanford M. *The Black American in Sociological Thought*. New York: Capricorn Books, 1972.
In this "sociology of sociology" Lyman examines the way different schools and various notables (including Robert E. Park) portrayed Black Americans and dealt with plight.

———. *Chinatown and Little Tokyo*, Millwood, NY: Associated Faculty Press, 1986.
Study of conflict and community among Chinese and Japanese immigrants in America.

Malamud, Bernard. *The Tenants*. New York: Farrar, Straus, and Giroux, 1971.
The interaction of a Black man and a Jew is the subject of this contemporary novel.

Malcolm X. *The Autobiography of Malcolm X*. New York: Grove Press, 1964.
The life story of the Black leader and, for a time, Muslim spokesman.

Newman, William M. *American Pluralism*. New York: Harper & Row, 1973.
Conflict theory as applied to examine many aspects of American life and, especially, to ethnic relations.

Novak, Michael. *The Rise of the Unmeltable Ethnics*. New York: Macmillan, 1971.
A lengthy essay on the place of Poles, Italians, Greeks, Slavs, and other "White ethnics" in American society and American consciousness.

O'Connor, Edwin. *The Last Hurrah*. Boston: Little Brown, 1956.
A description of Irish-Americans in politics. The setting is Boston.

Padilla, Elena. *Up from Puerto Rico*. New York: Columbia University Press, 1958.
A view of migration from Puerto Rico and settlement in New York City.

Parrillo, Vincent N. *Strangers to These Shores*. Boston: Houghton Mifflin,

2d ed., 1985.

A new text rich in historical grounding for a sociological analysis of racial and ethnic relations in the United States.

Petersen, William, et al. *Concepts of Ethnicity*. Cambridge, Mass.: Belknap Press of Harvard University Press, 1980.

Several entries from the Harvard Ethnic Encyclopedia dealing with "ethnicity" and its definition.

Pitkin, Thomas Monroe. *Keepers of the Gate: A History of Ellis Island*. New York: New York University Press, 1975.

A richly documented examination of the administrative side of "the Ellis Island story."

Polenberg, Richard. *One Nation Divisible*. New York: Pelican Books, 1983.

A critical examination of class, race, and ethnicity in the United States since 1938.

Puzo, Mario. *The Fortunate Pilgrim*. New York: Antheneum, 1964.

A novel about growing up Italian-American in New York City.

Quinley, Harold E. and Charles Y. Glock. *Anti-Semitism in America*. New York: Free Press, 1979.

The results of extensive studies conducted by the Survey Research Center of the University of California are analyzed as the major contribution to understanding anti-Semitism in contemporary America. The book is one in a series of volumes on "the tenacity of prejudice."

Report of the National Advisory Commission on Civil Disorders. New York: Bantam, 1968.

This is the famous "Kerner Commission" report on the urban riots of the 1960s and their causes. Includes comparisons of the experiences of White immigrants and Blacks.

Reimers, David. *Still the Golden Door*. New York: Columbia University Press, 1985.

A study of the new immigration to the United States, with a particular focus on those from Asia and Latin America.

Rex, John. *Race Relations in Sociological Theory*. New York: Oxford University Press, 1970.

An examination of the treatment of racial and ethnic relations by sociologists. The book ends with a statement about "race relations" as a distinct field of study.

Ringer, Benjamin B. and Elinor R. Lawless. *Race-Ethnicity and Society*. New York: Routledge, 1989.

A critical examination of the "We and They" character of racial and ethnic relations, supporting and expanding upon many of the arguments made in these pages.

Rogg, Eleanor Meyer. *The Assimilation of Cuban Exiles*. New York: Aberdeen Press, 1974.

Community and class are the critical variables in this study of Cuban exiles who settled in a New Jersey township.

Rose, Arnold M. *The Negro's Morale*. Minneapolis: University of Minnesota Press, 1949.

A study of self-identification of Black Americans largely based on material from the Carnegie Studies in the early 1940s.

Rose, Peter I., ed. *Working with Refugees*. Staten Island, N.Y.: Center for Migration Studies, 1986.

The proceedings of a conference on addressing the needs of refugees: from providing protection and assistance in "first asylum" countries to resettlement in "third countries."

————, ed. *Americans from Africa*, 2 vols. New York: Atherton, 1970.

Volume I, *Slavery and Its Aftermath*, deals with four controversies: the retention of "Africanisms," slavery and personality, family and social structure, and life in the North compared with life in the South. Volume II, *Old Memories, New Moods*, considers the roots of Black protest, the civil rights movement, Black Power, and changing self-images.

————, ed. *The Ghetto and Beyond*. New York: Random House, 1969.

Essays by the editor and others on Jewish life in America. Topics covered include culture, religion, politics, civil rights, and literary expression.

————, ed. *Nation of Nations*. New York: Random House, 1972; reprinted by University Press of America, 1981.

A volume of readings edited to accompany *They and We*. Includes essays, stories, excerpts from autobiographies, and sociological analyses of "ethnic experience and the racial crisis" in the United States.

————. *Strangers in Their Midst: Small-Town Jews and Their Neighbors*. Merrick, N.Y.: Richmond Publishing Co., 1977.

A study of small-town Jews, their neighbors, and their children over a 20-year period.

————. *The Subject Is Race*. New York: Oxford University Press, 1968.

A summary of the author's study of traditional ideologies and the teaching of race relations. Reports on hundreds of courses taught at American universities in the mid-1960s.

————, Stanley Rothman, and William J. Wilson, eds. *Through Different Eyes*. New York: Oxford University Press, 1974.

Original essays by 20 Black and White writers who examine race relations in the United States in the 1970s from varying perspectives.

Roth, Philip. *Goodbye Columbus*. Boston: Houghton Mifflin, 1959.

A prize-winning novella and several short stories about Jewish life in post-World War II America.

Ryan, Joseph, ed. *White Ethnics: Their Life in Working Class America*. Englewood Cliffs, N.J.: Prentice-Hall, 1973.

A collection of essays by social scientists including Andrew Greeley, Michael Novak, Joseph Lopreato, Herbert Gans, Nathan Glazer, and others.

Schermerhorn, R. A. *These Our People: Minorities in American Culture.* Boston: D. C. Heath, 1949.

Unlike most books on the subject this one includes discussions of Poles, Czechs and Slovaks, Hungarians and Yugoslavs in this country in addition to historical examinations of Blacks, Spanish-speaking Americans, Italians, Japanese-Americans, and Jews.

———. *Comparative Ethnic Relations.* New York: Random House, 1970.

Working papers on comparative ethnic relations, the author includes a commentary on the study of prejudice and the character of "victimology."

Schrag, Peter. *Out of Place in America.* New York: Random House, 1970.

A collection of Schrag's previously published essays on various aspects of American social life. Included here is his "Decline of the WASPs."

Seller, Maxine. *To Seek America.* Englewood Cliffs, N.J.: Jerome S. Ozer, 1979.

A brief historical review of U.S. immigration history with a useful annotated bibliography.

Senior, Clarence. *Strangers—Then Neighbors.* New York: Freedom Books, 1961.

A brief introduction to the Puerto Rican situation.

Sexton, Patricia. *Spanish Harlem.* New York: Harper & Row, 1965.

An excellent study of the Puerto Rican community in New York City.

Sherif, Muzafer and Carolyn Sherif. *Groups in Harmony and Tension.* New York: Harper & Row, 1953.

A series of essays on prejudice and a report on several fascinating studies of induced prejudice.

Shibutani, Tamotsu and Kian M. Kwan. *Ethnic Stratification: A Comparative Approach.* New York: Macmillan, 1965.

A textbook that raises a number of fundamental questions about the relations between peoples. Many sections are relevant for understanding the meaning of "integration."

Silberman, Charles. *Crisis in Black and White.* New York: Random House, 1964.

Anticipating many of the events of the mid- and late 1960s, Charles Silberman offers an examination of the struggle for and barriers to integration. His comments on Saul Alinsky's radical programs are especially significant.

Simpson, George E. and J. Milton Yinger. *Racial and Cultural Minorities,* 4th ed. New York: Harper & Row, 1972.

A widely used, near-encyclopedia text that deals with many different aspects of prejudice and discrimination from both a sociological and social psychological perspective.

Sindler, Allan. *Bakke, De Funis and Minority Admissions: The Quest for Equal Opportunity.* New York: Longman, 1978.

An analysis of recent cases concerning "Affirmative Action."

Skardal, Dorothy Burton. *The Divided Heart*. Oslo: Universitetsforlget, 1974.
    A history of Scandinavian immigration and settlement through literary sources.
Sklare, Marshall. *America's Jews*. New York: Random House, 1971.
    The entire volume deals with social history and group identity. Emphasis is on five social characteristics: family, community, education, interaction (and intermarriage), and the issue of Zionism.
Smith, Lillian. *Strange Fruit*. New York: Reynal and Hitchcock, 1946. The theme of this powerful novel is segregation in the deep South.
Sowell, Thomas. *The Economics and Politics of Race: An International Perspective*. New York: Quill, 1983.
    A comparative analysis of the relationship between economics and ethnicity which includes studies of the United States.
————, ed. *American Ethnic Groups*. New York: The Urban Institute, 1978.
    Analysis of the relationship between ethnicity and social inequality edited by an economist.
Steiner, Dale R. *Of Thee We Sing: Immigrants and American History*. New York: Harcourt Brace Jovanovich, 1987.
    A series of portraits of thirteen individual immigrants who represent different periods in American history—from John Winthrop, the Puritan leader, to Jamie Nguyen, a recently arrived Vietnamese refugee.
Stoddard, Ellwyn. *Mexican Americans*. New York: Random House, 1973.
    A controversial study which includes historical background and sociological analyses of Mexican-Americans.
Stonequist, Everett V. *The Marginal Man*. New York. Scribner's, 1937.
    The author applies Robert Park's notion of "marginality" to a variety of racially mixed peoples.
Styron, William. *Sophie's Choice*. New York: Random House, 1979.
    Set in the late 1940s, this novel is about intergroup relations and what Hannah Arendt once called "the banality of evil." The principal character is a survivor of Auschwitz now living in America.
Suchman, Edward A., John P. Dean, and Robin M. Williams, Jr. *Desegregation*. New York: The Anti-Defamation League, 1958.
    This book offers some propositions about research suggestions for understanding both the dominant and minority communities.
Sugarman, Tracy. *Stranger at the Gates: A Summer in Mississippi*. New York: Hill and Wang, 1966.
    An artist's commentary and sketches of the "Mississippi Summer" of 1964.
Sumner, William Graham. *Folkways*. Boston: Ginn, 1906.

A classic study in the sociology of culture, this book includes Sumner's definitions of "in-groups" and "out-groups" and a discussion of his conception, "ethnocentrism."

Takaki, Ronald, ed. *From Different Shores*. New York: Oxford University Press, 1987.
A fine collection of journal articles and excerpts from books offering varying sociological assessments of the successes and failures of American intergroup relations policies.
———, *Strangers From a Different Shore*. Boston: Little, Brown, 1989.
A new history of Asian immigrants to and in America.
Van den Berghe, Pierre. *Race and Racism*. New York: Wiley, 1967.
The author views the United States as a "herrenvolk democracy" and explains why in this comparative study of race and racism.
———. *Man in Society: A Biosocial View*. New York: Elsevier, 1975.
A controversial text that reopens the "nature" versus "nurture" debate.
Vanfossen, Beth. *The Structure of Social Inequality*. Boston: Little, Brown, 1979.
A text offering a good introduction to the study of social stratification.
Wagner, Nathaniel and Marsha J. Have, eds. *Chicanos* St. Louis: C. V. Mosby, 1971.
Contributed essays on social and psychological problems and perspectives of Mexican-Americans.
Warner, W. Lloyd and Leo Srole. *The Social Systems of American Ethnic Groups*. New Haven: Yale University Press, 1945.
One of the several volumes in the famous "Yankee City Series," this book deals with ethnicity.
Washington, Booker T. *Up From Slavery*. New York: Doubleday, Page and Company, 1901.
The Negro educator's autobiography.
Wax, Murray. *Indian-American: Unity and Diversity*. Englewood Cliffs, N.J.: Prentice-Hall, 1971.
One of the best among a growing number of studies of American Indians by sociologists and anthropologists.
Weinstein, Allen and Frank Otto Gattel, eds. *American Negro Slavery*, rev. ed. New York: Oxford University Press, 1973.
A modern reader which includes articles on slaves, masters and "the system."
Weisbrod, Robert J. and Arthur Stein. *Bittersweet Encounter*. New York: Schocken Books, 1972.
One of a number of volumes in which the relationships between Blacks and Jews are examined.
Weiss, Nancy. *The National Urban League, 1910–1940*. New York: Oxford University Press, 1974.
A history of one of the leading organizations fostering economic opportunities and social services for Black Americans.

Whyte, William Foote. *Street Corner Society*. Chicago: University of Chicago Press, 1943.
A sociological study of social interaction among the members of a group of men who lived in the Italian section of Boston.

Wilkinson, J. Harvie. *From Brown to Bakke*. New York: Oxford University Press, 1979.
A lawyer's analysis of the Supreme Court's decision regarding school desegregation from 1954–1978.

Wilkinson, Doris Y. and Ronald L. Taylor, eds. *The Black Male in America*. Chicago: Nelson-Hall, 1977.
An interdisciplinary set of essays on socialization, stigmatization, interracial marriage, and social status.

Williams, Robin M., Jr. *The Reduction of Intergroup Tensions*. New York: Social Science Research Council, 1947.
A quarter of a century ago, this little book provided a guide to understanding the dynamics of the intergroup conflict in the United States. Most of what was said then still applies.

———. *Strangers Next Door*. Englewood Cliffs, N.J.: Prentice-Hall, 1964.
A summary report on the Cornell Studies of Intergroup Relations conducted in the 1950s. Important chapters document group attitudes and minority reactions.

Wilson, William Julius. *The Truly Disadvantaged*. Chicago: University of Chicago Press, 1987.
An examination of the underclass in contemporary American society and a series of commentaries on social policy.

———. *The Declining Significance of Race*. Chicago: University of Chicago Press, 1978.
A critical analysis of recent trends in race relations and an analysis of the widening socio-economic gap in the Black community and its significance.

Wirth, Louis. *The Ghetto*. Chicago: University of Chicago Press, 1956.
A classic study of Jewish life in Europe and the United States with particular attention to responses to discrimination.

Woodward, C. Vann. *The Strange Career of Jim Crow*, New York: Oxford University Press, rev. ed., 1965.
The development of segregation from the withdrawal of federal forces from the South to the mid-1960s, written by the author of *Reunion and Reaction* (1951) and *Origins of the New South* (1951).

Wright, Richard. *Black Boy*. New York: Harper, 1945.
An autobiography of the famous Black writer, this book describes the impact of discrimination.

Wyman, David. *The Abandonment of the Jews*, New York: Pantheon Books, 1984.
A historical study of the policies of the American government toward Holocaust victims, 1941–1945.

Young, Donald. *American Minority Peoples*. New York: Harper, 1932.
    One of the first sociology texts to be devoted exclusively to the topic. Written by the person credited with introducing the concept "minority" into the sociological literature.

Ziegler, Benjamin M., ed. *Immigration: An America Dilemma*. Boston: D. C. Heath, 1953.
    A collection of famous papers on the immigration controversy. Includes Horace Kallen's early view of "cultural pluralism."

Zucker, Norman and Naomi Flink Zucker. *The Guarded Gate*. New York: Harcourt Brace Jovanovich, 1987.
    A critique of United States refugee policy and a set of recommendations for the future.

INDEX

(NOTE: Reference notes are indicated by "n." after the page number.)

Withdrawal, 147–148
Wright, Richard, 69, 111, 130n.,
   145–146, 154n., 229

X, Malcolm, 144, 160, 175n.,
   180

Yinger, J. Milton, 96, 107–108n.,
   144, 154n.

Young, Donald, 8, 12n.
Young, Whitney, Jr., 103, 109n.,
   167

Zangwill, Israel, 62, 80n., 151
Znaniecki, Florian, 225, 229,
   232n.